Africa Now

Africa Now is published by Zed Books in association Nordic Africa Institute. Featuring high-quality, cutting-edge research from leading academics, the series addresses the big issues confronting Africa today. Accessible but in-depth, and wide-ranging in its scope, Africa Now engages with the critical political, economic, sociological and development debates affecting the continent, shedding new light on pressing concerns.

Nordic Africa Institute

The Nordic Africa Institute (Nordiska Afrikainstitutet) is a center for research, documentation and information on modern Africa. Based in Uppsala, Sweden, the institute is dedicated to providing timely, critical and alternative research and analysis of Africa and to co-operation with African researchers. As a hub and a meeting place for a growing field of research and analysis, the Institute strives to put knowledge of African issues within reach of scholars, policy makers, politicians, media, students and the general public. The Institute is financed jointly by the Nordic countries (Denmark, Finland, Iceland, Norway and Sweden). www.nai.uu.se

Forthcoming titles

Cedric de Coning, Linnéa Gelot and John Karlsrud (eds), *The Future of African Peace Operations*
Tobias Hagmann and Filip Reyntjens (eds), *Aid and Authoritarianism in Africa*
Anders Themner (ed), *Warlord Democrats in Africa*

Titles already published

Fantu Cheru and Cyril Obi (eds), *The Rise of China and India in Africa*
Ilda Lindell (ed.), *Africa's Informal Workers*
Iman Hashim and Dorte Thorsen, *Child Migration in Africa*
Prosper B. Matondi, Kjell Havnevik and Atakilte Beyene (eds), *Biofuels, Land Grabbing and Food Security in Africa*
Cyril Obi and Siri Aas Rustad (eds), *Oil and Insurgency in the Niger Delta*
Mats Utas (ed.), *African Conflicts and Informal Power*
Prosper B. Matondi, *Zimbabwe's Fast Track Land Reform*
Maria Eriksson Baaz and Maria Stern, *Sexual Violence as a Weapon of War?*
Fantu Cheru and Renu Modi (eds), *Agricultural Development and Food Security in Africa*
Amanda Hammar (ed.), *Displacement Economies in Africa*
Mary Njeri Kinyanjui, *Women and the Informal Economy in Urban Africa*
Liisa Laakso and Petri Hautaniemi (eds), *Diasporas, Development and Peacemaking in the Horn of Africa*
Margaret C. Lee, *Africa's World Trade*
Godwin R. Murunga, Duncan Okello and Anders Sjögren (eds), *Kenya: The Struggle for a New Constitutional Order*
Lisa Åkesson and Maria Eriksson Baaz (eds), *Africa's Return Migrants*

About the author

Thiven Reddy is a senior lecturer in the Department of Political Studies, University of Cape Town. His previous publications include *Hegemony and Resistance: Contesting Identities in South Africa*.

South Africa, settler colonialism and the failures of liberal democracy

Thiven Reddy

Nordiska Afrikainstitutet
The Nordic Africa Institute

Zed Books
LONDON

South Africa, settler colonialism and the failures of liberal democracy was first published in 2015 in association with the Nordic Africa Institute, PO Box 1703, SE-751 47 Uppsala, Sweden, by Zed Books Ltd, The Foundry, 17 Oval Way, London SE11 5RR, UK.

www.zedbooks.co.uk
www.nai.uu.se

Copyright © Thiven Reddy 2015

The right of Thiven Reddy to be identified as the author of this work has been asserted by him in accordance with the Copyright, Designs and Patents Act, 1988

Typeset in Adobe Minion, Monotype Gill Sans Heavy by Sandra Friesen
Index: John Barker
Cover design: www.roguefour.co.uk
Cover image © James Oatway / Panos
Printed and bound by CPI Group (UK) Ltd, Croydon, CR0 4YY

All rights reserved. No part of this publication may be reproduced, stored in a retrieval system or transmitted in any form or by any means, electronic, mechanical, photocopying or otherwise, without the prior permission of Zed Books Ltd.

A catalogue record for this book is available from the British Library.

ISBN 978-1-78360-224-7 hb
ISBN 978-1-78360-223-0 pb
ISBN 978-1-78360-225-4 pdf
ISBN 978-1-78360-226-1 epub
ISBN 978-1-78360-227-8 mobi

MIX
Paper from responsible sources
FSC® C013604

Contents

Acknowledgements | vi

Introduction 1
1 Modernity: civil society, political society and the vulnerable 11
2 The limits of the conventional paradigm, modernity and South African democracy. 41
3 The Fanonian paradigm, settler colonialism and South African democracy. 63
4 The colonial state and settler-colonial modernism 83
5 Nationalism, ANC and domination without hegemony 107
6 Elites, masses and democratic change. 133
7 Crisis of the national modern: democracy, the state and ANC dominance. 151
Conclusion 187

References | 193
Index | 207

Acknowledgements

This book could not have been completed without the support and assistance of many people who contributed in large and small ways. I have been thinking about the issues raised in this work for over a decade. I had first decided to write on contemporary democratic politics in 2009, and I received funding support from the Oppenheimer Foundation Trust. Aspects of research from that project have found their way into this text.

In 2011, I received a Nordic Africa Institute scholarship. The Institute is a wonderful place to research and write. I thank Tor Sellström, Sonja Johansson, Inga-Britt Isaksson Faris and my fellow researchers Chibuike Uche and Mary Njeri Kinyanjui for their friendship and support.

The book began to look realisable when I confirmed a contract with Zed Books in 2013. As with most book projects, this one went through periods of frantic writing, excitement, flowing ideas and also uncertainty. I extend many thanks to Ken Barlow for taking this unusual argument on, spending many hours reading my drafts and being such a patient, encouraging and supportive editor. I thank Dominic Fagan and the anonymous reviewers for close reading of the manuscript and providing me with detailed questions and corrections. I want to thank those who read individual chapters, including Harry Stephan, Movindri Reddy, Ziyana Lategan, Harry Garuba and Shathley Q. Finally, I am grateful for my circle of friends and for the patience of my elderly parents, Jackie and Leela Reddy. My parents kept asking me when I would be finished, and now I can say that my excuses not to 'take them to the shops' have finally run out. I thank them for their love, support and sustained encouragement over many years.

Throughout, my strongest support and most consistent encouragement has come from my partner, Neetha Ravjee, who read all the different versions, made detailed editorial corrections and forgave me when I did not use all of them, and our son, Ché-Len, a saviour, my role model and an inspiration.

It is ironic that democratic South Africa continues to use the racial categories defined historically under Apartheid (African, Coloured, Indian/Asian and White). I reject this system of classification, and I would always place these terms within scare quotes if that were possible. Because it is not, I follow the convention associated with historical resistance practice and use the term 'Black' to refer to all those Africans, 'Coloureds' and 'Indians' whom Apartheid laws discriminated against, and I reluctantly use the historical racial group categories when referring to specific group political experiences.

Introduction

South Africa is a society driven by guilt, fear and anger. In a society that is so clearly a product of injustice for so long, the past cannot but be deeply etched upon everything. One part lives in a world of comfort, fear and guilt. The other, the vast majority, survives in a world of squalor, frustration and anger—a world of bare life (Agamben 1998). The two hardly meet except in the world of work, but this is a world of masters and servants. The democratic breakthrough in 1994 has not changed this division much. Now, another group, the emerging black middle class, has moved into the world of fear and guilt, but also comfort and, for a few, ostentatious wealth. Everywhere this division haunts all in this society; it never completely leaves even though most try to ignore its presence.

Ken Owen, a keen observer of South African politics, blamed 'the deplorable state' of contemporary South African democracy on the low self-esteem of the black leadership. He scathingly argued that 'we are dealing with a generation of black leaders who were severely damaged, men more than women, by the terrible humiliations of apartheid'. As a result the black political elite are prone to express 'insecurity, desperate greed, excessive concern for status and appearance, a sad reliance on paper qualifications, dishonesty, abuse of the weak, especially women and children, vain displays of wealth, and pomposity. Bodyguards, expensive cars, huge mansions, expensive whisky, business class flights—the symptoms of a sense of inferiority are everywhere'. By contrast: 'White South Africans are writing books, producing plays, defending causes, mending machines, teaching, even helping to govern badly like Alec Erwin and Jeremy Cronin' (2009).

Is this attack on a country that has only recently celebrated two full decades of constitutional democracy following the end of Apartheid, where the 'terrible humiliations' of this iniquitous system still remain raw, appropriate? Many would strongly disagree with Owen's view and especially his tone, but all his criticisms cannot be easily disputed. Perhaps we can accuse him of reductionist thinking, offering too simplified a conclusion to the problems that bedevil a complex society. After all, Owen would be remembered for the unintentional irony of his warning about the dangerous influence of 'Black Consciousness' as advocated by Steve Biko in the 1970s; he drew the Apartheid government's attention to the very issues that this ideology addressed, most importantly the psychological inferiority of the oppressed subject. Regardless, Owen's criticisms highlight an important aspect of contemporary South Africa's troubled, psychotic democracy. That theme is the focus of this book.

South Africa, a country known for Apartheid and Mandela, adopted a radical liberal democratic constitution after Apartheid. Unanimous praise for the peaceful transition from Apartheid between 1990 and 1994 came from all quarters of the globe. Hope, goodwill and a general sense of relief that Apartheid had been left behind prevailed. As Mandela eloquently said upon becoming the first democratically elected president of the 'new' South Africa, 'Never, never and never again shall it be that this beautiful land will again experience the oppression of one by another and suffer the indignity of being the skunk of the world' (1994). After those balmy moments of promise, new democratic rules of the political game were announced, new institutions were established, old institutions underwent change and the political landscape became arguably almost unrecognisable. The country experienced five elections, all relatively peaceful and 'free and fair'. Many parties competed vigorously against each other, the media extensively covered the everyday details of campaigning, and citizens phoned radio stations and took sides on key issues. On the surface, democratic institutions evidently functioned. Few observers disputed that democracy is close to being or has been 'consolidated' (Lane & Ersson 1997; Giliomee 1995; Lodge 1999; De Jager & Du Toit 2013). Drawing on democracy monitoring data comparing the health of democracy on a global scale, which was regularly announced by the US-based Freedom House Institute and other Western agencies, commentators labelled South Africa just 'another country' and 'an ordinary' democracy. It was held that democracy was on its way to becoming normal, or so the dominant ideology wanted people to believe.

At the time of Mandela's release from prison in 1990, heightened expectations for something better than the present, and believed to be closer to realisation, were immediately discernable. As mainstream US media outlets covering Mandela's walk from Victor Verster Prison repeatedly warned, the majority, millions of black and poor South Africans, expected with varying degrees of patience that the many legacies of Apartheid would be addressed. Commentators repeated assessments of this growing pressure when the last white president of South Africa announced a negotiated path to end state-legislated racism a few months earlier: the mass of ordinary citizens, who bore the brunt of Apartheid, would expect and demand 'the world'. Many predicted that if these expectations were left unrealised, the accumulated frustration would produce instability and violence. Two decades later, despite popular frustration, South Africa continues to witness political institutional stability even though a tenuous politics is manifest. This situation can be credited, in large part, to the historical nationalist appeal of the African National Congress (ANC) government.

Yet a culture of violence permeates so much of South African society that it is widely considered endemic. South Africa's democracy seems to be in permanent trouble. Contradictorily, the public sphere exhibits both political system stability and everyday violence or threats. Everywhere we see the unravelling of the dreams of post-Apartheid expectation, general disappointment and political malaise replacing the optimism and enthusiasm of 1994. There are many signs: high unemployment, high rates of crime, massive inequality, and millions living in desperate poverty. Collective demands from students, trade unions and communities highlight the state's inability to deliver on campaign promises. And fragmentation and factionalism within the ruling party are leading to a political discourse that relies on threats of violence. These manifestations of popular frustration express not only a decay of political order or stability, or more directly a weakness in the structure of the state, but also point to the rise of a kind or mode of politics that the political theorist Andreas Kalyvas labelled 'the politics of the extraordinary' (2009, 6).

Kalyvas distinguished between 'normal' and 'extraordinary' politics, deriving the latter from late nineteenth- and early twentieth-century economic and political theorists who were sceptical of reading politics off from the economic, like Max Weber, Carl Schmitt and Hannah Arendt. Normal politics is 'monopolized by political elites, entrenched interest groups, bureaucratic parties, rigid institutionalised procedures, the principle of representation, and parliamentary electoral processes'. It consists of low popular participation 'in the deliberation about common affairs and decision-making'. While these features may be present, the key features of extraordinary politics are 'high levels of collective mobilisation, extensive popular support for some fundamental changes; the emergence of irregular and informal public spaces; and the formation of extra-institutional and anti-statist movements that directly challenge the established balance of forces, the prevailing politico-social status quo, the state legality, and the dominant value system' (Kalyvas 2009, 6). While the characteristics turn on matters of degree, most if not all the features of extraordinary politics are identifiable in post-1994 South African politics. Democratic features reflected in the constitutional order certainly did not fully incorporate the 'slumbering popular sovereign'. The anti-Apartheid struggle, especially of the 1980s, was a commonsense cause awakening the mass political subject. The 'rights-based' official discourse post-1994 has been unable to steer the popular sovereign in the direction of 'normal politics.'

Partha Chatterjee, drawing on Antonio Gramsci's work, made a similar distinction between a politics dominated by civil society and by political society. According to conventional democratic theory, civil society should be the primary site for dispute regulation. Chatterjee (2003; 2004) argued persuasively that the orthodox division between the state and civil society in Western political theory inadequately applies to postcolonial societies. It is more constructive to think of a domain of mediating institutions between civil society and the state. Only a small part of the population, 'the nationalist elite', participates in modern associational life with the rights and obligations discourse characteristic of civil society. In places like contemporary South Africa, political society assumes the terrain for poor people to articulate their concerns. Non-hostile, orderly civic-legal relations, which are the bedrock of middle-class values, have not become dominant although they are enshrined in the constitution and dubiously pronounced by the political elite. Following Chatterjee's analysis, what we witness instead is the assertion of political society and a subaltern politics of social mobilisation.

The troubled state of democracy in South Africa directly relates to the broader questions of modernity in postcolonial situations, and specifically how was modernity imposed? Modernity was imposed through settler colonialism, which should be conceived as distinct from the generic 'colonialism' written about in the postcolonial theory literature. Settler colonialism as it played itself out in Southern Africa (South Africa, Mozambique, Namibia, Zimbabwe and Angola), especially its enforcement with the most extreme forms of violence and by the consequent forms of nationalist struggles, has contributed to this mode of politics. I will argue that, in societies imprinted by settler colonialism (or the imposition of modernity through violence), democracy characterised by 'normal politics' becomes a messy, unpredictable and perhaps impossible process. What we have in post-1994 South Africa are battles for hegemony under democratic conditions. In other words, in societies like South Africa that are marked by a particular type of modernity, captured in the category of settler colonialism, we witness a mode of politics that intrinsically involves power struggles over resources, recognition and ultimately who prevails in establishing the foundations of evaluation. The mode of politics expected of and associated with liberal constitutional democracy fails to obtain a dominant foothold. In such postcolonial situations, mainly but not exclusively in Southern Africa, rigid distinctions between state, political and civil society, pivotal concepts and assumption of mainstream analysis are conceptually inadequate. A mode of politics that is characterised by pervasive battles of influence constitutes all these terrains. These spheres become terrains of conflict not only over the basic distribution of resources and political offices, but also over the 'unfinished business' of the very constitution of the political community and the emergence of the modern political subject (Gramsci 1971, 160; Samaddara 2010).

Thus the South African experience offers a unique lens through which to observe the global story of modernity. It raises questions about how we study and understand modernity in general and political modernity in particular. As Karl Marx poetically described this revolutionary process, 'all that is solid melts into the air' (1978, 476). In Southern Africa and especially South Africa, the experience of modernity is traumatic and violent; the changes are far-reaching and involve many communities. It has taken place in short bursts and over long periods, spanning some three hundred years. The large settled white population was unable to decimate, but also unwilling to culturally assimilate with, the local populations. Slave, feudal and capitalist relations entrenched themselves over long periods. The discovery of large mining deposits further transformed the society, drawing South Africa into a global capitalist system. Mining also intensified the centrality and awesome capacity of the state and produced conditions in which grotesque violence was not hidden behind the veil of the market.

In such colonised societies, settled by large numbers of Europeans, the tensions and contradictions come from three processes: state-building and the imposition of racial capitalist relations and dominant values. A product of colonialism, which became known as South Africa, inherited the largest population of European settlers in Africa. As in the United States, Canada, Australia and New Zealand, settlers avoided integration with the diverse majority of local inhabitants from their arrival in 1652. But unlike these countries, where the large-scale killing of the 'natives' and continuous immigration provided different conditions for the constitution of the national community, in South Africa whites laid claim to an unchallenged indigenous South African identity and citizenship on the basis that they had settled over three centuries ago. The white community adopted white supremacist policies and culturally 'dis-associated' itself from the native majority, contributing to complex questions of identity dividing the society. The history of white supremacy, and the consequence that blacks were politically excluded, economically deprived and culturally despised, kept constitution of the political community unsettled.

A distinctive feature of South African modernity turned on the settled minority both relying on the majority's labour and lands and excluding blacks from the political community since the period of colonial conquest. The necessary black acquiescence for its capitalist modernity was acquired largely through a monopoly of violence enshrined in the modern bureaucratic state, and the exercise of force. Prompted by the mining industry, the structural and organic incorporation of South African society into a growing global trading network in the late nineteenth-century introduced capitalist economic relations, wage labour and large-scale proletarianisation, based on extra-economic coercive measures. In addition, the dominant's close interaction with and systematic cultural negativity towards everything associated with the dominated, which is another key feature of settler colonialism in Africa, historically characterised the political, ideological and cultural aspects of South Africa's unfolding modernity.

Some characteristic features of settler-colonial modernity formally ended with the overthrowing of the Apartheid-colonialist political system in 1994. The black majority's struggle under the banner of nationalism and a campaign for democracy oriented itself towards acquiring state power. This struggle assumed many forms, but ultimately the monopoly of violence waged by the state was counterbalanced by the mass mobilisation of the majority. The changing global environment at the end of the Cold War and internal tensions within the established political elite produced a negotiated settlement and a new constitution. The nationalist struggle, another crucial element of South Africa's modern experience, had two significant implications: contributing to a conception of politics as a means to achieve some goal and creating a fighting political subject constituted ultimately by forces in conflict. So, although the period of white supremacist privilege enshrined in law was brought to a formal close, the cultural idioms associated with the emergence, formation and constitution of the mass political subject, subjected to colonial violence, continue to resonate today.

Over two decades after the democratic breakthrough, battles grounded in old racial narratives are continuing, just in a different political context and with new actors and conflicting discourses whose rage is pushing democratic engagements to their limits. The battles are taking place on multiple fronts in what Gramsci called a 'trench-warfare' of close combat (1971). One sphere of society seems to resemble a Western-type democratic system. The institutions hammered out during the almost four years of negotiations, from 1990 to 1994, reflect values associated with democracy. They were crafted with citizens in mind, giving them access to the political system and making it difficult (though not impossible) for leaders to rule arbitrarily. In practice, this dimension of South African politics is dominated by the middle classes and their demands for rights, accountability, engagement in public discourse, participation in associational life and non-violent governmental channels (law, public media, debates, civil institutions, etc.). But even within this formal democratic framework, discursive battles rage: put simplistically, between the nationalist-struggle paradigm claiming to represent 'the masses' and that of 'Western' liberal democracy largely representing the middle classes, who were mainly white, but also Apartheid-classified African, Coloured and Indian elites. The politics of the majority lies outside this sphere. In the main its collective action relies on mass demonstrations, violent and threatening discourses to indicate impatience, criminality and disrespect for the law, and collectivism that relies on both organisation and informality.

As a case study for the understanding of modernity and its implication for politics, South Africa raises questions for analysing democracy in the conventional paradigm of comparative politics. In analyses influenced by American schools of political science, the democratic change in South Africa is a significant case study of third wave democratisation, which Samuel P. Huntington termed 'third wave democracy' in 1991. It encompasses the establishment of democratic regimes around the world from the early 1970s to the late 1990s and simultaneous emergence of competitive electoral politics with the end of the Cold War. Huntington (1991) identified the first wave as 1828–1926, when twenty-nine countries became democratic, and the second as 1943–1962, when another thrity-six (mainly in Africa and Asia) transitioned. Both were followed by a 'reverse wave' towards authoritarian regimes. The third wave includes Spain, Portugal and Greece in the 1970s, Latin American countries in the 1980s and Eastern Europe and additional African countries in the 1990s. The interest in third wave democracy meant that, by 1994, a toolkit of concepts and theories were 'ready at hand' to apply to South Africa. The roots of this dominant approach can be traced to 1950s modernisation theory. In this view, the Western liberal democratic framework of politics serves as the foundational and uncritical assumption motivating the analysis of political practice and theory. This assumption has long dominated the study of South African politics. Further, influenced by modernisation theory, the third wave literature associates modernity with the transition to democratic institutions (in South Africa this implies black majority rule) but ignores the particular features of settler-colonialist modernity. It emphasises a uniform, linear conception of history while dismissing the past as an analytical legacy that is not constitutive of the present. In my analysis, I emphasise that the modern in South Africa was first introduced by settler colonialism and that the specifically South African features were consolidated under Apartheid and continue along this trajectory in the post-Apartheid system. This singular process, despite the different internal political struggles that constitute different cultural terrains, describes the approach followed here and is neatly summarised in Marx's idea that the present congeals the past.

Interestingly, dominant paradigms in South African studies defend South African colonialism as a positive intervention to 'develop' society along modern lines. After World War II, when many African and Asian countries were ending foreign rule and colonialism was beginning to be universally condemned, scholars of South Africa debated the reinvigoration of Apartheid colonialism under Nationalist Party rule. Despite intensified debate and internal differences, both liberal and Marxist paradigms viewed Apartheid as an aberration and an impediment to developing full, 'normal' modernity. These approaches believed that modernisation was partially developed, incomplete because racially structured. They assumed that, as modernity spread, stabilising democratic institutions would allow the black majority to 'catch up'. This inadequate thesis will be critiqued. In following the rich analysis of Frantz Fanon, I argue that settler colonialism is a very particular form of modernity, encountered and implicated in continuous violence, presenting a condition that undermines the presumed linear trajectory towards liberal democracy. Given this very different path to the modern, particularly the manner with which old social relations and institutions were destroyed in Europe and in Africa, South African political modernity will be different and necessarily unlike that of Europe. Certainly, the assumptions of the Western liberal democratic model as an inevitable process, a desirable end goal, and a standard of evaluation must be questioned.

The dubious claim found in some Western media that South Africa is another failed attempt at Third World modernity allows us to revisit old theoretical questions from the perspective of this last of freed colonies. What was wrong with the conceptual model of modernisation predicting that all countries once formerly independent and free from colonialism would inevitably end up looking like the advanced capitalist democracies? What features of settler-colonialist histories make that prediction false? How and why do leaderships embrace ideologies that seem forced and incommensurable with citizen values? These questions are not considered to explain the 'failure' of establishing liberal democracy in South Africa against an imagined western and liberal democratic standard, but to understand how imposing this model produced a contradictory, hybrid system infested with contradictions: an idea of the rule of law, yet with widespread violations by leaders and citizenry; the existence of democratic institutions that work against democratic values, both internally and externally; competitive multiparty systems that produce dominant party outcomes allowing for the rule of a benign despot; and a 'security' sensitivity towards rights, ideas and alternatives from the state, which is controlled by a party that responds to legacies of which it itself was a product. The subject of this book is the apparent contradiction of modernity and the 'non-modern' as it plays out in contemporary South African politics.

I present five key elements of the argument in this book. First, the conventional approach to studying contemporary South African democracy identifies the South African problem as not conforming to the standard template of democracy, which was established elsewhere. Second, I propose another approach. Borrowing from David Scott's (1999a) analysis of Jamaican politics, I interpret the dilemmas of politics in the current conjuncture in South Africa as part of a larger problem relating to the crisis of the national-modern project, which is represented by the nationalist elite. Third, I argue that this is really a crisis of the nationalist elite being unable to establish hegemony over society, a central point developed in Chatterjee's work (2004). Chatterjee drew on Gramsci (1971) to focus on the historical tension between the nationalist elite and the subaltern mass to understand how the former carve out a struggle of nationalism against colonial power. Fourth, I draw on Fanon's powerful analysis of how and why settler-colonial modernity has a specificity that cannot be ignored. He raised important questions about the nature of power, capitalist modernity in colonial society and the complexity of colonial subjects. Fanon put on the analytical agenda the relationship between universal claims and its dismissal of particular, local histories and believed that without acutely rethinking this relationship, a mass subject of political change in the colonial situation will remain unfulfilled. Lastly, I explore how the mode of politics engaged in by the subaltern masses in contemporary South Africa, which relies on the extraordinary politics of social mobilisation, can be understood as a response to everyday vulnerability captured in Giorgio Agamben's (1998) concept of *'homo sacer'* (Latin: 'protected but ostracised man', literally sacred/cursed man). Agamben's work contributes to a general critique of the limitations of liberal capitalism. It seems that Agamben's *homo sacer* has a stronger resonance in democracies whose modernities are traceable to settler-colonial violence.

The analysis is organised into seven chapters. In chapter 1, I map democratic politics in contemporary South Africa by identifying two modes of politics (civil society and political society), identifying the crisis of the nationalist middle class over compromised democratic transitions in societies with settler-colonial histories and presenting an expanded discussion of the theoretical influences behind these arguments. In the discussion of civil society and democracy, I consider the relationship between settler-colonial modernity and a politics of bare life in which vulnerable subalterns demand basic services through the extraordinary politics of mass mobilisation.

The thesis that South African 'democracy' and its 'consolidation' rely on the modernisation paradigm of the 1950s is taken up in chapter 2. This conventional approach to politics in the Third World pervades academic and journalistic accounts of everyday South African politics. The broad modernisation thesis, discredited in the mid-1970s, bounced back with the current study of democratic transitions based on regime changes in the 1990s; in this literature, the South African transition is a paradigmatic case. I criticise the central assumption of historicism, a dominant view of Western thought in which the liberal democratic political systems of Europe and North America are used as the ideal universal standard against which Third World and African politics are considered exceptional or incomplete, as if in continuous transition. It is troubling that the key concepts, which developed out of a particular regional European experience, are presented as scientific, neutral and universal (Chakrabarty 2000). Stuart Hall (1996), who provocatively spelled out the discourse of 'the West and the Rest', had in mind the modernisation approach as a good example of such a discourse. It is difficult to think of a counter-discourse of political change of 'the rest' in terms separate from this dominant discourse; at the conceptual level the modernisation discourse is so powerfully insidious. My critique draws attention to how we 'read' South African politics after Apartheid in a particular way, identifying the problem in the simple terms of a dominant party thesis or related to the latter, the culture and values of the political elite. This unconvincing approach excludes the main actors and the structural conditions that produce particular behaviours from elites. Instead, I emphasise the configuration of settler colonialism as a central category to understand South African politics after Apartheid, a notion the conventional paradigm ignores or leaves marginalised.

A reading of modernity that includes settler colonialism as a central concept to understand the particular conditions of how modernity is imposed in South Africa as well as the emergence of the mass political subject directly relates to how I understand democratic politics, which is the central thesis of this book. In chapter 3, I explain how it is impossible to understand the dynamics of settler colonialism, of which South Africa serves as the paradigmatic case, without looking to Fanon. As yet few theorists have been able to describe 'the ordering and geography of power in a colonial situation' in such accurate detail as he does (1963). Fanon's attention is on the organisation of power and also power's constitution of the identities of the dominant and dominated, coloniser and colonised; a major contribution is his understanding of modern social relations based on violence and not legitimacy. He captures the different dimensions of violence—open physical violence and the more subtle impressions—on the consciousness of dominant and oppressed, a situation leaving no subject untouched or outside its ambit. The latter's legacies do not end with the hoisting of the new flag announcing the new nation. Fanon traces the vulgarities of politics after independence to colonial legacies and the processes of decolonisation. This is different from mainstream approaches that easily dismiss the political, economic and psycho-cultural features uniquely inherited from the settler-colonial situation rather than creatively confronting them.

In chapter 4, I apply Fanon's analysis to South African state and society, relocating the concept of settler colonialism to the centre of analysis and its feature of domination without hegemony. I trace the historical features of modernity's birth, its reliance on physical violence and the organisation of civil society on the basis of race. This allows me to more strongly grasp the contemporary pitfalls of identity that bedevil contemporary democratic politics and help reorientate the understanding of South African politics away from the restrictive 'democratic transition framework'.

In chapter 5, I focus on another modern idea: nationalism. I look at how the relationship between colonised elites and subaltern masses was historically fraught with tension over the nationalist elite's aim to dominate, control and represent 'the struggle'. The nationalist elite approached this cautiously and in ways that varied so highly over time that it was not always clear that it was serving its own class interests in the long term.

In chapter 6, I trace the key processes of the democratic transition as it unfolded in South Africa. But instead of approaching this topic in the conventional manner by emphasising the ideological and tactical differences between the Apartheid government elites and those from the nationalist movement, I ask what was in their common interest. I identify their need to control the 'unruly mass' by aiming to re-direct popular mass mobilisation into a mode of politics that was considered 'normal' and acceptable, a particular normative form of political rationality. This form of politics, encouraged by elites from both sides, desired mass demobilisation and the subaltern to uncritically accept a discourse of rights, sovereignty and the law.

In chapter 7, I focus on the democratic state and its challenging goal to 'de-racialise' state and society and how these efforts manifest in the crisis of the national-modern project.

1 | Modernity: civil society, political society and the vulnerable

The aim of this study is to understand examples of the extraordinary politics of the mass collective subject of post-1994 democracy in relation to the civil politics of the middle classes. This dual mode of politics is a salient feature of contemporary South African politics. I contend that the conventional analyses represented in third wave democracy studies and approaches to modernisation are limiting and inadequate because they view collective action by national popular sections as exceptional illustrations only of state failure or an ongoing or incomplete democratic transition. I have pieced together a new theoretical framework to argue that, instead, they are integral to liberal democracy in a society marked by settler colonialism. This allows subaltern unease, as manifested in the politics of social mobilisation, to be understood not in the terms of the liberal democratic framework and its emphasis on civil society but by locating South Africa's history in the terms of its own experience of modernity. This makes it necessary to trace back the features of colonial modernity as expressed historically in South Africa as settler colonialism and analyse how expressions of settler colonialism, including legacies of violence, Othered subjects and racialised capitalism, present new contradictions to its liberal democratic project.

Unlike the elites, the masses practice a mode of politics in which they are key participants of mobilised protest but remain loyal supporters of the governing party. This chapter explores how this mode of politics tests the limits of liberal democracy and reveals the contradictions expressed in its politics. By examining salient examples of mobilised politics, it affirms that liberal democracies must radically confront the histories and legacies of settler colonialism—the historical production of subject identities under conditions of violence—so that citizens can see and interact with each other on equal terms. It argues that the fundamental restructuring of established property relations and fostering conditions in which 'the Other' is recognised within oneself forces us to think of an alternative modernity.

In order to spell out the big picture of the book, trends in post-1994 democratic politics and the elements of the theoretical framework used, the discussion is divided into four sections. The first illustrates a type of politics and one way that mass politics interacts with a weak national bourgeois leadership that dominates without hegemony. It draws on case studies that represent the diversity of expressions of this extraordinary politics: the Marikana massacre, protests against *The Spear*, social delivery community protests and xenophobic attacks. The second discusses the anxieties of dealing with the past and the crisis of the present among the nationalist elite, as well as debates surrounding unfinished national liberation and the establishment of liberal democracy. The third brings these perspectives to the core problem of identifying and explaining the two modes of politics, that of the elite in civil society and that of the masses in political society. The fourth uses this new assessment as the basis for a new theoretical framework. As the argument unfolds, it draws on work by Antonio Gramsci, Frantz Fanon, Partha Chatterjee, David Scott, Michel Foucault and Giorgio Agamben.

Elite vs mass politics

Marikana and 'uncritical solidarities' In August 2012, police killed thirty-four striking miners at the Lonmin mine in the North West Province. The tragedy was televised. For weeks, the events featured on South African and global television, the names and forms of the now dead bodies permeated all forms of media (Alexander et al. 2013). The long-seething dispute over wages for rock-drill operators, coupled with the belief that the National Union of Mineworkers (NUM) had become a 'sweetheart' union of the bosses, motivated thousands of workers to join a rival breakaway union, the African Mineworkers and Construction Union (AMCU) in 2012. The week-long strike itself went through a violent period, with NUM and AMCU reporting that their members were being intimidated, even killed. The striking AMCU workers gathered at a nearby *koppie* (hill) of the mine and faced a mounting and belligerent police presence. Just before the police opened fire, it was reported that Cyril Ramaphosa, then deputy president of the African National Congress (ANC) (and shareholder of Lonmin), had described the strike as 'criminal' and asked the police to take 'concomitant action' (Patel 2013). The following month, the government established a commission of Inquiry under former Appeals Court Judge Ian Farlam to investigate the massacre. After many delays and changes of its terms of reference, the Commission finally submitted its report to President Jacob Zuma in 2015; after further delays the 400-plus page report was released for public discussion in which its main findings exonerated key individuals in government and business but called for improved public order policing. The families of the dead victims were extremely disappointed and felt let down by the entire commission process.

Nearly two decades after the first open election in 1994, the black middle class has visibly grown. However, the stark overlap of class and race continues; the majority of the poor living in squalor are black, while most of those who are well off are white. The related discourses of separation and suspicion, coupled with fear, frustration and anger, result in a politics of Gramsci's 'trench warfare', often using rudimentary symbolic weapons. Moeletsi Mbeki argued in 2009 that 'the ANC is faced with a revolt at the bottom and it is about inequality. And how do you explain to those people protesting what causes the inequality? You explain they are left behind because they are discriminated against by whites' (Roussouw 2009). He fears that the next phase, counting the number of black Africans in each sector of societal leadership under affirmative action policies, will soon deteriorate into counting black African ethnic identities and thus pave the way for dangerous tribalism and lead to a closed, parochial future.

As Fanon predicted, the nationalist bourgeoisie (in the ANC and its Tripartite Alliance) relies on a racialised discourse that emphasises the idea of the 'indigenous majority' (black people, or those with more narrowly conceived African identities, who are seen as victims of the colonial and Apartheid past) that are morally deserving of recognition through representation. This past explains why the majority continue to live in squalor and endure what Agamben calls a 'bare life' always vulnerable to death (2011): mere biological survival, ever precarious, without political significance. It is also why subaltern protests are increasingly prevalent, occurring outside the rules of civil discourse, and exhibiting multiple and contradictory features. They are controlled and uncontrollable, unregulated and regulated, strategic and opportunistic, political and sometimes bordering on the criminal. They occur with increasing frequency outside courts, churches and taxi ranks, in shantytowns, informal urban settlements and townships, and in rural and farming communities. In every instance, the state has reacted with accusations of criminality, criticising the subaltern classes of disrespecting democracy.

Njabulo Ndebele offers a nuanced and close reading of South Africa's present conjuncture. After two decades of democracy, both blacks and whites engage dishonestly: 'The whites are pretending it [Apartheid] didn't happen; the blacks are pretending to forgive' (2009). Strikingly, he does not see this pretence as entirely negative. In racial situations when one is unable to behave truthfully, he suggests that it can serve as a positive 'coping strategy'. Emphasising the psychological quandary in which white and black find themselves, he sees whites as experiencing unease when they realise that they were not only complicit in Apartheid, but also that they continue to enjoy its material benefits and may suffer from corrective practices. Whites thus live in pretence, in what Ndebele calls a 'space of anguish', rather than working to find a lasting solution that would negatively impinge on their accumulated material privilege (2009). Blacks also live in anguish, but from material deprivation in the rough and violent life of townships, which themselves are reminders of Apartheid that treat their residents as objects without dignity. The hope of a non-racial future, inspired by the transition to a liberal democratic constitutional order, has wrestled against the guttural anger and hatred that also motivated and sustained the struggle against Apartheid. Inequalities of the past are reproduced, and despite a superficial black cultural assertiveness, blacks are still subordinate in all the areas that matter, from economics to media, literature and the arts. Their response is to fall back 'to the alluring hatred of the past and their call for activism' (Ndebele 2009). But after a while, says Ndebele, 'you pause' and ask 'is it the whites who are responsible for my anguish or is it a black government that is not providing the requisite leadership and delivery, the heaven it promised?' (Ndebele 2009) He criticises the failing black government, the co-option of the democratic transition that gave further advantage to the elites, the emphasis on 'redistribution over creation and invention' and the demobilisation of the masses. Most importantly, Ndebele objects to 'uncritical solidarities'. For instance, blacks abandon 'good sense' to defend the indefensible, such as siding with fellow blacks, no matter what they have done, merely because they were criticised by whites. It will be argued that the role of 'uncritical solidarities' of blacks and whites that mark liberal democracy in South Africa, its availability in the political field, cannot be explained outside settler-colonial history.

'Uncritical solidarities' and The Spear   The public's reaction to Brett Murray's painting of President Zuma, *The Spear* (2012), demonstrates the idea of uncritical solidarities and its availability in the political field exceptionally well. The depiction of Zuma in the guise of Lenin in Victor Ivanov's iconic Soviet propaganda poster *Lenin Lived, Lenin is Alive, Lenin Will Live* (1967), but with his penis exposed, was deliberately provocative. Publication of the painting in the *City Press* weekly newspaper immediately took it from a bourgeois gallery public to many different publics, and widespread mobilisation ensued against the painting, the artist, and gallery, fuelled and egged on by the senior ANC leadership. They emphasised that the painting was not about free expression, but about racism, and that it expressed the disrespect that whites continued to harbour towards black people in general; the president became, in this case, the symbol of 'the people'. The controversy ended after the ANC organised a march to Johannesburg's Goodman Gallery, the painting was defaced (on a separate occasion), and the gallery and the painter apologised. Steven Robins observed that debates about unflattering representations of political elites by artists or cartoonists had previously pitted freedom of expression against cultural beliefs about dignity and respect, but that the question in this case was 'how leaders ... ought to act when, for various reasons, the 'raw emotions' of citizens become available for populist mobilisation' (2012).

Achille Mbembe writes that this painting of Zuma's private parts served as the 'outlet of deep-seated, repressed, or denied racial anger, which itself is, paradoxically, the expression of a deep longing for a community worthy of that name' (2012). How do we explain the anger expressed over the 'intersection of art, sexuality and power?' Mbembe asked, and he suggested that the reaction to the painting relates to the different worlds inhabited by blacks and whites. Three factors coalesced. Firstly, the ANC was exerting subaltern control via culture in the context of the 'intellectual decay' in the ruling party. It promoted a form of 'official culture' to domesticate the subaltern masses by demarcating the lines between the acceptable and the permissible, or normal, by 'depoliticising' the arts. As Mbembe said, 'From its citizens, it is requesting subordination to authority in the name of culturalism' (2012). Secondly, Zuma's stature and patriarchal power symbolised, by contrast, the powerlessness of young men and the threat to their historical sense of manhood; in a powerful visual, it expressed that younger generations of men could not 'enjoy the privileges of patriarchy'. And thirdly, the Spear controversy illustrated the anxieties of the white world impressed on the black body in new art forms. Mbembe understands Murray as part of a new group of artists who identify in the 'black body ... the repository of all the anxieties, neuroses, phobias and sense of estrangement of white South Africa' (2012). Generally, he continues, South African art lacks original concepts, and its art boils down to endless collection and 'repetition'. And this unimaginative mimicking of what is believed to be current and/or fashionable in Europe and the US is not an uncommon South African practice in the arts, in politics, education and the economy.

Regardless, the cultural and political meanings of the protestors' 'raw emotions' cannot be understood without reference to South Africa's settler-colonial history. Robins (2012) traced the basis of these raw emotions to the settler-colonial experience with its Christian 'civilising mission', which demanded that those who they considered 'heathens' (and 'backward') had to cover their bodies, especially their genitals. But the black body was not only violated by the missionaries; it was also the object of 'scientific' discourse: investigated, measured, tested and studied to support theories of racial hierarchies. Political elites drew on these colonial humiliations to mobilise thousands of supporters against the gallery and the painter. The artwork's supporters were mainly white and some in the black middle class who viewed the episode as one of cultural expression, artistic taste and free expression, all of which are necessary in a democratic society.

Murray's painting thus attempts to critique the political elite and patriarchy using ideas that can be related to the past, which would have been unthinkable outside the settler-colonial archive of domination. Cultural scars from Apartheid, which cannot necessarily be distinguished from the scars from colonial settlement, continue to drive protests against its sources and its manifestations. Here, the mobilisation of the subaltern classes was spurred by ANC elites against an identifiable target, representing meanings of the past traceable, to racism and settler-colonial wounds. Robins's and Mbembe's analyses of how the masses reacted to it also explain the similar, near-daily demonstrations; although they take the form of targeted material needs, such as poor sanitation, the lack of running water, frequent electricity cut-offs, unaffordable rents and inefficient local councils. They are demonstrations against racism of the past that continues today and reasons why the ANC could be both target and facilitator in this scenario.

According to Fanon, these examples signify the 'consciousness of the black body as non-human' (1963). Essentially, this is Agamben's *homo sacer* (literally sacred man). In Roman antiquity, the term was used for men who were ostracized (literally, excluded from the city or stripped of citizenship; in practice, excluded from all forms of society) but could not be killed. The punishment did not regard the body as insignificant or undervalued, but as the key means of extending the ultimate torments. It is a very rough equivalent of solitary confinement in prison today. Agamben defined it more as 'undervalued body', referring to life so precarious that the killer of a modern *homo sacer* does not have to fear prosecution. He also, it seems, stretched the original meaning to question the 'sacredness' of life of members or citizens of democratic societies, which is preached in modern political theory. I use *homo sacer* in Agamben's sense. This notion resonates with Arendt's (1986) reference to the 'abandoned' stateless people after World War I despite commitments made by states to the Declaration of the Rights of Man. I want to highlight the idea that the black body has inhabited an ambiguous site between potential rights and Agamben's precariousness (see chapter 3) in the age of the capitalist world system, that this situation describes the contemporary moment of South African politics, and that this bigger picture exposes weaknesses of modern democratic political theory.

The politics of bare life: extra-ordinary politics Whether due to a lack of state capacity, inefficient and corrupt practices, neo-liberal macroeconomic policies, the dominance of the ruling party over the state, or as I will contend, a consciousness of being treated as non-humans, citizens' frustrations with receiving poor services have grown since the late 1990s. Poor communities, mainly resident in 'informal settlements' and some townships, mobilise protests against local councils for failing to deliver on election promises or realising rights for housing, water and electricity. This is another illustration of the subaltern mass's unease with formal liberal democratic politics in South Africa.

The first community protests occurred in the late 1990s (primarily while President Thabo Mbeki, 1999–2004, was in office) and increased substantially from 2002 (Alexander 2010). How do we make sense of protests that remind so vividly of the running battles between poor communities and the Apartheid state in the early 1980s? The term 'community' has been contested, particularly around who claims to represent 'the community'. And databases of media reports, such as the South African Local Government Association (SALGA), Briefings Reports and the Municipal IQ Hotspot Monitor, give a good sense of the empirical trends despite their varying definitions of the 'social delivery protests'. Municipal IQ's definition, 'those protests where communities oppose the pace or quality of service delivery by their municipalities', is so narrow that it excludes local protests targeted at the national government (Karamoko and Jain 2011). This distinction has important consequences: Municipal IQ data identifies 32 and 27 'major protests' for 2007 and 2008, respectively, whereas Karamoko and Jain count 96 and 118. The South African Institute of Race Relations (SAIRR), also drawing on Municipal IQ data, found that social protests increased by 96 per cent from 2010 to 2014 and that 176 major service delivery protests took place in 2014 alone (Polity 26/05/2015).

Regardless of the data source or definition of terms, it is clear that the number of protests has risen since 2007, which had 8.73 protests per month. The monthly average was 9.83 in 2008; 17.75 in 2009; 11.08 in 2010 (the FIFA Soccer World Cup explains the relative calm for the remainder of 2010, with only 6 protests per month); 8.80 in 2011; 13.1 in 2012; and 11.2 in 2013, and reaching an all-time high of 18 per month in 2014 (Powell, O'Donovan and Visser 2014). There are also more protests in winter (June and July) than in summer: 2007 saw 8.1 protests per month in summer but 12 during winter; 2008 averaged 5.67 in summer but 10.67 per month in winter. The most common grievances are over basic resources, such as water, sanitation, toilets and electricity. These claims about lack of dignity are often associated with claims of abuse by local government officials, who are accused of corruption and failing to respond to previous complaints. Typically, the number of protestors range from small groups of fifty to two hundred to large gatherings involving thousands of participants. Most recorded protests take place in Gauteng (31.46 per cent), followed by the Western Province (17.05 per cent) and the North West (11.09 per cent). The fewest are recorded in Limpopo (5.3 per cent), Free State (4.9 per cent) and the Northern Cape (1.82 per cent). In the middle, are the Eastern Cape (11.09 per cent), Kwa-Zulu Natal (9.27 per cent) and Mpumalanga (7.95 per cent) (Karamoko and Jain 2011).

An increase in violent protest is traceable to April 2009, which corresponds to growing unemployment figures and the global recession. More protestors have defended themselves against an increasingly aggressive police force and actively targeted symbols of the state or council representatives. Whereas 36.86 protests were violent between 2007 and March 2009, slightly more than half (53 per cent) were violent from March 2009 until 2014. Often the targets were African immigrants, so these collective actions were classified as xenophobic attacks. But social delivery protests are not the only cases of mobilised communities voicing anger, frustration and alienation from the formal system of politics. SAIRR quoted a South African Police annual report in which it is clear that even the classification and wording of the protests is politicised to play down anti-state sentiment: in 2014 it recorded 11,668 'peaceful crowd-related incidents', 1,907 'unrest-related incidents' and 1,691 'public violence incidents' (Polity 2015).

Interestingly, the protesting citizens participate in elections, mostly voting for the ANC, while engaging in community protest against ANC-controlled local municipalities. But popular protest is common outside social delivery protests. There are daily reports of students, workers and other interest groups who protest to demand lower tuition rates, higher wages, better working conditions and cultural or religious recognition. From taxi owners and drivers who demand reduced state regulation to shack dwellers who claim proper housing and protest against forced removals, a recurring theme is the demand for the kind of recognition that formal politics seems to undervalue. This recognition is reducible to a demand for rights, as in the state provision of proper housing for shack dwellers, and it is also a form of identity politics related to dignity, which is repeatedly reflected in the speeches made at these protests.

This 'new' social mobilisation (Ballard 2005; Hough 2008; Grobler 2009) often evokes continuities in cultural practice—the slogans, songs, dance, posters and style of speeches—with the discourses of the 1980s mass uprisings in South African urban townships (Gunner 2008). These patterns resurfaced after a few years of democracy, as continued racist practices, feelings of alienation in white-dominant institutions and social spaces, state inefficiencies, macroeconomic policy and corruption frustrated and angered the many who remained poor or whose material and symbolic lifeworlds worsened. Yet, obvious differences in political systemic contexts between the 1980s and the post-1994 period exist. Under Apartheid, racial divisions and inequalities presented specific conditions for social mobilisation; blacks at a minimum demanded full democratic participation in the political system. It is significant that the cultural strand of the 1980s social mobilisation, which was symbolically influenced by military (guerrilla) action, resurfaced in post-1994 protests. The previous opposition to a clearly delineated enemy, reliance on force and use of symbolic practices associated with militarist campaigns have resurfaced more vigorously under democratic conditions. The citizen participation encouraged by the democratic system—electoral politics, lobbying of interests, and reasoned and rational public deliberation to influence the national agenda—demonstrates elements of a developing civil society discourse. These operate alongside the politics of mobilisation, which mirror the often inchoate patterns of the 1980s and are relevant to subaltern claims against the ANC's statism.

This increased social mobilisation has pressured the ANC, both as the government and as the nationalist organisation having a long history of mobilising against Apartheid. It has responded ambiguously: although it has condemned protests at the national level, it is not unusual to find some ANC members or ANC-aligned structures at the local level, such as the extended protest in the Khutsong township between 2006 and 2009. In this small and poor community, residents protested for three years against the redrawing of provincial boundaries that moved them from Gauteng to what they saw as the inefficient and corrupt North West province. Though an ANC stronghold, the Khutsong community boycotted schools, burnt the local library, torched cars, chased away the ANC national leadership and boycotted the local government elections until the area was rezoned back to Gauteng. On the one hand, the ANC as a political party portrays itself as pursuing the 'national democratic revolution' that encourages party-led political and social mobilisation. On the other, the ANC as a ruling party falls back on a defensive approach that emphasises the 'rule of law' or 'law and order'. The ANC's knee-jerk reaction is to draw attention to ongoing racial divisions, thus evoking the anti-Apartheid history of struggle that is, and remains, the provisional and unreliable basis for its legitimacy and popularity. This response has thus far worked to secure the position of the ruling party, but it also contributes to a continued racialised political discourse that risks further confusing and alienating the already discontented.

The slow pace of change and the ineffective delivery of services, which were initially blamed on the conservative bureaucracy of the Apartheid era, are increasingly identified as the result of a 'lack of capacity'. The phrase refers to the ANC's own appointees in what is now an overwhelmingly black civil service. The idea of transforming the state has been narrowly interpreted as replacing white personnel with black staff, most often party members. The redeployment of these party appointees for positions in the state machinery, together with access to valued state resources such as tenders, have fuelled factional battles within the ANC. In recent years, these internal conflicts have become more vicious and sometimes violent.

The 'people' and the mob

'They beat you with anything they find, like a rock', says Eugene Cukana, a construction worker who lives nearby. 'Then they put a tire around your neck and they burn you'.... In the past year, Mr. Cukana witnessed a killing by a mob of 100 people. The victim was a suspected criminal. They dragged him unconscious to the 'field of death'. 'Nobody bothered to call the police … It was quite a sad thing', Mr. Cukana said in an interview on the edge of the field. 'He's still a human. But if you call the police, they don't come. So we take the law into our own hands' (York 2014).

This sentiment, expressed by a resident of Khayelitsha (one of the large barren townships and squatter camp areas of the Cape Flats facing Table Mountain), reflects the reality of the situation in the squatter camps and townships. It also introduces us to a familiar pattern of social mobilisation in South Africa. Between April 2011 and June 2012, seventy-eight people were reportedly killed in such 'vigilante violence' (York 2014). The number of 'illegal mob deaths' could be increased many times over if it included other parts of the country, xenophobic attacks on 'foreign' African nationals or factored in the extent of under-reported crimes among the poor in South Africa (and by the police themselves in crime statistics reports). These events are regularly in local papers and sometimes the global media, and they have become normalised in poor communities. They are the third illustration of mobilisations that place participants ambiguously in relation to the law and nationalist and struggle discourse; the nationalist middle class struggle rejects them due to their ambiguous criminality.

In addition to these forms of social mobilisation protecting the community from crime, local government corruption and service delivery failures from 2000, South Africa began experiencing major waves of xenophobic attacks on foreign-born Africans in May 2008. A woman who witnessed a man burning in the street, one of the first to be killed by an angry mob, reported the extreme horrors:

> After seeing a gang douse a Mozambican immigrant with petrol and throw him into his burning shack, a woman from Zimbabwe told the BBC she had decided to leave Johannesburg and return home. 'The screams of the burning Mozambican still haunt me. When I close my eyes to try to sleep, I see the man screaming for help. But no one helps him.… I have never seen such barbarism' (BBC 2008).

The type of violence has continued largely with individual attacks, which are reported regularly. But a flare-up in April 2015 involved street battles in Durban and Johannesburg between mainly Zulu speakers, who had heeded the Zulu monarch King Zwelithini's warnings about foreign migrants draining 'South African' public resources. Here again, the xenophobic attacks took the same form as 'normal community protests': they were mass-based, open, political and violent.

Before these events, community activists, journalists and academics warned of rampant xenophobia against Africans from other African countries and recent immigrants from Pakistan, China and India. Andile Mngxitama (2009) appropriately labelled this black self-hatred externalised onto other poor blacks 'negrophobia' and called for direct state intervention. The government failed to revisit existing policy and practice or educate South African citizens, so the tensions persisted and migrants remained easy targets for Othering. It actively worsened the problem. In official policy and action, and in political speeches, state officials voiced anxiety about the increase in the number of new immigrants (Crush 2000a; Crush 2000b; Worby, Hassim, and Kupe 2008). The police, together with Home Affairs officials, adopted a program to find, detain and repatriate 'illegal immigrants' to their 'home' countries. Recurring police anti-crime campaigns targeted non-nationals. Foreign-born applicants complained that the Department of Home Affairs, which is responsible for population control and notorious for bureaucracy, inefficiency and corruption, treated them with disrespect, and the department offices had to be guarded by twenty-four-hour private security. Still, clashes between security staff and immigrants remain commonplace and contribute to xenophobic discourse.

The origins of the xenophobic attacks in mass mobilisation is significant, as is their resonance with the culture of the popular protests of the 1980s (Crush 2000a). They were openly conceived in the public sphere. In some planned mass meetings, community leaders warned foreign-born residents to leave the area and even read aloud a list of names. Often 'the mob' formed immediately after the meeting ended, moving to the houses of foreign-born residents while singing songs associated with the anti-Apartheid struggle that were suggestive of organised, systematic mobilisation. The much-discussed civic and democratic values of post-Apartheid South Africa, which emphasise the Pan-Africanist solidarity of Ubuntu and the protection of liberal individual rights in the constitution, were absent.

This kind of violent collective action, ostensibly following moral codes, has precedents in South African history. In the 1980s and early 1990s, 'black on black' violence in the townships was common. 'Mini wars' raged between ethnic communal groups throughout the colonial encounter, as did the 'faction fights' in the mining industry (Murray 1987; Sisk 1995). These prejudices and resentment remain common. The xenophobic or negrophobic attacks against non-nationals must be understood in the context of such previous violent clashes. A defining characteristic of the 1980s was brutality, including shooting, raping, burning bodies and 'necklacing' (placing a burning car tyre around the victim's neck). Much was blamed on the 'Third Force' (the clandestine units of the Apartheid state), but local residents were also sometimes actively involved.

In places such as Alexandra in Johannesburg, an important moment in the nationalist struggle was the ANC's campaign to take control of townships from the Apartheid state. Local activist structures claimed to have organised 'street committees' (Neocosmos 1998). In a fluid local power dynamic, 'popular justice' was meted out to transgressors of community codes. Some popular structures directed extreme punishments, like necklacing, at those accused of cooperating with the Apartheid police and working against the community's political agenda. This community violence during the last days of Apartheid points to the depth of community organisation, the ever-present possibility of vigilantism, and the history of internal conflict arising from alienation from the state. The more recent protests and xenophobic attacks mimic this pattern, although the targets and expressions of violence are different.

These forms of 'citizen' action, namely forms of popular action by poor people, point to a mix of elements that reflects post-1994 democratic politics in South Africa but is also traceable to the past. They are different to the politics of affirmative action or Black Economic Empowerment (BEE), which evoke the law, human rights and the constitution. These elite expressions of politics manifest on the surface of power; rights, for instance, are denied or applied according to double standards. In contrast, the underlying forms of disciplinary power that constitute subjects as 'non-human' drive a different politics, a discourse of anger in the domain of political society that can be categorised as everyday or extraordinary. Post-1994, the subaltern realised that winning a struggle for a new democratic constitution may not change the way in which power operated 'below the edifice of law and sovereignty' (Cohen and Arato 1994, 257). This realisation prompted urgent social mobilisation, which was made even more desperate when former members of the community flaunted their newfound wealth and status.

These illustrations of subaltern mobilisations reveal a glimpse of politics driven by a realisation of a life without political significance, a 'bare life' that functions as a constitutive element of non-being and being, a 'zone of indistinction' between man and beast (Agamben 1998). Two layers and conceptions of politics we can identify in contemporary South Africa, one working with and through the formal channels, the other expressed through informal strategies and mass mobilisations. They feed off each other and often interact, and they cannot be adequately understood within the framework of 'democratic politics' (at least, in the paradigm of liberal democracy). The anxious, uncertain, intermediate role of the national middle class is crucial to this development, as is the equally uncertain status of national liberation movements (NLMs) that claim radical independence from colonial domination only to find themselves in severely compromised transitions. In both cases, the gap between the radical ideologies and the inherited states' precarious capacities has not prepared this class well for internal criticism. A crisis of the national modern is their lot.

National-modern crisis: the 'intermediary class', national liberation and compromise

Monday, 13 February 2014: the first day of the annual parliamentary session. Two helicopters circulate over Rondebosch and Newlands, the neighbourhoods housing the president, not too far from the parliamentary buildings in the Cape Town city centre. The main highway linking the southern suburbs of Cape Town to the city centre is closed during the busy midday commute and traffic is rerouted to Main Road, now congested for kilometres in both directions. After a long lunch, members of parliament and celebrity guests walk along the red carpet. President Jacob Zuma makes the

State of the Nation speech, reflecting the main theme of the ANC election campaign, that South Africa has 'a good story to tell', because it 'is a much better place to live' today than under Apartheid:

> Our message has been loud and clear. Twenty years of freedom and democracy have changed the face of our country. The last five years have further advanced change and a better life for all, especially the poor and the working class. Our country is a much better place to live in now than it was before 1994. The freedom-loving people of our country, led by the African National Congress, put an end to Apartheid, established a thriving constitutional democracy and laid a firm foundation for progress towards inclusive growth and prosperity. Indeed, we have a good story to tell (Zuma 2014).

Zuma dots all the '*i*'s and crosses the '*t*'s in the tired nationalist narrative. After three hundred years of colonial oppression, Fanon's predictions for and disappointment in this 'intermediary' class could not be more accurate for South Africa's nationalist elites. The pomp and pageantry associated with this class, as well as the fact that its ambitions are driven by self-interest and garnering recognition from the white power structure, is recognisable at all levels of society, symptoms of a 'wounded civilisation'.

Even established members of the political elite recognise the challenges posed and inadvertently express this crisis of the nationalist project. For example, almost two decades after the negotiated settlement, Winnie Madikizela-Mandela expressed her reservations regarding the democratic transition. In an interview with Nadira Naipaul reported in the *Evening Standard* (London), 8 March 2010, 'the mother of the nation' criticised her former husband for negotiating 'a bad deal for blacks' and appeasing the Apartheid leadership.

> I cannot forgive him for going to receive the Nobel [Peace Prize] with his jailer, [F. W.] de Klerk. Hand in hand they went. Do you think de Klerk released him from the goodness of his heart? He had to. The times dictated it, the world had changed, and our struggle was not a flash in the pan; it was bloody to say the least, and we had given rivers of blood. I had kept it alive with every means at my disposal (Naipaul 2010).

She subsequently denied having said that she found Mandela's willingness to negotiate with his former oppressors abhorrent. Patti Waldmeir also accepted that the past cannot and should not be forgotten, but she offered a different interpretation of the South African democratic transition (1998): 'Why did the Afrikaners do what so few ruling groups had ever done in history, voluntarily relinquish power?... Why did the Boers give it all away?' She ends her account with a powerful lesson:

But the future is another country that I cannot hope to visit. The present is quite extraordinary enough. For a girl who learned her race politics on the top of Tiger Stadium, South Africa was a dream impossibly come true. It was a powerful rebuke to the memories of my girlhood, a chance to do what South Africans had taught me: to liberate myself from my past (Waldmeir 1998, xiv).

Her personal revelation is also a national question. Is it possible for South African politics, with its violent legacies carved out of settler-colonial modernity, to 'liberate itself from' its past? Current political developments suggest not. Despite the dominance of the ANC's political system and general praise for the transition, the new government has found it difficult to deliver on the liberal democratic project of modernity. Regardless, Waldmeir's conclusion that whites gave up power is problematic, as relinquishing control of governing power or even of the state does not necessarily translate into fundamental shifts in power relations. She wrongly assumes that the 'old order' was defeated; a more pressing question may be what kind of victory the subaltern can claim.

The ANC does not see itself in the mould of an orthodox political party, but rather as a broad organisation for national liberation (Maharaj 2008). As a nationalist movement, it sought to bring about the liberation of oppressed people to enable a non-racial, non-sexist, democratic society; that was its party platform in the 1994 elections. While the advent of the democratic constitution established a critical beachhead, the tasks of liberation remained incomplete. There was a need to maintain the Tripartite Alliance, which had changed from the Congress movement in the 1950s, now composed of the ANC, SACP and Cosatu, that had mobilised resistance against white domination in the 1990s. The Tripartite Alliance, together with a broad spectrum of organisations, contributed towards a widely defined nationalist agenda. This diversity of paradigms and a broad conception of nationalism enabled the ANC to mobilise mass support against colonial power. This South African development of broad social mobilisation differs significantly from the predominance of decades-long military struggles after the mid-1960s in the rest of Southern Africa. Once in control of the state, the ANC defined its challenging tasks in national-modernist terms: 'nation-building', 'democratic institutional development', 'socio-economic development' and 'party system development' aimed at discouraging threats of racial and ethnic societal divisions.

But this paradigm has run aground. One explanation derives from the Southern African experience of the role of the national liberation movement (NLM) in establishing democratic societies. Marina Ottaway (1991), Henning Melber (2009) and Roger Southall (2003) concluded that NLMs are unlikely to establish democratic societies. They argue that, in their fight for liberation, NLMs develop undemocratic political cultures. Once in power, the NLM leadership promotes its own self-interests and reasserts the cultural patterns of anti-settler-colonial struggle, undermining state structures and democratic values. In this suspicious context, the nascent ruling party does not see its main goal as achieving democracy, but rather as making progress in the nationalist struggle. The struggle remains vaguely defined but revolves around reversing the power relationship between whites and blacks or the superiority-inferiority complex associated with settler-colonial rule.

Henning Melber (2009) presented a nuanced version of this argument. He began with the empirical observation that, in Southern Africa, where societies were historically established out of settler-colonial experiences, the dominant NLMs that became governments have found it impossible to establish robust democratic systems. He identified two types of discourses that coexist but are incorrectly thought to be the same: one associated with the struggle against oppressive colonial regimes and the other associated with democracy. The notion of 'the armed struggle', in particular, produces a conception of politics of 'winners and losers'. The prevailing belief is that victory is all-important—there is an inbuilt reluctance to compromise—and the individual's personal values and morality should be suppressed in favour of the collective and final outcomes. He contrasted this with 'democratic discourse', in which the key priorities are the 'search for the common good', compromise and 'the search for consensus, in pursuit of the public good' (Melber 2009, 45).

Given that all Southern Africans were involved in struggles against settler colonialism, Melber emphasised that this kind of conflict produced its own dynamic; in other words, these violent systems promoted counter-violence. Emphasis was placed on military-like guerrilla networks that created particular cultural patterns: power was rigidly hierarchical, patronage networks between patrons (commanders) and their supporters (ordinary members) became entrenched, the conditions of endemic resource shortages encouraged 'rough survival strategies and techniques', and these legacies of armed struggle took root and were 'permanently nurtured' (Melber 2009, 453). Such deprivations motivate the postcolonial elite to act no differently than their previous colonisers, using the resources of the state for themselves and effectively using the state to remain in power. They assume that the sacrifices they made in the resistance struggle would morally justify any rewards they receive once they are in control of the state. One is reminded of the famous response of Smuts Ngonyama, ANC's former head of communications, when he was asked about his involvement in a BEE deal: 'We did not struggle to be poor'.

In Angola, Mozambique, Zimbabwe, Namibia, and to a much lesser degree, South Africa, the dominant nationalist organisations participated primarily in armed warfare to overthrow minority white rule. Once in power, the nationalist elite immediately undertook to narrate the country's history from the perspective of the struggle for independence. Further, the new power holders marginalised the role of old nationalist rivals and undermined the influence of new opposition groups, aiming to secure an uncontested legitimacy. As soon as serious competitors arrived on the scene, the dominant ruling organisation assumed a 'war footing', demonising the opposition as fronts promoting imperialist interests. The new situation was likened to the old independence struggle. This has transpired in Namibia with the opposition Rally for Democracy and Progress (RDP), in Zimbabwe with the Movement for

Democratic Change (MDC), in Mozambique with the Mozambican National Resistance (RENAMO), and in South Africa with the Congress of the People (COPE) and, more recently, the Economic Freedom Fighters (EFF).

Zimbabwe, Namibia and South Africa have different dynamics than Angola and Mozambique because their conflicts ended differently. They ended colonialism through negotiated settlements, leaving many issues unresolved. In South Africa, the negotiated outcomes remain particularly tenuous. Its nationalist elite regularly evokes the idea that the 'struggle' continues, in waves that vaguely correlate to the intensity of societal criticism faced by the dominant party as well as its perception of the security of its hold on the state. Melber is unsure about South Africa because it both fits and differs from the regional pattern; he believes it is too early to arrive at firm conclusions. While the political culture of members who came from exile to join government tend to fit the regional model, most in the ANC came from political backgrounds (e.g., the internal civil revolts of the 1980s or long imprisonment terms in Apartheid jails) with no direct experience of clandestine exile politics. The leading parties thus have different cultures and attitudes towards democratic politics (Melber 2009).

The settler-colonial dynamic and legacies make the subaltern mass in South Africa a politically significant figure in politics because it's permanently mobilisable, at least for the purposes of the nationalist middle class. Any opposition party, especially with even tenuous cultural ties to white citizens, is viewed as illegitimate and a possible threat to the security of the new order. When black parties oppose government, they are often discredited by the leading party with accusations of standing up for the former white minority. The enduring dominance of whites in the major economic and cultural institutions comes in part from their historical ties to the former colonial powers. The dominance of these countries in the international system makes available a discourse that targets a potential scapegoat. Much political tension comes from blacks asserting political dominance but not hegemony; the ideological, cultural and aesthetic realms remain illusive. This serves as a worrying reminder to the black middle class of its own weakness, in that as a promoter of modernity it cannot lay claim to be its authentic subject or unchallenged representative. Societies emerging out of settler-colonial histories face so many legacies that unblemished modernist discourses are not available for new ruling elites. The reminders of the past are always available in the present. Unless elites make Herculean efforts to move beyond the serviceable and the instrumental, and also distance themselves from reminders of the painful past that they think will bring short-term gains with the popular subaltern mass, a democratic discourse of government and opposition cannot easily settle in a place found legitimate by both sides.

This thesis about NLMs and democracy has been challenged by assertions that the empirical evidence is not sufficiently overwhelming or entirely lacking. The existence of the modern United States refutes the claims that a war of national liberation cannot produce democratic institutions. Further, organisations like the ANC had many components, not just armed wings. A minority of the ANC's total membership were in exile, and only a smaller number of them were active combatants in the military side of the organisation. According to Tom Lodge (1992), in the mid-1980s, at the height of its exile years and when thousands of young people joined its ranks, only four thousand of the nine thousand–ten thousand ANC members were associated with the military. The majority of new recruits to the armed wing joined following the experiences of the 1976/77 Soweto revolt. That period was strongly influenced by Black Consciousness (BC), with its emphasis on popular mobilisation and identity politics. Moreover, the ANC assigned a considerable percentage of its exiled members to do organisational work in democratic countries, an experience that would have influenced their politics. It is inappropriate to lump all NLMs together, Raymond Suttner argues, because they differ significantly in terms of the length of time they operated, the ideologies that they espoused (Marxist, radically nationalist, ethnic nationalist and so on), the kinds of political activity that they engaged in (for example, operating in the open or clandestinely, adopting civil protest or armed struggle). Other differences include their social bases of support and organisational techniques: mass activity to prepare for revolution or negotiation, extensive organisational structures or narrow and controlled institutions, a loose or close-knit relationship with followers, and forming alliances or refusing to engage with other social movements (Suttner 2004).

To understand the complexity of the ANC, it must be acknowledged that its old heritage includes both democratic and undemocratic institutional practices. Talking about its undemocratic practices does not mean focusing only on its armed struggle. It also repressed critical opposition inside its ranks, detained members who reported torture, crushed two mutinies in military camps in Angola and Tanzania (Shubin 2008) and violently attacked potential competitors, such as Inkatha and the BC groups (Murray 1987). Suttner has a problem with explanations that emphasise how the anticolonial struggle is waged; rather, he argues, it is important to appreciate that settler colonialism and its violence have a bearing on nationalism and other countercultures. It is impossible to overthrow settler colonialism without a degree of violence, yet this same violence, according to these explanations, ultimately 'prevents' democratic outcomes. It becomes an ouroboros, the ancient mythical snake that eats its own tail.

The crisis of the national-modern and civil and political society

Why are there increasingly violent and uncontrolled protests in a country whose relatively peaceful democratic transition from Apartheid is touted as a great example? Can the regular occurrence of protests and instances of subaltern social mobilisation that are similar in form and character to the Marikana protest help make sense of the failing nationalist and democratic project in post-Apartheid South Africa?

The liberal democratic constitution functions more as an idea of the future, a discourse and a metaphor, than a serious empirical manifestation of modernity or outline of legal rules to regulate the polity. Nearly two decades after the celebrated negotiated settlement of the early 1990s, the past remains ever-present. Political malaise and a sense of disillusionment are widespread, in stark contrast to the periods immediately following the unbanning of nationalist organisations and then the first elections in 1994.

Two decades later, incessant public coverage of unethical politics among the political elite has taken its toll. The new political class is composed of participants in the black-nationalist struggle who were admired for their sacrifice and heroism but are now scorned and face public ridicule. Citizen complaints of bureaucratic inefficiencies and poor service plague everyday public administration, and many now expect that government services will be unfit for purpose. Passing legislation does not guarantee that laws will be effectively implemented. The media widely publicises conflicts among the political elite, who accuse and counter-accuse each other of corruption; though this contributes to a robust public sphere, it also promotes disillusionment and frustration. The dominant party faces an internal crisis: factionalism is rife, it is fed by an increasing reliance on state resources and the politics of patronage, and this is evident at all levels of the organisation.

The features of democratic politics in South Africa and the crisis of the nationalist project, I contend, require that the legacies of settler-colonial modernity be recognised—a modernity ushered through state violence, racialised capitalism and subjects whose identities thoroughly depend on relations with the Other. These legacies, like the type of resistance required to overcome them and the continued cultural and economic dominance of whites claiming to represent European modernity, continue to shape politics. The anxieties of the nationalist elite as an intermediary class contribute to the alienation of the popular groups that ambiguously draw on moral and tactical notions of anti-colonial struggle discourses, to register its recognition in democratic politics.

Civil society and democracy: beyond the Western standard Conventional democratic theory and political science conceive of civil society as the site for dispute regulation. From the seventeenth-century, when social contract theorists understood civil society as that all-important area separate from and suspicious of state encroachment, it has been considered necessary for democratic freedom. Thomas Hobbes, John Locke and even Jean-Jacques Rousseau viewed civil society as that space within which citizens interact with each other with no constraints and which those citizens define according to their understanding of when s/he reasonably feels interfered with. This is similar to the manner in which Isaiah Berlin defines freedom as non-interference where a 'frontier must be drawn between the area of private life and that of public authority' (Berlin 2000, 124).

In the democratisation literature on civil society, the term 'civil society' covers an enormous range of attributes. In Nelson Kasfir's (1998) summary of the key theories, the core is easier to identify—the concept includes some state aspects, reciprocity through social solidarity or economic exchanges, self-interested rules and voluntary organisations—but the periphery is fuzzy. For instance, according to Michael Bratton, 'In its broadest reach, civil society can be conceived as including all public, political non-state activity occurring between government and family' (Kasfir 1998, 4). Michael Walzer's definition is 'the space of uncoerced human associations and also the set of relational networks—formed for [the] sake of family, faith, interest and ideology—that fill that space'. Others (Kasfir 1998, 4) include 'civil activity', such as strikes, boycotts, riots and demonstrations. Alfred Stepan (1988, 3–4) defines it as an 'arena where manifold social movements ... and civic organisations ... attempt to constitute themselves in an ensemble of arrangements so that they can express themselves and advance their interests'. Stepan divides these formal and informal organisations into seven categories by purpose and activity (economic, cultural, informational, interest based, developmental, issue-oriented and civic) and excludes those that are not 'voluntary, self-generating, autonomous and rule-abiding'. He sees organisations of civil society as different from other social groups in five respects: they are public and state-related, have specific interests and partialness, and are not attempting to win power (see Stepan 1988). From this brief overview, it can be gleaned that there is only vague agreement on what civil society is (space outside structures of the state) but little consensus on what is part of civil society and what is not. Thus this concept must be applied to the developing world with caution, and to settler-colonial societies in particular with careful analysis and rich empirical evidence.

Kasfir (1998) criticizes recent third wave democracy literature on Africa for its generalised view, based on a small group of non-state associations rather than the history of the individual societies, that civil society is the key instrument for the consolidation of democracy. He identifies the following problematic assumptions: that civil society will resist authoritarian states and support democratic regimes; that the most effective means of controlling government abuses is to build civil society; and that supposedly civil society performs a variety of tasks that contribute towards democracy. These claims lead to exaggerated possibilities for democracy in Africa, giving rise to the false belief that authoritarian states have been weakened and are 'less dominant than it was previously thought to be' (Kasfir 1998, 2). This literature further selects particular types of 'new' associations believed to act as sources of political pressure, yet it is not clear that they do create political democratic agendas. International donors favour these non-government associations because the donors want to build a European/American type of civil society (Kasfir 1998, 2–3). Kasfir debunks the notions that civil society is becoming fully fledged, as per the West, and that this naturally bodes well for the stability of electoral democracy in Africa.

But a concept of civil society drawn from the 'Western experience' cannot be applied to the Third World, and especially to countries that are products of settler-colonial modernity. Sudipta Kaviraj and Sunil Khilnani gave a strong warning:

> Thus, it is hardly surprising that with the coming of the modern state—with its enormous potentialities of collective action and equally vast dangers—this conceptual language began to be used outside the West. The historical result has been a strange paradox—which political scientists analysing non-Western societies cannot ignore. Actual political processes in the Third World are mostly very different from

political life in the West, yet strangely, the language used to describe, evaluate and express the experiences of politics are the same everywhere. For historical reasons nearly all societies of the Third World speak, as far as politics is concerned, a Western language. It is the language which identifies states and civil societies, speaks of bureaucracies, political parties, parliaments, expresses political desires for the establishment of liberal, Communist or socialist political forms, and evaluates political systems in terms of democracy or dictatorship (Kaviraj and Khilnani 2001, 5).

Understanding civil society: Gramsci's important influence The mainstream state–civil society literature conceives of civil society in opposition to the state and as a means through which civilians increase their power with respect to state authority. This understanding, as is shown above, presents the state as imposing and domineering, whereas it conceives of civil society as the space and arena of freedom and autonomous citizen activity. Following Gramsci, I propose that we view civil society as related to the state while rejecting A) the notion of oppositional separation and B) the ensuing necessity of examining how civil society was historically formed and investigating the ways in which its practices and culture were constructed through consent, conflict and ambiguity. Historically, Kaviraj and Khilnani emphasise, civil society consists of 'sets of practices and possibilities' (2001).

Gramsci (1971) approaches the 'separation' of state and civil society cautiously, emphasising the 'mediations' between different spheres of capitalist society that organise power to keep the ruling class in power and to prevent radical social transformation. Because his focus is on relations of power and how they operate, Gramsci is much more helpful for our analysis. His understanding of power is preoccupied less with the repressive apparatus of the state (the army and police) and more with what makes the 'lived experience' of the oppressed and exploited a battlefield etched into its subjectivity that instils into them a common-sense, 'taken for granted' perspective. This shift opens up for analysis the institutions of civil society and its settled rules and practices, methods of stabilising power relations in society. Of course, he never assumes these relations of domination to be static, and he approaches them as always potentially contestable 'moments' in an ongoing fight. The everyday practices and the institutions of civil society that the dominated take for granted as 'common-sense' and as part of everyday life can be contested, and the battle itself accounts for the 'fragmentary' and complex consciousness of the subalterns.

A racialised 'civil society' in South Africa The weakness of institutions that emphasise elite culture (Putnam 1993), state patrimonialism (Clapham 1985) and demands for increased institutionalisation (Huntington 1968) explain both the desire and failure to establish orderly civic relations—the bedrock of middle-class values—as the dominant and official political culture in South Africa. Yet they are also why conventional civil society remains the standard and political society is defined so narrowly that it is reduced to electoral and party politics. Focusing on patterns of politicisation—on the collective mass subject of democratic politics in South Africa—allows civil society to be understood differently.

Blacks in settler-colonial situations were never truly part of civil society; as non-beings, they were the targets of the state, which used violence or its threat to regulate life and death. The colonised blacks of South Africa had no protected sphere; even their most private zone was potentially vulnerable. The state desired to control black people and their bodies—their movements, interactions, thoughts and even self-conceptions. In such circumstances of racial oppression, the absence of threats (including state surveillance) from the 'private domains' of consciousness creates a dynamic of outward/inward behaviour in public and private domains. Around the turn of the century, W. E. B. Du Bois (2008) identified this experience of African-Americans as 'double consciousness'. After World War II, Fanon (1963), Biko (2005) and Paul Gilroy (1993) further developed it by offering political interpretations of the complexities of agency of blacks who had to look at themselves through the eyes of others in a never-ending internal struggle.

In settler-colonial states, the discourses of the dominant and dominated encounter each other in schools, churches, universities, newspapers, popular journals, the law, drama and sports activities, and everyday situations. Technically, though, we cannot really speak of civil society in its European sense. The idea of 'radical difference' officially operating in settler-colonial situations meant that the capacity to reason necessary for participation in civil society was absent, given that blacks were treated as 'non-human' or 'subhuman'. In South Africa, the organisation of civil institutions on the basis of 'race' and ethnicity makes it reasonable to speak of perhaps 'two civil societies' (Ekeh 1975). Historically, in South Africa, settler colonialism divided the key institutions of civil society along lines of 'race': white churches and black churches, jobs for whites and jobs for blacks, schools for whites and schools for blacks, etc. However, and astonishingly, studies of third wave democracy ignore the specificity of the settler-colonial situation. The belief that democracies require civil society to be 'consolidated', as in Europe, denies the peculiarities of settler colonialism, as well as the interstices of race, class and gender in the production of subjects and the power distribution of such subjects in the social hierarchy. While some might go so far to recognise two civil societies under Apartheid in South Africa, none have fully unpacked the role of race as a 'master narrative' precisely because law and its exceptions are an intrinsic and 'normal' feature of politics under settler colonialism. The sovereign does not suspend the law to protect the polity in exceptional moments of history, as Agamben wrote. Instead, the state continuously targets black life in general, which is experienced within the law but 'without rights' and outside of civil society.

Empirically, the area of civil society historically became the domain in which the organisations of nationalism operated; especially after World War II, these organisations wanted to be closely associated with the awakening mass popular subject, where black nationalist elites saw themselves as representing the area of 'indigenous' culture

(Chatterjee 1999, 10). Popular sectors rapidly became politically aware in the 1970s due to the influence of BC, and schools, universities, factories, churches and sports bodies became sites of organised resistance. This was spurred in the 1980s by the United Democratic Front (UDF) and National Forum coalitions. In the early 1990s, this popular pressure from below, driven by a politicised collective subject, enabled the negotiated settlement between government and nationalist elites. The compromises produced the liberal democratic political system currently in place. However, the mass subaltern subject continues to target sources of power that do not recognise the political significance of its black bodies, as in Agamben's *homo sacer*, and it thus constitutes political society and extraordinary politics.

I argue that settler colonialism has an abiding influence on civil and political society under electoral democracy. Chatterjee's (2004) reworking of Gramsci's state-civil society analysis to understand subaltern-elite politics in the Third World makes sense of competing modes of politics in South Africa. I agree with Chatterjee that civil society is constituted by a mode of politics that is framed largely within rules and that privileges constitutional and legal discourse. His argument that subaltern groups in the developing world engage in action *to be recognised* does apply to South Africa. However, it is not necessarily a vulgar form of protest, as Chatterjee assumed, but a concerted, conscious effort to articulate a meaningful politics of mass mobilisation in the political terrain that uses tactics (often subjugated knowledges) from the 1980s. This idea builds on Sydney Tarrow's (1994) interpretation of Charles Tilly's (1993) theory of *repertoires* of contention, which includes historical lessons, accumulated experience and prevailing standards of rights and justice. Although the political elite attempts to demobilise subaltern-inspired politics to *domesticate* subalterns according to a different political rationality that is confined to civil society, these attempts have proven unsuccessful. Instead, there are two different but related modes of politics, operating on two terrains, with two registers (civil and political society), which amount to a social formation of domination without hegemony. I contend that the particular manifestations of these elements of the political sphere in South Africa have their roots in settler-colonialist modernity; settler colonialism thus continues to define the post-Apartheid system and frames the constitution of state and civil society.

The recurring possibility of violent clashes and discourses of anger characterises the public sphere. It is not uncommon to witness or read about threatening and aggressive language being used between parties and/or key political actors; recently parliament has become known for such engagement between the dominant ANC and some opposition parties, like the Economic Freedom Fighters (EFF). Direct attacks on key aspects of democratic politics, such as the media, courts, judges and state-associated 'Chapter 9' institutions provided for in the constitution to 'enhance democracy', are widespread. Political parties, especially the ruling party, stretch constitutional rules to protect its own members. Demonstrations often turn violent, with protesters relying on old anti-Apartheid tactics like burning tyres, throwing stones, constructing rudimentary roadblocks and aggressively presenting demands. In the public sphere, subalterns' protests for rights or to support opposing factional leaders often bear the brunt of violent police responses. These mobilisations of the poor ought to be interpreted also as demands for recognition

Following Chatterjee and Gramsci, these developments, or better, these modes of politics, can be understood in terms of the 'terrains' of civil and political society. They partially overlap with race and class: the black and white middle classes cluster around civil society, whereas the subaltern masses aggregate and articulate their interests in political society. The types of engagements and articulations differ: the former unreservedly value the regulatory rules of the system, whereas the latter rely on techniques to exhibit force and strength, so the demonstration and symbolic discourse of anger matters more. The historic causes for tension of this relationship, which is suggestive of Guha's idea of domination without hegemony (1997), include the structural legacies of the violence of settler-colonial modernity, which were left unanswered in the democratic transition. In the official and dominant discourse of change, the nationalist elite represents the democratic transition as victorious, 'the struggle won', rather than as the outcome of significant compromises. Finally, the assumptions that were intrinsic to 'the struggle', such as the interests of the national elite coinciding with those of the masses, did not begin unravelling until the Marikana massacre in 2012 made it abundantly clear.

To summarise, contemporary South African democracy is contradictory. Rather than being driven by formal rules established in the political system, as predicted, politics is characterised by increased social mobilisations of disgruntled citizens, who rely on mass action to articulate their grievances and obtain recognition from formal political structures. The deepening economic inequality, which is historic but has been recently exacerbated by neo-liberal state policy and the ANC's factionalisation cannot be isolated from the broader structural features of settler-colonial modernity and the struggle to overcome it. The political alienation of the subaltern masses, a key manifestation of the nationalist project running aground, has encouraged a mass politics in which political society, rather than civil society, has become the main terrain for expressing conflict 'when the state can influence the life chances of many social groups' (Kohli 1990, 10). In short, the idea of nationalist-modernity represented by the ANC and nationalist elites has been unable to control the subaltern masses in the terms of the old nationalist discourse and archive of techniques, and a different 'moral register' between elites and masses has come into play.

The argument expanded: national-modern crisis and two modes of politics In South Africa, political society presents a different terrain, one that hosts conflict, mostly over the distribution of resources, the recognition of rights of historically subjected groups and the expression of subjugated culture, and relies on a violent, desperate and threatening discourse. Inequality is increasing, and the majority feels frustrated as the white and black middle class flaunt their wealth. Elective democracy creates the conditions for increased social mobilisation; in South Africa, it is also influenced by the ANC and the dominant discourse, which presents the state as the source of social improvements and population welfare: the 'pastoral' state and biopolitical power together, as Foucault (1980; 1994) wrote.

The poor have constituted *political society* as their terrain, through which they seek to articulate their concerns. Chatterjee described this as bringing into the 'hallways and corridors of power some of the squalor, ugliness and violence of popular life' (Chatterjee, 2004, 74). The daily violence, material deprivations and alienation of the black subject under settler-colonial modernity cannot be articulated within a purely rational mode of politics or the legal discourse of civil society. To quote Chatterjee again, 'if one truly values the freedom and equality that democracy promises, then one cannot imprison it within the sanitised fortress of civil society' (Chatterjee, 2004, 74).

The ANC finds itself caught between having to accept and encourage this kind of political engagement and/or domesticating it within the confines of civil society and a political discourse based on law and order. In the new democracy, the ANC encourages mobilisation when it suits its own or factionalist interests but domesticates subalterns through demobilisation. No doubt, the persistent factionalism that plagues it and its decline as the main integrating institution with its democratic discourse of rights influence this volatile politics. This has been exacerbated by the political elite's drive to accumulate the material rewards of public office and the consequent weakening of key political institutions as party and state collapse in the formal political system.

The political practice of the nationalist elite has moved dramatically from a politics of community service and values associated with popular struggle and self-sacrifice to self-seeking special interests. This has inevitably made key political institutions weak or even ineffective, including the ANC; significantly, the new political ruling class is unable to establish hegemony. Historically, the nationalist elite highly valued the state and its dominating role in society (given its organised violence and resource capacity), but the state and its new political class have been crucially unable to garner the 'spontaneous consent' of the popular classes on the basis of its nationalist-modern project. This access to the state by the nationalist elite takes place in the context of popular mobilisations from 1976 through the 1980s, which first enabled this elite to take control of the new democratic state.

Kohli accurately identified these two key factors, the central organising role of the state and the opening up of democratic space to historically marginalised groups, as 'the patterns of politicisation that result when the state can influence the life chances of many social groups and when this state is accessible via democratic politics' (1990, 11). They are especially relevant to contemporary South African civil and political society, in which different groups have influence over political outcomes and access to state resources. The 'patterns of politicization' (Kohli 1990) that came with democracy are apparent in the daily confrontations between the state and the poor majority. These confrontations occur in an arena of contestation over power and unfulfilled promises, mostly to claim political significance beyond bare life, and they are influenced by the assumption that the democratic state is the main instrument for social and economic improvement and upward mobility. That was also a dominant message to the popular sectors during the nationalist struggle, and it contributed to the formation of the mass popular subject. The nationalist leadership portrayed the state as the main target for 'capture', so its replacement with a national-democratic state was the struggle's goal. The nationalist elite aimed to mobilise the masses with the moral agenda of fighting an unjust and oppressive state. They also expected them to continue following their lead and confining themselves to a political rationality, which Mbembe (2012) identified as narrowly defined as 'the acceptable' and permissible normative order once state political power changed hands.

The nationalist middle class, in part due to its structural weaknesses and realisation that it lacks universal cultural power, is almost compelled to approach objective structures and impersonal institutions as mere strategic tools for instrumental use. In order to retain state power, nationalist leaders inevitably gravitated towards mobilisational politics and promised state favours in electoral periods, aiming to strengthen the link to their followers. This mode of engagement, in which popular support is filtered through charisma and loyalty to individual personalities and/or factions in the party, encourages personalised forms of political interactions. However, power-holders suspect and denigrate those outside the circle, contributing to the uncivil discourses that have become increasingly prominent within the dominant party and its relationship to its supporters.

This politics of social mobilisation gives political society, as defined above, more prominence. At least for subalterns, it becomes the main terrain or arena in which political battles are fought, which in turn makes civil society less important for the majority of the population. All the while, civil society continues to be valued by the established and emerging middle classes. Committed as they are to an abstract 'constitutionalism', they remain hopeful that a civic culture will eventually take root in the society. Using the avenues they have available, they condemn the 'unruliness' of the popular sectors. 'The mob' shows disrespect for individual rights and flouts the rules of acceptable civil action. This rhetoric is tricky. The middle-class's protests about subaltern behaviour show that they are aware of the ever-present risk of slippage between condemning such mass actions and being accused of fuelling the spectre of racism and justifying class privilege.

The situation in South Africa is complicated by the fact that social mobilisation for political ends—in other words, demanding recognition and resources from the state—is expressed in violent and threatening protests. Putnam's notion of the level of trust and social capital that is intrinsic to civil society is at best superficial (1993). In the trenches of political society, as Chatterjee observed in the case of India, the poor and marginalised groups who are desperate to access goods and services from government 'must succeed in applying the right pressure at the right places in the governmental machinery. This would frequently mean the bending or stretching of rules, because existing procedures have historically worked to exclude or marginalise them' (Chatterjee 2004, 66). The divided ANC, driven by a politics of patronage and corruption yet needing desperately to control the historically marginalised but political conscious majority (whose lives have been materially devastated by historical legacies of deprivation and worsened by unfriendly national and global economic policies post-1994), makes a democratic civic tradition all the more elusive in South Africa.

Theoretical apparatus

In my aim of understanding the contradictions inherent in the liberal democratic moment in relation to South Africa's long history of a politics of 'race consciousness'—i.e., settler-colonial modernity—I have been drawn to an eclectic range of sources and brought together key ideas drawn from Fanon, Gramsci, Chatterjee, Scott, Arendt, Foucault and Agamben. However, the argument is not strictly linear. The work of Gramsci and Chatterjee help to identify and interpret key features of post-Apartheid democratic politics and Scott is used to give it a name or label it as a crisis of the national-modern project of postcolonial societies, while using Fanon, Arendt, Foucault and Agamben assist in the expansion of the 'explanation' of settler-colonial modernity. To understand empirical trends in post-1994 politics Chatterjee's interpretation of Gramsci allowed me to identify two modes of politics, divided broadly along class and race lines. To explain the important role of settler-colonial modernity in producing this dual politics under liberal democracy I have relied on the work of Fanon, Arendt, Foucault, and Agamben.

I utilise Fanon's analysis of power in Manichean society to understand the indelible settler-colonial markings of South African society. He identified two important implications: the first is that settler colonial modernity produces subjects who have to deal with permanent 'incompleteness' in a world dominated by the idea of the 'whole subject'; the second is that the nationalist bourgeoisie as a weak product of setter colonialism will be unable on its own, or with only a 'half-hearted' commitment to the masses, to succeed in its anti-colonial project. Because of its ambiguous position in settler-colonial society, the national middle class is placed in a complex relationship with the subalterns—its desire and need for modern education cuts it off from the people and historical culture—and yet it is unable to overthrow colonial rule without mass social mobilisation. Both legacies are evident in South African politics but have not been adequately addressed.

To understand the nationalist struggle, Chatterjee developed Gramsci's ideas to draw attention to the project of the nationalist elite, which is to 'win' the consent of the masses to represent and control them. The degree to which this hegemony is achieved has a bearing on the nationalist-modern project. Starting with this premise, Chatterjee proposed that in the opposing domains of civil society (occupied by the middle classes) and political society (the domain of the subalterns) a generalised Third World experience accounting for the complexities of politics is manifest. This framework helps to understand the politics of the collective mass subject under liberal democratic conditions. In an earlier section of this chapter, I drew heavily on Gramsci's conception of civil society in the broad organisation of power in capitalist society to present a descriptive and analytical account of civil society in South Africa under settler-colonial conditions, then during the reorienting of civil society in nationalist resistance, and finally under democratic conditions today.

David Scott's (1999) idea of the crisis of the national-modern project in Jamaica has contributed to this explanation. He expands upon the Fanonian idea that the failures of the nationalist bourgeoisie produce deep political alienation from the masses. In his analysis of Jamaican post-independence politics, Scott explains the erosion of the taken-for-granted leadership of the political arena by the educated middle class. From the time of the national struggle, mass support had given credence to the nationalist-modern project and to its values of progress and political modernity. The endeavour to 'catch up' to Western modernity, which was assumed to be the standard, also reflected the desire to promote 'an enlightened, humanist, and morally and socially reforming modernity'. The socialist ideals and humanist alternative emphasis of the Bandung moment of 1955, in which Third World revolutionaries articulated 'an ethos of egalitarianism and social justice, and a faith in its own basic reasonableness and decency', represented the radical version of this nationalist-modern project (Scott 1999, 191). When promises of the national project proved illusive in Jamaica, the masses broke with the cultural strictures cherished by the educated middle class and articulated a national-popular culture reflective of their desperate social and material conditions.

The liberal nationalist-modern project built itself upon a cultural repertoire of its own parochial colonised middle-class values, which Fanon analysed so profoundly. As the masses found their lives becoming more precarious and marginalised, due in part to globalised neo-liberalism and the effects of structural adjustment programs imposed by nationalist leaders, the 'national-popular' sectors identified with alternative cultural values, thus causing 'anxiety' among the middle classes. Typically, and following a long history of class division, the middle classes of modernity (and particularly settler modernity) find their national-popular sectors losing their 'moral code' by behaving in ways considered 'debased' and uncouth. This is similar to, and not too distant from, Chatterjee's point about the masses in the domain of political society: they 'bring into the hallways and corridors of power some of the squalor, ugliness and violence of popular life' (2004, 74).

Rather than seek to understand these patterns through the perspective of the middle classes and their anxiety about confronting a more volatile and uncontrollable majority post-independence, I trace elements of subaltern political alienation from a liberal democratic modernist project from the very beginning of nationalist struggle. A pattern in the South African case is the sustained effort of the national middle class to impose a political rationality on a reluctant and mostly suspicious subaltern sector faced with a dominant white society that also claims to represent (different) versions of modernity. The relationship in struggle discourses involved a constant back-and-forth about domestication and loss of control between the national middle class and subalterns, which suggested a middle class anxiety about its leadership of the subalterns and its claims to represent the nation.

The recurrent 'poo wars' (Robins 2013) of 2013–2015 between state structures and poor residents over access to proper toilets, which illustrate countless conflicts about human dignity, are difficult to ignore and open up questions around bare life, political life and political power. The work of Agamben (1998) is indispensible for understanding the politics of bare life, which is intrinsic to liberal democratic modernities, but it is made especially visible in post-settler-colonial societies like South Africa. Agamben did not reduce the crisis to the collective culture of the middle classes, conservative neo-liberal economic trends, the implementation of reforms and or completion of the liberal democratic modernist promise. Instead, he proposed that modernity's 'totalitarian features' and the ever-present possibility of death are neither exceptional nor openly sanctioned but features of liberal modernity that are 'excluded/included' grey areas permanently at its core. The idea of the politics of bare life in *homo sacer* (Agamben 1998) resonates strongly with the current political conjuncture in South Africa. The front pages of newspapers are filled with death and struggles over basic conditions for sustaining life. It also complements the theoretical framework, from the settler-colonial analysis of Fanon to the elements of Chatterjee and Scott on the crisis of the national-modern.

By going back to Plato and Aristotle in Western political thought, Agamben (1998) identified how the Western political philosophy tradition separated 'bare life' (*zoe*) from the good life (*bios*) and focused exclusively on the latter. He considered this an ambiguous division whose conceptual tension has haunted society ever since, arguing that bare life is always both excluded and included in modern understandings of the political community. According to Agamben's reading of the dominant Western tradition of political thought, the exclusion of the idea of bare life is necessary for its understanding of the good life; the *polis* always required an unacknowledged Other to substantiate the concept of the good society. Agamben wrote that Plato and Aristotle did not concern themselves much with 'the simple natural life' but examined 'how we should live'. Agamben found that this concern with the ideal life has been a major theme of Western philosophy; Hobbes, Locke, Rousseau, Machiavelli, Hegel and Marx all addressed it. The social contract theorists left bare life to the state of nature, before the proper formation of the political community.

Foucault (1990) and Arendt (1986) broke with the exclusion of bare life from traditional political thought by bringing it into their analysis of modern power and its operation. Agamben observed that they recognised this exclusion but did not integrate it into their philosophies and that Foucault did not consider his reliance on Arendt. In his studies of modern power, Foucault thought it best to describe modern politics as biopolitics because natural life was no longer outside the focus of power but central to its exercise in disciplinary discourses. Governmentality aims to regulate systematically whole populations (totalising procedures) and target individuals' micro-behavior (individuating bodies) so that they 'self-police' according to societal moral codes, especially of sexuality. Arendt addressed 'bare life' in her studies on modern labour, focusing on the life of work and its links with biological life. Her analysis of the 'refugee problem' in the period before and during World War II pointed to the absolute vulnerability of 'stateless' persons, left without the protection of the law due to the modern state system. She explained the failure of states to conform to the values of the Rights of Man to protect and give sanctuary to refugees. The focus on political significance, the preservation of the rights of persons as citizens and the focus of the state meant that 'life' itself outside this discourse has neither meaning nor protection and individuals were left vulnerable to death. The meaning of 'bare life' has been historically undermined and excluded from the modern value system.

Agamben thus introduced the figure of *homo sacer* to denote the extreme Other. *Homo sacer* was defined in Roman law as a man who was so vulnerable, whose life precariously bordered on death, and that he could be killed—but whose killer could not be prosecuted. Today, it refers to a person with no practical rights; all she has is her bare life, which is not valued, insecure and open to attack and abuse. Agamben applies this complete vulnerability to the concentration camp inmate, and, following Arendt, to the modern-day refugee. In Agamben's detailed and complicated argument, where bare life functions as a 'state of exception', he is driven to the troubling conclusion that modern society makes every man 'potentially *homo sacer*'.

This term can also be applied to the politically excluded blacks of settler colonialism, who were historically not incorporated into the political community, who remained rights-less and whose bare life had no meaning inside colonial discourses. They were vulnerable to modern power from the time of conquest, and their status has hardly improved under liberal democracy, which now gives them the semblance of political significance. And in modern capitalist society, the citizen-person always has merely a semblance of political significance. The term encapsulates the condition of subalterns in South Africa, who live on the margins of society in squalid informal squatter camps and townships. Under democratic conditions, South Africa's *homo sacer* battle daily against vulnerability; hence extraordinary politics is normalised.

The social mobilisations—against 'foreign-born' Africans, competition for material goods, demanding basic services such as electricity, housing, sanitation, water and health care—can be understood as the vulnerable, quasi-human *homo sacer* demanding political significance. They have become more desperate because the new perpetrators are fellow blacks of the middle class who historically preached solidarity against settler-colonial domination. It partly explains why the demonstrations invariably demand recognition, from calling officials to receive memoranda of demands to renewing previously legitimate actions of cultural struggle (burning tyres, throwing stones and singing and dancing to articulate subjecthood), and enact a modern politics of the spectacle. This interpretation of current political modes under liberal democracy offers an alternative understanding, unrelated to the minimalist model that relies on rights and the law and is dominant in the mainstream democratisation literature.

Conclusion

In this chapter, I drew on four case studies that represent key trends in post-1994 democratic politics in South Africa. The demonstrations associated with *The Spear Painting*, Marikana strike, 'social delivery' protests and xenophobic attacks point to two different modes of politics: 'normal' politics that follow the constitutional order and the extraordinary politics of subaltern mobilisation. Conventional approaches emphasise the role of civil society as the foundation of a rationally deliberative democratic politics, but they overlook that politics reliant on social mobilisation stem from 'uncritical solidarities' from South Africa's settler-colonial history. To understand the centrality of settler-colonial modernity and its influence on politics in South Africa, I proposed and followed a radically new theoretical framework that includes an eclectic range of sources, from Gramsci to Fanon to Agamben.

2| The limits of the conventional paradigm, modernity and South African democracy

The study of historical and contemporary South African politics is dominated by a political development discourse rooted in a broad modernisation paradigm. This perspective is inadequate because it under-appreciates the centrality of settler-colonial domination as a path towards modernity, which is the characteristic feature of the South African social formation. Drawing on critical scholarship that questions the European experience's role in the understanding of global modernity, this chapter highlights the key ideas that have strongly influenced the analysis of South African politics. In the first section, I examine the influence of modernisation discourse on third wave democracy, in which South Africa serves as a crucial case study. In the following section, I introduce and critically review the key approaches in the modernisation literature in terms of the post-World War II context and US imperial domination. This expands the concept of political development, which is the main theme of structural functionalism and modernisation revisionism in comparative politics. In the third section, I examine how deliberately omitting the specific features of settler-colonial modernity and assuming the unfolding of a universal process of liberal democracy in South Africa makes the modernisation paradigm inadequate. I conclude by presenting elements of a new critical framework to understand unfolding politics in South Africa.

South African democratic studies and the influence of modernisation theory

Studies of Apartheid legacies, the democratic transition and democratic consolidation are stamped by the conventional approaches of the modernisation paradigm. Media, politicians, journalists and analysts regularly refer to these categories of third wave democratisation literature, a discourse that was entirely absent in studies of South African politics prior to the 1990s. They serve as a new frame of reference for post-Apartheid politics and of modernisation discourses in the field of comparative politics. In this framework the experience of western Europe and North America serves as the template, 'democratic politics' is narrowly conceived to mean 'electoral practice' and emphasis given to economic-managerial notions of government, capitalist economic growth, political stability and liberal-individualist values.

More surprising is the strong but subtle influence of the post-World War II modernisation paradigm on third wave analysis and its promotion by the nationalist elite and the black and white middle class. It holds that South Africa follows the preferred model of change, in which moderate elites negotiate a political transition and institute a liberal political order. Given South Africa's past political order of entrenched racism, this was seen as a miracle. The new constitution recognises far-reaching individual as well as social rights, the latter atypical of many older democracies. When asked to share advice on democratic constitutional writing processes on a visit to Egypt in 2012, Associate Justice of the Supreme Court of the United States Ruth Bader Ginsberg angered American conservatives by suggesting that Egyptians emulate the South African constitution (Sacks 2012). The nature of the transition, the goals promised in the liberal vision and the enormous historical legacy of three centuries of systematic racism all assign the process of democratisation in South Africa a special place in third wave studies.

Since 1994, the discourse of third wave democratisation has replaced or been set uneasily alongside older discourses of the politics of Apartheid and resistance. Its literature, formal studies in disciplinary political science and comparative politics, exercises influence beyond the academy, framing processes through key concepts that move seamlessly from scholarly journals via the media to the public realm and eventually become regular political discourse. Fragments of the 'scholarly literature' that consider modernity as a linear progression through recognisable stages, which are often packaged in accessible popular beliefs, have been absorbed by 'common sense' worldviews. For instance, South African radio and TV often feature politicians and ordinary citizens who mention concepts such as 'democratic consolidation', 'democratic transition' and 'emerging democracy'. ANC politicians frequently retort 'We are not a banana republic', using this discourse as a standard of evaluation, and in 2014 Jacob Zuma appealed to Johannesburg residents who refused to pay e-tolls on city highways that 'We can't think like Africans in Africa generally. We're in Johannesburg' (Fabricius 2013).

Some claim that third wave discourse is scientific, neutral and objective. It is not. In the political sphere, it provides but one frame for understanding the world. Despite the advent of democracy, power relations between the state and its citizens, especially those traceable to the old regime, remain unchanged. Yet third wave discourse can ill afford to recognise continuity, as it depends on marking regime differences according to differences in the sources of legitimacy, not by power relations and everyday practices. For example, the labels 'a new democracy' and the 'new South Africa' ideologically emphasise the novelty of the present; they reduce continuities of political practices to 'subjugated knowledge' unless they have been ordered, monitored and promoted by the nationalist elite of the ANC. This is visible in the everyday policing of subalterns, which is sometimes even worse than that under Apartheid. Similarly, government departments continue to treat subalterns coldly and bureaucratically, as they did in the 'old South Africa'.

The third wave literature interprets South African politics within a linear narrative of political modernity: colonialism to Apartheid to democracy. In 1994, the road ahead was clearly mapped out. Post-World War II modernisation theorists praised capitalist modernity as the preferred model for the Third World, so post-Apartheid South Africa was seen to be joining (or maybe rejoining) the normal path. The 'promised land' entailed a complex bureaucratised state, capitalist production relations, vibrant civil society, 'modern' value orientations and the rule of law. In the last decade, in keeping with global trends, democratic elections and neo-liberal economic policies were added to this checklist. This narrative is increasingly, but still contradictorily, reflected in popular notions of political change.

Disciplinary knowledge, the post-World War II context and imperial power

The conventional understanding of post-Apartheid politics draws on third wave democracy studies that are traceable to earlier modernisation frameworks. These earlier managerial and economic approaches prescribed what ought to be done, established criteria for evaluation and explained failures to meet the goals of modernisation. In the human sciences, debates in the 1950s about the comparative method and scientific methodology created an aura of credibility while critics condemned them as ideological (Kesselman 1973; Sklar 1993; Mirsepassi 2000). The scientific pretence masked its promotion of US national and imperial interests by sustaining postcolonial dynamics through a discourse of development. The idea was that few would argue against 'development', a palatable goal of societies coming out of prolonged violent colonial rule, and that the intermediate postcolonial elite would be allies who managed independence and disciplined citizens.

From the mid-1950s, a desire for a systematic comparative study of Third World politics appeared (Bill and Hardgrave 1981). An early advocate, Harold Lasswell, spoke candidly of the role of intellectuals in the service of national and imperial interests:

> It is, I think, evident from available studies of intellectual history that when imperial powers are part of a civilization, rather than of a tribal or folk culture, they encourage some study of comparative government, even though some of the results may be buried in intelligence archives and not made available to private scholars (1968, 4).

After World War II the US's new status as the hegemon in the global imperial system motivated the comparative study of postcolonial societies. Expanding politics beyond legal institutions made sense and was strategic for imperial state interventions. Traditional political studies were biased towards power as sovereignty and not social forces, so the new pseudo-scientific approach explored the political behaviour of institutions and actors. This remedied omissions of the traditional focus on legal constitutionalism, for example examining why actors behaved in particular ways and anticipating how and why institutions changed over time, especially concerning the rise of fascist ideology in 'advanced' European civilisations.

Ironically, in foreshadowing Kuhn (1970), Lasswell claimed:

> Once the professional core of political science is established, there is no mystery about how it is maintained. Vested and sentimental interests are generated in its transmission. Since the overwhelming fraction of those who receive professional training do little subsequent research, once a given conception of comparative government is crystallized, it provides the frame of reference within which subsequent teaching and consultation is carried on (1968).

Lasswell anticipated Kuhn's seminal analysis (Kuhn 1970), which explains how paradigms reproduce themselves in what is now considered disciplinary reason and how normal science sustains itself. His appeal fell on sympathetic ears. A flood of formative articles reiterated his call for a new approach. The Social Science Research Council (SSRC) established the Committee on Comparative Politics in 1954. Gramsci's idea of traditional intellectuals accurately describes its aims to be 'objective and scientific' to serve national interests. The claim of scientific rigor and practical relevance shaped the structural-functionalist framework that it promoted, and the unipolarity of the world with the US hegemon accounts for the confidence with which younger comparative politics scholars applied it. Under the chairmanship of Gabriel Almond (Macridis 1963), the committee produced a conceptual, scientific framework for systematic comparative politics. It received extensive funding from government and private foundations (particularly the Ford Foundation) and served as Lasswell's 'institutional base', the 'central core' he considered important in the early organisation of disciplines. Riggs criticises the mutually beneficial relationship between corporate funders and 'political development', which rears its head only in advanced capitalism:

> In the context of the day, when international technical cooperation was widely hailed as a means to bring the advantages of modern industrial society to the relatively deprived countries of the Third World, the action-oriented word 'development' clearly opened more doors than did its near synonym, 'modernization', which carried more academic and behavioural connotations.... When it became a question of securing generous financial support for the preparation and publication of an important series of books, they were prepared to adapt (1981, 307).

Changes in the worldview from the imperial centre, which moved from Lisbon in the sixteenth-century to Madrid in the seventeenth, Paris in the eighteenth, London in the nineteenth and (during the high point of capitalist imperialism) to Washington, D.C., after World War II, reveals trends in the organisation and production of knowledge. The US recognised the strategic importance of acquiring knowledge about territories coming out of decades of colonialism (Riggs 1981). Huntington, an influential contributor to modernisation theory, admitted this: 'After World War II scholarship followed the flag into the Cold War against the Soviet Union and then into the expansion of the American presence in Asia, the Middle East, Latin America and Africa' (Huntington in Greenstein and Polsby 1975, 1). The newly independent states in

Africa, Asia and the Middle East became targets of US foreign policy, as America attempted to extend its sphere of influence beyond Latin America. If the older European powers relied on history and anthropological knowledge for imperial domination; the US relied on social science (Mazower 2013).

When countries in Africa, Asia and the Middle East were incorporated into the global capitalist system as independent states, political science became interested in political stability, especially its impact on similar political institutions in different country-contexts. The unit of analysis and the focal point was the European model of the state, considered as the institutional matrix of authority, the site of sovereignty and the regulator of the law between state and society and between citizens. The committee's promotion of the study of the Third World made it an attractive area of research. Newly established university departments in the social sciences offered funding from government agencies and corporate foundations to students, while faculty and graduate researchers found in the new independent states an expanded and ready-made 'laboratory' for research. As these societies established 'modern' state structures to transform themselves, a new literature about 'developing areas' grew rapidly in various disciplines.

The processes of how societies 'modernise' (in other words, how they 'progress' from 'backward' agricultural to industrial forms) were observable in the new states. It was believed that this modernisation would come through a series of revolutions or reforms, as it had in Europe, and that had been catalysed by key social groups, such as the capitalist class (according to Marx) or an emerging middle class (for liberals). To these influential paradigms of Enlightenment thought, liberalism and Marxism, the idea of 'progress', closely intertwined with 'civilisation', morphed in the post-World War II context into 'development'. The view that societies moved inevitably through what Walter Benjamin called 'empty homogenous time' toward higher stages was taken for granted. Today, people have a different understanding than their predecessors of the now-conventional Enlightenment idea of social and historical change as linear, progressive and willing itself forward on some foundational notion, for example Kantian reason, towards a perceivable end; Latour (1993) argued convincingly that the non-modern notion of cyclical change could make equal sense. Now, the accepted metaphor of 'progress' as a Hegelian 'endpoint' broadly embraces growth in economics and politics (in terms of the post-World War II obsession with political development and liberal democracy) and a society regulated by law. Fukuyama somewhat famously celebrated it, adding US cell phones, DVDs and Hollywood movies (Fukuyama 1989).

Yet it has not been recognised that the advanced economies of North America and Europe implicitly function as the endpoint and model of evaluation in comparative approaches to progress and development. The disciplines of sociology and political Science develop from the special value assigned to the experience of Europe and North America, as did their main theories, concepts and general understanding of societal change (Hall, 1996). Even Marx, who was ever critical of the dominant capitalist order and its thought systems (but also sensitive to local context, as his writings on modernity in Russia and

India indicate), agonised over the formulation of a universal model, eventually settling on the claim that 'the nation that is more developed industrially only shows, to the less developed, the image of its own future' (Marx 1978, 296). Will South Africa, having transitioned into liberal democracy, follow in the footsteps of the advanced economies, or will its violent experience of modernity since its formation produce radically different outcomes? The democratisation literature that is drawn from discourses of modernisation will surely identify failings in South Africa's unfolding democratic project and just as surely explain them in terms of culture, elites or incomplete transitions rather than as *aporias* of modernity and its dominant understanding itself.

The idea of political development?

In this section I analyse the varied meanings of the concept of political development, the central idea of the modernisation perspective, from its beginnings in Easton's elementary system to Huntington's emphasis on political stability and institutionalisation. By the 1970s, confidence was declining in the post-World War II modernisation viewpoint, which was strongly associated with vulgar representational differences between the West and the rest in both popular ideology and the knowledge sphere. Along the way, the Bandung 'peoples'' vision garnered support in the Third World opposing the US support for authoritarian governments. The American defeat in Vietnam was an especially significant (Mazower 2013) contribution to this shift (Sartori 1970). The voluminous output of cross-national comparative analyses (Przeworski and Teune 1970) that came out of US political science departments mostly arrived at familiar conclusions that were predictable within the dominant discourse and turned out to be interesting less for their 'scientific' generalisations than for revealing US cultural insularity, the superficial liberalism of its social science scholarship and a reliance on 'theories' that were meaningful only from a standpoint internal to imperial interests. Edward Said's classic *Orientalism* (1978) critiqued the glaring prejudices and historicism in Orientalist discourse, exposing the charade of dominant discourse and opening up space for alternative knowledges, interpretations and, least of all, views that put the humanity of the Third World more to the centre of analysis. The appeal of neo-Marxism and dependency perspectives in the Third World increased, allowing many to conclude that modernisation theory was dead. But was it?

The aim of arriving at a grand theory of modernisation (an indication of the swelled egos of the time) depended upon an agreed set of concepts, and 'political development' held out the possibility that it could serve that unifying purpose (Chilcote 1994; Eckstein 1963; Stepan 2001; Wiarda & Skelley 2007). The study of social change, democracy, nationalism, stability and political system dynamics, which attracted the most interest, were approached as different expressions of political development. Political development was the focus on 'the political aspects and political effects of social, economic and cultural modernization' (Huntington 1965). The definition of 'political' received little attention partly because it was already assumed from the study of politics in the US and Europe. On the other hand, 'modernisation' received much interest, and scholars were at pains to define which elements constituted its core features.

The modernisation process involved economic growth, industrialisation, urbanisation, mass media expansion, widespread literacy of the general population and increasing mobility of social groups between occupations (Bill and Hardgrave 1981). Most researchers of politics considered politics derivative of the larger process of modernisation (Huntington 1987). Curiously, 'political development' referred to many different goals (Sartori 1976) and had as many definitions as scholars writing on the subject (Randall 1985; Greenstein 1975; Migdal 1983; Huntington 1987): democracy, stability, national integration, and governmental effectiveness, legitimacy, participation, mobilisation, institutionalisation, equality, capability, differentiation, identity, penetration, distribution, integration, rationalisation, bureaucratisation, security, welfare, justice and liberty (Riggs 1981). Geographically, the term applied to the 'lesser-developed countries' of Asia, Latin America and Africa.

Pye (1966) tried in vain to clarify the concept and end the confusion surrounding political development. But he identified ten meanings that further added to the perplexity: the prerequisite for economic development, a description of politics found in the industrial societies, a synonym for modernisation, what modern nation states do, the building of state organisations and related institutions, mass mobilisation and increased participation, the establishment of a democratic polity, the management of stability and order, the demonstration of popular and symbolic mobilisation of the people, and one aspect among others in the process of social change. In 1970, Almond noted that those who used the concept believed that political development was desirable and happening, albeit quite slowly, that the movement was from 'traditional' to 'modern' political systems, and that it would resemble features of a modern Western liberal democracy.

These features, when framed in structural functionalist terms, made the political system the central focus, while the approach sought to gather data on equal access, capacity and differentiation of roles and structures in cross-national studies. Whether all goals were achievable in the same process, or whether they complemented or contradicted each other became topics of debate. The functionalism of Almond and Powel had proposed that political development was found where the attributes of modern society functioned properly or, in other words, political development was found only in functionally modern societies. As political parties are found only in modern societies, it could be reasonably concluded that they were functional to modern but not traditional societies (Riggs 1981). Huntington made waves by arguing in response to this influential structural functionalism that modernisation brought with it political decay, and that even traditional societies could produce strong political institutions (Huntington 1965) and express modern features.

The structural-functionalist approach claimed to provide a scientific model, namely a universal framework to study the politics of the 'developing areas' becoming the pre-eminent approach of the discipline in the 1950s and early 1960s. Parsons's reading of Weber and the systems analysis of David Easton (Easton 1957; Easton 1965) acted as strong influences on Almond's structural functionalism. Easton (1957) argued that political theory dealt with normative questions and the study of the 'great books'. It ignored empirical manifestations of politics, which he considered central to developing a science of political behaviour. The idea of a 'system' when applied to the sphere of politics would thus be analogous to an inorganic, self-regulating system like that found in electrical engineering, a practical and scientific area of study widely acknowledged for its internal coherence.

The concern with how systems survived indicates bias towards stability rather than interest in social change, sowing a weakness that runs throughout the modernisation approach. This implicit disinterest in social change made little sense especially since the driving force of politics in the postcolonies was a narrative of change. Because a political system responds to changes in its environment due to its adaptive capacity, Easton argued that the function of a political system was to preserve the 'authoritative allocation of values for society', which also defined what a system was (Easton 1957). The values themselves, which are often fought over in the activity called 'politics', did not concern Easton. The values from the environment, which he called the inputs (demands and supports), work their way through the political system, ultimately becoming outputs (legislation); these in turn fed back into the political system as new input demands, thus allowing the system to monitor and adjust its performance. This model is like a mechanical thermostat, and it may seem too vague and simplistic to study the complexity of politics, unless it is defined minimally in managerial and economic terms. A study of politics that banished political theory to the margins with the aim of becoming a technical discourse is shortsighted and more likely to work as a handmaiden of power. The approach defines inputs, outputs and the system broadly. The category boundaries are not easily distinguishable, so they offer very little analytical value. Such an abstract framework can apply to just about any context. It does not reveal much about a country's specific politics. Easton's scientific model turns out to be neat and parsimonious, but ultimately uncompelling. More troublingly, it assumes the consensus of the major rules and values of a society, which applies to some Western political systems in particular historical periods but is highly unlikely in postcolonial countries.

Almond embraced Easton's commitment to developing a 'scientific model' of politics with a global reach to enable the systematic comparisons of the politics of all states, although in reality it amounted to the implicit comparison of Third World states against the standard established in the West. His ambitious and grand project was conceivable only from the shores of the global hegemon and its major universities. Edward Said would later label this a typical illustration of the 'imperial gaze' towards the Third World, representing its Other in Orientalist discourse (Said 1978). Besides system theory, Almond also drew on Talcott Parsons's (1968) idea of society as constituted by the interdependence of the contributing parts of various social systems. In framing society as a system of parts and functions, relations between parts or relations between parts and the whole, identifying and comparing functions becomes the researcher's main task to understand modernising society. Whereas Easton's system drew on the thermostat, Parsons's system followed what LaCapra described as 'the biologically driven mimetic epistemology of positivism' (LaCapra 1983, 76). Social systems approximated biological organisms, Parsons believed. His system found a way to perform the necessary functions for its survival, but the new categories generated to analyse systems (integration, adaptation, goal attainment and pattern maintenance) betrayed the bias towards stability.

In distinguishing between traditional and modern societies, the social roles of the 'traditional' village sat in sharp contrast to that of the 'modern' town. This is demonstrated by five dichotomous 'pattern variables' that enable Parsons to define his understanding of the modern: affective/affective-neutral, particularistic/universalistic, collective orientation/self-orientation, ascription/achievement, and functionally diffuse/functionally specific. The first of the pair reflects features of modern European society, while the second and opposite are characteristics of the traditional Third World. The so-called modern sector is the centre of activity, where the action of politics and economics takes place. By contrast, passivity and being acted upon describe the traditional sector (Migdal 1988). In studies of political development, Parsons's pattern variables, biases towards functional integration (stability) and reproduction of societies through 'pattern maintenance' (values) left their mark. The pattern variables built on sedimented historicist ideas that worked their ways even into the writing of the founding 'fathers' of social science, Marx, Weber and Durkheim, whose work also relied on distinguishing 'traditional' from 'modern' societies dichotomously.

Almond's is a paradigmatic model for analysing political development in the Third World. His correction of the main criticism levelled at Easton, that the political system was an empty 'black box', was to fill it with categories describing inputs and outputs. The input functions included 'political socialisation' (ways in which individuals acquire attitudes about the political system, e.g., through families, schools, etc.), 'political recruitment', 'political articulation' (informal associations) and 'interest aggregation (the roles of parties). The political system processes these inputs from society, making general rules (rule-making as outputs) through the legislative process. They become laws implemented by a civil bureaucracy, and impartial courts adjudicate disputes about them, constituting the judicial system. The political system of structural functionalism thus turns out to be the classic separation of powers between the executive, legislative and judiciary, following the contract theory of Hobbes, Locke, Rousseau and, in the modern colonial period, John Stuart Mill. The function of the media is to communicate political values to citizens. In Almond's hands, the American and most western European political systems become the 'universal' model of politics against which all 'developing countries' are evaluated. The narrow focus on formal, institutional politics reduced politics to sovereignty and the law; it did not approach how power constituted subjects through violence and radical difference, which is the key characteristic of settler-colonial modernity.

Researchers used this toolbox to conduct primary and empirical research in diverse and exotic lands, producing a vast body of work. This early work, first-hand descriptive accounts of societies embarking on national paths as independent, sovereign states and their general observations expressed in a 'universal language' of politics, became rich sources from which later research departed. In the comparative study of politics, some countries represented types of political systems having political or social features considered sufficiently significant to attract research interest that generated a body of concepts, literature and debate. For instance, Nigeria represented the case of regionalism and tribalism associated with sub-Saharan Africa, Mexico and Brazil stood for the neo-patrimonialism of Latin America, and Great Britain or France were positioned at the top of the pyramid of political development as case studies of the advanced liberal democracies. This remains the standard format and approach of introductory texts to politics.

The imperial necessity of developing a universal, scientific model for understanding politics in the Third World, as in Almond's structural functionalism, depended upon a contrived narrative of the West. The dichotomous categories encouraged only a particular kind of change, the adoption of Western values and practices of modernity, which was assumed to be the only possible version of modernity and to which all rational minds would logically accept as the best and most advanced. It did not entertain possible alternatives of modernity, the contribution of other culture-zones to Western modernity or try to explain or perhaps overcome the systematic exploitation that came with an ever-expanding Western imperialism. The norm is a conception of politics as about deciding, voicing and implementing rules, but this narrow view ignores vast areas of politics. Lukes (1986; 2005) writes that the real battles of politics occur around power's capacity of agenda setting and that it was as important to keep certain issues off as on the political agenda. Marxists have always warned about how ruling classes de-politicise issues by restricting them to the purely economic or technocratic, and they criticise this as a form of 'economic reductionism' used strategically by the ruling class to undermine working-class struggle. In postcolonial societies like South Africa that are typically marked by histories of glaring inequality and defined by large swathes of poverty, the structural-functional framework obscures the politics of bare life. That is where subalterns fight over the 'acceptable' ideas and values circulating in society, which dismisses them as politically insignificant. This study of politics ignores these messy terrains of conflict in favour of rules and the interests of elite groups. Where in Almond's theory is the state, which can and often does initiate and design what are to become inputs? Where is the coercion often unleashed by states in their aim to control the population?

Yet, despite questions surrounding Eurocentric assumptions, logic, policy and ideology, modernisation theory experienced a boost from the democratic third wave. The democratic trend coinciding with the end of the Cold War presented an opportunity for comparative politics discourse to bring back ideas associated with the earlier literature on political development. The same 'end goal' was assumed. Even though the political changes were occurring in different regions of the world and amidst different circumstances, the wish for Western liberal democracy with political stability remained consistent. An enthusiasm for spreading democracy replaced the insecurity of younger scholars who had been concerned about Orientalist assumptions, as Said highlighted. By the 1990s, democracy had lost much of the radical meanings of the popular upsurges for social justice of 1848 and 1871 (the publication of Marx's *Communist Manifesto* and the Paris Commune, respectively) and become compatible with elite interests by incorporating earlier notions of political development.

The key figure in current democracy studies coincidentally happened to be a key theorist of political development and defender of the anti-democratic regimes of the 1960s and 1970s. Samuel Huntington, whose work stands out for its link between political development and democracy studies, dismissed the cultural variables in structural functionalism and the historical structuralism implicit in Marxism. His revised modernisation thesis avoided what he saw as society-centred approaches that undermined the role of the state as merely a 'black box'. Instead he advocated an early institutionalist view, attributed to the influence of Weber and Hintz, who also believed approaches that marginalised the state were inadequate. Weberian insights emphasised Europe's differences in Orientalist and historicist terms. Weber saw economic conditions as necessary but insufficient for developing modern capitalist democracy because they required an appropriate ethic, which was packaged most appropriately in European Protestantism. His novel classification of legitimacy (rational-legal, traditional and charismatic) to account for obedience to power (Migdal 1983) depends on a specifically European construction of itself. What made Western modernity unique in Weber's view had very little to do with influences outside the West.

Huntington takes on board these ideas. He concluded that modernisation could not come to the Third World without political development, and that this essentially meant political order. He argued that the sovereign must be preserved by whatever means necessary, exactly what Agamben found to be the classical problem. To Agamben this would require the suspension of the law in order to preserve the law, a position that views government rather than the people as the sovereign and that reveals the economic-managerial bias of modern political theory. Huntington believed stability came before democracy. The government's suppression of popular politics was not a problem, as he admired political order over everything else (1968). A critical failure of previous modernisation studies was its reliance on what he labelled the 'compatibility thesis', which held that all development goals would be realised simultaneously (1987) but effectively ignored the challenge of political order in the new states. Latin American, Middle Eastern and African militaries frequently overthrew democratic governments in the 1960s. Single-party or military rule based on authoritarian repression and charismatic ideology characterised the period. This empirical trend led to the questioning of modernisation advocates; conventional wisdom that economic development would lead to social stability and democratic culture. The opposite occurred. Rapid economic changes led to political instability and even decay.

Huntington attributed the cause to popular politics, in which the citizens demanded greater political participation to address social inequality. Their heightened expectations were an unavoidable part of modernising processes, and their increased social mobilisation should come as no surprise, he argued. However, these outcomes were preventable. The important variable was the weakness of political institutions in these countries, which were unable to maintain control and lacked capacity and institutional strength. The strength of institutions could be measured along axes of adaptability, autonomy, coherence and complexity (Huntington 1968). Weaknesses in these areas would translate into the inability of new state's political institutions to withstand popular pressure, resulting in widespread social unrest. By focusing on only domestic concerns, such as social mobilisation, the role of the lower middle class in the military and elite patron-client relations in weak political parties, he excluded the significance of imperialist interests to social instability in postcolonial states. Huntington believed authoritarian-type regimes were necessary, at least in the early processes of modernisation, and his advice to political elites was to take seriously the need for political institutionalisation and develop strong political parties to channel popular frustrations and prevent social revolution.

The specificity of settler-colonial relations as a path towards modernity

Settler colonialism characterises the history of South Africa. Under this form of domination, the state gradually imposed itself by spreading its influence through law while capitalist relations of exploitation unfolded and citizen identities formed and eventually gelled into 'races'. All were held together by and rooted in systematic violence. Precisely because it ignores this mode of domination and this particular variant and path of modernity (Hall et al. 1996), the mainstream paradigm inadequately analyses post-1994 democracy. A discourse of difference, called the 'West and the Rest' discourse by Stuart Hall (1996), is embedded in mainstream studies. Similarly, Chakrabarty (2000) referred to it as a 'habit of thought' translated as 'first in the West, and then elsewhere'. The 'West and the Rest' discourse relies on an uncritical Eurocentric understanding of modernity, argued Hall, and such historicist frameworks viewed in relation to the Third World reproduce global imperial networks in the sphere of knowledge.

Why is the concept of settler colonialism excluded in studies of post-1994 South African politics and Apartheid, yet the legacies of that long experience of systematic racism are so easily visible? Why is the past limited to Apartheid, defined as a set of racially discriminatory policies implemented by the Nationalist Party between 1948 and the onset of negotiations in the early 1990s? What is the relation between settler colonialism and the formation of the state and subject identities, in other words, settler colonialism and modernity? The historicist and Orientalist framing organising the study of politics in disciplinary political science and comparative politics provides one, albeit limited, answer to these questions.

Modern colonialism has two imperatives: to suppress the native culture and to create or replace it with something narcissistically reflective. Colonial power approaches these projects like a mission, utilising all effective means. This unmaking and different remaking—like the breaking and putting together of Humpty Dumpty—concerns the hidden 'spirit of colonialism'. And here Fanon proves indispensable for understanding the subtle layers of identity specifically from settler-colonial domination because they become less discrete with time; only flashes and traces of cultural attributes from the past constitute the basis of 'authentic' identity claims. The Fanonian analysis is discussed in more depth in chapter 3, but its key features are salient here.

The mode of power's operation underlying settler colonialism can be distinguished from other forms of colonialism, yet students of colonialism tend to collapse the different types into a generic, homogenous category. Few are interested in classifying different types of colonialism; even the classical studies of colonialism, like that of Fanon, avoid it. This failure is surprisingly evident in two opposing discourses on colonialism: the historicist modernisation paradigm and postcolonial theories that critique dominant discourses. Both assume a universalising generalisation: the former holds that all paths to modernity are reducible to the European experience, the latter that colonialism's common features throughout the Third World defend generalisation. The abundance of postcolonial studies on India, which question uncritical modernist discourses and have influenced postcolonial theory literature globally, are unhelpful if applied uncritically to the unique settler-colonial forms of domination in Southern African societies, especially to South Africa. Even within Africa significant expressions of colonial domination must be acknowledged. Surely, the length of the colonial experience has some not-so-insignificant bearing on state and society, as for example, the difference between Nigeria (formally colonised in 1900 and politically independent in 1960, as much of west and east Africa) and South Africa (colonised in 1652 and formally ending legal minority privileges with its first democratic elections in 1994). Fanon seemed to describe the settler-colonial type in his references to colonialism, but he never made that explicit. It would not be incorrect to infer that, for Fanon, settler colonialism functions as the ideal type from which various approximations can be arrived at empirically.

Modernisation theory and recent democratisation studies dismiss any negative impact or ignore the colonial experience. Lucian Pye's (1966) studies of political development illustrate this conclusion. Pye viewed colonialism positively, namely for bringing modernity to Africa (and to other colonised areas) from the outside; he did not see any internal dynamics towards modernity in precolonial Africa, but social formations outside history, which Hegel described in racist terms as statically 'passing time' and awaiting enlightenment. By introducing the rudiments of modern administration, the colonial state creates the foundation from which a modern, independent state can be built. Pye completely ignored the violence surrounding the initial conquest, the exploitation of labour and land, the deliberate undermining of local culture and institutions, the forced creation of subjects that would fit into the colonial order and the everyday violence required to maintain this social formation and have it reproduce itself. Rather, he described the unfolding of a benign process that is mainly progressive despite blemishes of racism. He emphasised institutional foundations, continuity, administrative procedures and management rules, all of which are modernising products of colonialism, and envisaged they would lead to the efficiency in consciousness necessary for general governance.

The colonial state faced the complicated, daunting challenge of a small group administering a 'foreign land' and its many inhabitants, and it soon realised that developing efficient structures was minimally necessary to accomplish this task. Although Pye valued the importance of a 'science' of administration to governing in colonial situations, he did not analyse its particular forms or legacies. That is Mamdani's (1996) important conceptual contribution about the bifurcated state. According to Neocosmos (2006), Mamdani highlighted the institutional dimension by understanding the internal structure of the colonial and postcolonial state as bifurcated, thus effectively 'interpellating' urban and rural inhabitants into different subjects. Separating rural from urban subjects, Mamdani argued, is a generalised practice of all African states and the constitution of African society that both marks a legacy that few post-independence states have been successful in dismantling and partially accounts for the persistence of alarming identity politics.

By 'colonialism', Emmanuel Eze (1997) wrote, we should understand the crisis disproportionately suffered by African peoples in their tragic encounter with the European world over two centuries. His more 'clustered concept' refers to three forms of violence towards Africans: slavery, direct colonialism and Eurocentric knowledge (1997, 4). Eze's broader understanding connects slavery to direct occupation and forced administration, and, in his words, 'the resilient and enduring ideologies and practices of European cultural superiority (ethnocentricism) and "racial" supremacy (racism)' (1997, 4). Eze deliberately emphasised violence as a defining core of the European 'Age of Enlightenment', which is typically presented as neutral and unrelated to the empirical and imperialist history of violent conquest. He challenged the conventional uncoupling in Eurocentric knowledge of the abstract concepts associated with the Enlightenment, in particular Kantian reason from Kantian racism, and their close relations to the brutality experienced by colonised people. Eze's remarkable contributions suffer from some analytical impreciseness; by not classifying types of colonialism, his generalisations of certain empirical topics are better distinguished from each other. Eze treated all of African colonialism as if it was the same. For a critique of the large abstractions of philosophical thought this makes immediate sense, but there are drawbacks to lumping together the colonial experiences of Nigeria, Kenya and South Africa when it comes to empirical and historical questions.

Osterhammel (1997) offered a detailed analysis of the classification of the colonial concept, as distinct from related concepts, within a useful typology. He admits that the term 'colonialism' has been overused and abused because it is essential in practical politics and current and historical ideologies. Even if his exaggeration of the difference between the concept's ideological and analytical uses were rejected, his classificatory scheme would remain useful. He claimed that classification was difficult because, historically, vast areas and peoples have come under outside control and colonial 'reality was multifaceted'. In addition, diverse forms, expressions and outcomes did not always follow colonisers' designs. Further, in situations of intense close combat, power is always shaped by multiple struggles and varied contexts. These dimensions ought to be considered with 'a central focus on both perpetrators and victims' (1997, 4).

He explains that the process of acquiring territory, colonisation, is not the same as establishing a colony, which refers to a type of sociopolitical organisation. 'Colonialism' refers to a system of domination; the distinguishing features for analytical purposes are process, organisation and system. Importantly, all three share 'the notion of expansion of a society beyond its original habitat' (Osterhammel, 1997, 4). However, the varied forms of expansion beyond the 'original habitat' point to significant differences in number, intention, attitude, history and institutional conditions.

Osterhammel (1997) identified six types of 'expansion'. In total migration, entire populations are forced or choose to leave an 'original habitat' (an exodus); though colonies may not necessarily result, they often do. The group might use conquest to remain in another place while also settling in new territory. Examples of this include the forced resettlements under Stalin and the Great Trek of Afrikaners from the Cape to establish the Boer Republics of the Orange Free State, Transvaal and even Natal. The latter have elements of an exodus, but because many Afrikaners also chose to remain in Cape Town, it is not a pure case. In other kinds of mass migration, people might leave as individuals; collectively, though, the result of an exodus is that a large number of people are relocated. The mass individual migration of Europeans to America illustrates the voluntary type, whereas the forced, violent imposition of slavery from Africa and the transport of captured slaves to America, like the large-scale indenture of Chinese and Indians on plantations of the New World, represent the involuntary type. Large numbers of people moving and colonising areas across a 'border', as in the frontier movement in North America, is yet another example of mass migration into new areas, which Osterhammel (1997) called 'border colonization'. He distinguished between the empire-building wars of conquest, citing the Romans in much of Europe and the British in India, and the naval networks of, say, the Portuguese, where the emphasis was on remaining in harbour areas with little effort made at internal settlement.

The large-scale overseas settlement colonisation is most relevant to the South African experience, and here Osterhammel identified three types. One is the initial English settlement of North America and Australia, in which the settlers and natives were separated territorially. They had less direct contact initially, but eventually the indigenous people were completely subjugated. A second type is that of South Africa and Kenya, in which settlement was large-scale and colonial society relied on the labour of local Africans. In the Caribbean, an example of the third type, the distinguishing feature was the employment of locals in a plantation economy. He further categorises colonies into the exploitation, maritime-enclave and settlement types. Colonies often witness invasions, new political organisations and the persistence of precolonial features while relying on the 'mother country'.

The two important elements of modern colonialism are domination and cultural dissimilarity. Modern colonialism made racism its distinctive feature. In large settlement communities the colonial state was often bifurcated, dividing the polity according to race to privilege white settlers at the expense of native Others. The colonial society was organised along a relationship of masters and servants. The dominated are effectively robbed of their historical line of development. The communities already inhabiting the land are externally manipulated and ruled in the interests of the colonisers. For Osterhammel, it is crucial that the colonial rulers are unwilling to make any cultural concessions to the subjugated people; rather than assimilating into the local culture, the dominant refuse to 'borrow' and consciously take on very little from the dominated. They vilify local cultural practices and distance themselves from them. Interpretations of this situation can lead to deeply opposing viewpoints. The colonisers view their presence as a project of modernity, namely as the imposition of an outside modernity to civilise the backward savages. Osterhammel (1997) made the telling points that 'any definition of colonialism must take into account this lack of willingness to assimilate on the part of the colonial rulers' and that 'modern colonialism is not only a relationship that can be described in structural terms, but also a particular interpretation of this relationship' (1997, 16). Thus the study of colonialism should not exclude or marginalise ideologies. In modern colonialism the colonisers assumed their cultural superiority and, as Arendt (1986) pointed out, associated this expression of imperialism with their 'race' is the key feature of this form of domination. In Osterhammel's words, 'only in modern colonialism did this kind of ethnocentric arrogance take an aggressive expansionist turn' because the spirit of colonialism is central; he concludes that, 'this spirit has outlived the reality of the colonial era' (1997, 16).

From whose perspective we are to interpret what is a situation of conflict and power is relevant. Fanon, as will be discussed in chapter 3, chose to write this history from the place, experience and viewpoint of the colonised. His method of understanding colonial modernity is to approach everything in this deeply divided and conflictual society from the particular location and standpoint experience of the colonised. More often than not, postcolonial democratic politics perpetuate these differences. From that perspective Fanon committed himself to fundamentally changing the colonial order of state and society with a revolutionary passion and commitment to practical struggle.

Some elements of radical critique

Europe's historical experience of modernity defines the conceptual understanding of modernity (Berman 1988; Dussel 1998; Gilroy 1993; Mitchell 2000; Scott 1999). I use the term 'historicist' to refer to a conception of history drawn from the European experience with the endpoint of modernity defined as Western liberal democracy. In historicism the Western experience of the modern serves as the universal template. It occupies a space of privilege and functions as the reference point against which other histories are understood. In its aim to demonstrate a universal process, a historicist frame emphasises those attributes familiar to the Eurocentric historical narrative while marginalising or excluding features that do not fit this narrative. In the historicist body of thought, settler colonialism as written about by Fanon (which is key to the South African experience) disrupts historicist reasoning and its narrative. This approach conceives of a European modernity isolated from non-Western influences. A silence about the non-Western role in modernity prevails (Mitchell 2000) based on the belief that modernity will travel in space and time to the non-West after having established itself in the West (Chakrabarty 2000).

An important period for the development of modernity, the Enlightenment, relates to scientific approaches to knowledge that established specialised disciplines. The study of politics reveals a particular structure of thought, conceiving of political modernity as a singular universal process in which all societies will eventually arrive at a society of laws closely resembling European democratic societies. The following section critiques this dominant, Western approach to political studies in the Third World.

It is nearly impossible to think of comparative politics as a field outside the framework of established theories of modernisation. The approach 'requires one first to establish the nature of modernity in general, as a standard against which the variations among different world regions could be measured' (Mitchell 2000, xxi). Though questionable, the single standard posited by the dominant paradigm 'was always by default the history of the West' (Mitchell 2000, xxi), a characteristic feature of disciplinary knowledge haunting our understanding of the non-West. In our thinking and political practice, Western modernity is so deeply ingrained that even radical critics fail to break with its influence. For example, the critical dependency school, despite importantly exposing 'the peripheral position of the non-West', 'still represented the non-West in terms of its difference from the West, and thus [remains] within the West's universalizing narrative' (Mitchell, 2000, xxi). A discourse of progress constitutes customary practice in Third World and in particular African Studies, where the 'dark continent' signifies the extreme Other to identify 'difference' from the Western standard and explain the deviations in these societies.

In South African studies, the pervasiveness of 'race' alongside the development of capitalism poses the key challenge. Liberal and Marxist debates dominate the literature. Both accept that South Africa was an exceptional (not normal) case and are wedded, to different degrees, to historicist thinking and core notions of Western modernity. Unlike in other industrial capitalist countries, the denial of political rights to the majority black workforce and its systematic exclusion from the dominant political institutions (Trapido 1971) made South Africa a deviant case of normal modernisation. In the 1970s, when the relationship of capitalism to racism drew much scholarly attention, terms such as 'archaic', 'backward', 'underdeveloped', 'fetter' and 'dual economy' were used to make sense of persistent racism. On the question of modernity and its normal path, liberals and Marxists disagreed as to whether capitalism contradicted or complemented the racial hierarchies that had become so deeply ingrained in the society.

In the study of the non-West, which is framed in historicist and Orientalist discourse, the problem is not limited to the subtle racism underlying remarks about 'late modernisers'. In the conventional discourse of comparative difference, the privileging of the European experience manifests itself in the key concepts and theories, so it seems impossible to write about modernity without reference to the West. How then can the politics of the 'non-West' be written? Can there be a narrative that breaks with the historical positioning of modernity in the West and, if so, what would it look like? The complexity increases when elites seek to emulate the 'Western original' in their national postcolonial development projects (Kaviraj 2000). Clearly these challenges have implications not only for studies of the Third World, but also for the practical political demands of Africanist curricula and decolonising institutions such as universities, which are profoundly influenced by settler-colonial histories.

I present a critique of the discourses of comparative difference, drawing on the work of Hall (1996), Chakrabarty (2000) and Mitchell (2000). Hall warns that thinking about an alternative narrative for the non-West entails awareness that the modern always requires and interacts with the non-modern and that colonial difference was essential to the emergence of and to the understanding of the modern. This point is wonderfully illustrated in Arendt's (1986) fascinating study of the emergence of the Nazis in Europe, which she relates to imperialist expansion, 'the mob' and the influence of the politics of 'race consciousness' in South Africa. Yet, typically the generic concept of the 'West' is constructed in isolation from and without acknowledgment of interaction or influences from other parts of the world, especially African colonies. For Hall, the distinction of the 'West and the Rest' in dominant discourse remains deeply embedded in the disciplinary discourses of the social sciences. Even when the key notions have been attacked in studies of the non-West, they are subsequently resuscitated under new labels, as in the recent studies of third wave democratisation.

The 'West' is partly about geography (though there is a politics about boundaries and inclusions and exclusions) but mostly about the deployment of ideas, representations and discourses. Nevertheless geographic disputes persist and are related to Eurocentric discourse. It is common to include the US, Canada, Australia and New Zealand (in the past white South Africa was also included, although white South Africans still refer to themselves as 'Westerners') under the spatial category of the 'West', whereas including parts of Eastern Europe and the former Soviet Union raise eyebrows among some. It is worth noting that Camus (2013) consistently argued for a division on cultural grounds between northern and Mediterranean Europe. On economic size and capacity for production, a case can be made for Japan's inclusion. But for Hall, the West is a product of historical, economic, political, cultural, and social processes, or of the material, pedagogical and symbolic; the place and the 'idea' or representation are closely intertwined and difficult to disentangle.

The 'West' refers to a type of society that is 'developed, industrialised, urbanised, capitalist, secular, and modern' (Hall, 1996, 187). It equals the modern, a notion that functions in the discourse of the 'West and the Rest' in particular ways: to classify, to characterise, a structure of thought and knowledge, a set of images to simplify and represent. As a system of representation, it complements other systems of thought and images/representations by providing a standard for evaluation or a template for (often implicit) comparison. It aims to explain difference by providing positive or negative attitudes that function as ideology (Hall 1996, 186).

The Enlightenment 'treated the West as the result of forces largely internal to Europe's history', Hall wrote (1996). Yet its modernity was a global phenomenon of European expansion, imperialism and the discourses of power representing the Other. The internal cohesion and silence about violent relations towards outside forces represent the West in a 'family of ideas' or archive whose varied sources include classical knowledge, religious texts, mythology and, importantly, travellers' accounts (1996, 206). By comparing Europeans with its Others, they exaggerated contrasts and eventually influenced scientific accounts.

These representations, which Europeans identified, came together to form 'regimes of truth' and reduced complex ideas to simple images: 'savage' societies displayed very little social organisation and certainly no civil society; native people lived in a pure state of nature; women were 'sexualised' in exotic images; and the territory and environment were untouched by human labour. The last point, Ellen Wood (2003) wrote, serves as the basis of the *res nullius* principle, a Roman law that John Locke drew upon to argue that unused land justified conquest as it could not legitimately be claimed by inhabitants. The settler colonialist contributed to humanity as a whole by exploiting the land through the labour of defeated communities. Based on radical contrasts, the representation of rational Western man was consolidated. It helped answer questions that Enlightenment philosophers raised about how Europe reached such heights of development but these Others did not. Kant based his answers on the anthropological discourses later known as the 'West and the Rest', to which he contributed greatly in his own anthropological studies, yet 'scholarly forgetfulness of Kant's racial theories' and his racism pervades Kantian studies in the philosophical canon (Eze 1997). Hall wrote that the 'West and the Rest' discourse gradually worked its way into how modernity is understood even in the writings of the founding fathers of the social sciences, Durkheim, Marx and Weber, and remains influential through their work.

Historicism is a 'habit of thought', where the idea 'first in the West, and then elsewhere' prevails (Chakrabarty 2000, 6). In this discourse, history is a linear process in which Europe represents the endpoint. Having experienced development first places it at the centre of analysis, and it assumed that all countries will follow in its footsteps. In the colonies, political modernity and historicism come together through the concepts of development and progress as expressed in the modernisation perspective. Chakrabarty warned:

> The phenomenon of 'political modernity'—namely, the rule by modern institutions of the state, bureaucracy, and capitalist enterprise—is impossible to think of anywhere in the world without invoking certain categories and concepts, the genealogies of which go deep into the intellectual and even theological traditions of Europe (2000, 4).

When applied to the study of the politics of individual Third World countries, these concepts are inevitably found to fall short on criteria related to the conception of Europe as the ultimate end (a metaphor for the universal) and the end of the process of development (or modernity). The belief that the Western experience will or ought to serve as the universal model for all countries overlooks Europe's internal diversity by considering it a region and does not acknowledge other pathways to modernity. This template of polar opposites contrasting the West and the non-West paves the way for universal claims and the 'totalising' knowledge of capitalist modernity. A conceptual enterprise such as this creates boundaries that demarcate an exterior, exaggerates cultural differences and imagines a Europe stripped of its rich diversity. Such historicist analysis of South African politics identifies failure to establish political stability, democracy and economic development and offers explanations based on comparative analysis against the European standard.

The conventional discourse of comparative difference allows for the reading of the empirical in the non-West in particular ways, least of all as in a situation of permanent transition. It explains away complexity by relying on elements of radical cultural difference. And, unsurprisingly, it explains this within the same discourse that emphasised the differences in the first place. It is better, following Agamben (who was influenced by Arendt and Foucault), to understand *aporias* of modernity within the Western modern experience itself without forgetting the impact of imperialist violence in the colonies.

Agamben (2011) writes that Western 'democracy' has two primary meanings, both related to power: of what and how the body politic is constituted and executive and techniques of governing and administering the political community. In the former, power legitimates itself through the idea of popular sovereignty, although this meaning has steadily declined in significance as it has been reduced to mean shallow election exercises at regular intervals. 'Democracy' thus refers to the manner in which power is administered by government, not through the one or the few, but on behalf of the many. Under conditions of modernity, the legitimating juridico-political and constitutional aspects have become confused with the economic-managerial of the executive government and administration of power. It is not easy to untangle the constituent from the constituted power, since, as Agamben observed, both have been entangled in the idea of the government or the sovereign since Plato and Rousseau contributed significantly towards the acceptance of this confusion by uniting 'sovereignty' and 'government' to define 'modernity': 'Today we behold the overwhelming preponderance of the government and the economy over anything you could call popular sovereignty—an expression by now drained of all meaning' (2011, 4).

In the colonies it is significant that the distinction that Agamben discussed, the constituting of the body politic and the constituted power, is not evident in either the emergence or process of consolidation of the colony, a point originally declared by Fanon. The constitution of the people and the legitimating of constituted power related to the governed are forever absent; instead, an initial violent encounter constitutes the political community and a permanent state of violence ensues. Fanon analysed this in detail and defines the relationship of the government in its exercise of power over the people as permanent war. The focus is on the economic management and administration of the people to create docile bodies, utilising a mixture of power discursively as repression and positively constitutive, while the settlers serve as a collective, citizen police force. Hence Agamben's distinction between the two aspects of democracy, which was evident during the mature phase of European modernity, was absent at the dawn of capitalist imperialism in its administration of its colonies. In the postcolony, the subaltern continues to live as Arendt's interwar refugee or 'stateless person' or Agamben's *homo sacer*, precariously meeting the needs of life.

Conclusion

In a review of the democratisation literature, Hagopian wrote, 'The two great trends at the century's end—globalisation and third wave democratisation—have led scholars to return to the large question of the nature of the relationship between economic and political development and even to revive modernisation theory' (2000, 882). If any scholar illustrates the link between the earlier modernisation discourse, with its Orientalist and historicist assumptions, and recent studies of democratisation, it is Samuel Huntington. His *Political Order in Changing Societies* (1968) significantly altered the reception of earlier modernisation studies, and his examination of the causes and outcomes of the waves of democracy, culminating in a third wave introduced many of the key concepts in this new field. It made comparative politics scholars, who are now more aware of the cruder claims and assumptions of the early modernisation paradigm with which many were socalised, become interested in third wave democratisation.

In this chapter, I identified the discourse of modernisation and its conception of political modernity. It claims to be 'scientific' by being based on comparative studies, published in established, reputable journals and presented at all the major conferences of the discipline. Yet modernity as it unfolded in the West was intricately linked to modernity as it unfolded in the non-West. The discourse of the 'West and the Rest' influenced the field of democratisation studies. The transition in South Africa followed closely the classical model of democratic transitions in terms of this discourse. The relatively peaceful transition and the promulgation of a constitution that enshrines progressive individual rights (the democratic values that are associated with the endpoint of modernisation) make South Africa a useful starting point for engaging critically with this discourse. The failure of conventional approaches to appreciate the historical context, i.e., the importance of settler-colonial modernity marking South

African society, is a significant weakness. Consequently, studies of democracy in Southern Africa, and in particular South Africa, have assigned very little analytical value to established social relations that are traceable to settler-colonial modernity (which is the focus of chapter 4). In the chapters that follow, I draw attention to the specificities of settler colonialism as a particular variant of modernity, which has an important bearing on why liberal democratic formal politics sits uneasily with citizen-subjects who have been constituted through settler-colonial violence.

3| The Fanonian paradigm, settler colonialism and South African democracy

In the previous chapters I proposed that South Africa is the 'paradigmatic case' of settler-colonial dynamics. But settler colonialism is also a particular form of modernity and type of domination. This chapter expands on this claim and makes a case for relocating the concept of settler colonialism to the centre of political analysis. It returns settler colonialism to political analysis to better understand contemporary South Africa's troubled democracy, in which competing modes of politics present themselves: that of the middle class focuses on a discourse of rights in the terrain of civil society and that of the subaltern mass a discourse of recognition in political society. Its framework moves beyond the restrictive third wave democratic paradigm, which excludes the settler-colonial mode as a factor of analysis. The methodology draws upon Fanon's prescient analysis of the organisation of power and power's constitution of the identities of the dominant and the dominated, or the coloniser and the colonised under settler colonialism, because it illuminates the unique features and legacies of settler-colonial modernity. The discussion begins by recalling the moment of Steve Biko and Black Consciousness (BC) in the 1970s and exploring how subaltern conceptions about politics were mediated by these BC ideas and thus indirectly influenced by Fanon. It focuses on Fanon's definition of the 'colonial situation'; domination without hegemony; the centrality of violence; the constitution of the subject by colonial discourse; resistance; and the *aporias* of postcolonial politics. By doing so, it explains how Fanon's approach helps to understand the crisis of what David Scott called the 'nationalist modern' in Jamaica, and which I apply to the project of the African National Congress (ANC) in South Africa.

Biko and the limits of non-racialism as antidote to the white power structure

The weakening of the Apartheid state's capacity to maintain social control due to the subaltern social mobilisation of the 1970s and 1980s enabled South Africa's negotiated transition to democracy. But how did this popular mobilisation come about? The straightforward answer is the emergence and spread of BC, which is traceable to the Biko generation from 1968. BC directly influenced the emergence of mass politics in South Africa, and this arguably amounted to a qualitative change in resistance politics. Realising its own political agency, this new assertive urban black subject, spurred on events such as the 1976 Soweto revolt (Kane-Berman 1978). The Soweto revolt opened the floodgates for urban protest that fed into the uprisings of the 1980s, which further radicalised urban blacks. This internal resistance led to the negotiations and, ultimately, the democratic settlement in 1994.

Just as the mass political subject was expressing itself in popular forms of people's power, nationalist elites and sections of the Apartheid leadership changed the mode of politics to impose a different political rationality. It stymied the development of BC. The black subject of colonial oppression had not completely realised its psychological transformations; the white had gone no further than awareness of guilt. And the idea of legal subjects that came with democratic and non-racial discourse was inadequate to address the deeply layered (dialectical) legacies of white and black subjects formed from violent settler-colonial relationships over three centuries.

The negotiations and the emphasis on producing a legal subject were a logical outcome of the non-racial, liberal-universalist tradition, which was grounded in historical South African politics. Many texts describe the dominant non-racial tradition of the ANC. The African Claims and the Freedom Charter come to mind, but Nelson Mandela's 1964 Rivonia Trial defence speech (his 'I am prepared to die' speech) is equally relevant because it foregrounds key differences with Biko. Mandela's defence for Umkhonto we Sizwe (MK) and the ANC taking up arms lies in black leaders finding themselves in a political situation in which they had few choices. Given the immoral laws of Apartheid and the terrible material conditions it compelled Africans to live under, we could anticipate mass violence by Africans towards the state and whites. Mandela believed Apartheid promoted race hatred and that its logical outcome would be race war. Black leaders were caught between an intransigent government and a rising, impatient, impoverished people. He warned that the black leaders, even if they wanted to, would not be able to control the subaltern black masses much longer. They decided that rational, pragmatic and targeted violence of sabotage (i.e., acts that cause no civilian deaths, as opposed to guerrilla warfare or terrorism) applied reasonable pressure and hoped the Apartheid government would come to its senses and negotiate. The prevention of race war (the same argument that Hendrik Verwoerd used to justify 'the separation of the races') was uppermost in Mandela's mind, although he argued to end Apartheid and supported non-racialism as the best means for preventing race war. He believed that strategically targeted sabotage would assuage African anger, hence it was a strategy to control and direct that anger. He envisaged a negotiated settlement towards parliamentary democracy and non-racialism (values he believed the Congress movement placed high on its agenda) would prevent white or alternative black domination and create a single civil society whose laws would be equal and applicable to all.

Mandela wanted the court to appreciate that, in the complex political context of South Africa, strategic armed struggle was enlightened and rational, compared to the irrationality and irresponsible monopoly of violence at the hands of the Apartheid state that was then charging him with treason. Although Mandela identified the emergence of South African society as the outcome of colonial wars and portrayed his struggle as a continuation of this conflict, the political problem was the discriminatory laws targeted at indigenous Africans, Coloureds and Indians. Apartheid was the enemy. The nationalist struggle's goals to overcome racially discriminatory norms and laws and obtain a democratic system included recognising non-whites as citizens, granting them the rights to vote and determine the laws, and ensuring the applicability of laws regardless of race. Mandela presented the leaders on trial, caught between a hostile, insensitive and irrational government and a downtrodden mass, which was likely to be driven by their pent-up emotions, as willingly accepting the higher responsibility to steer South Africa away from the abyss of racial war. After careful consideration of all the political, economic and moral factors, the leaders rationally calculated the best cause of action. Mandela painstakingly defended the choice of carefully targeted sabotage over civil unrest and terrorism. The leaders arrived at this conclusion after having advocated peaceful protest against discriminatory laws for decades, only to see the introduction of harsher ones. Still, Mandela left the door open for the government to come to its senses and embrace modern parliamentary democracy. In this Apartheid court, faced with the death penalty, Mandela reversed the roles to make the white government represent irrationality and blacks (rather, the national middle-class leadership of African nationalism) Kantian reason and liberal enlightenment.

The struggle narrative describes the post-Sharpeville period, following the killing of 69 protesters at an anti-pass demonstration in 1960, as a political vacuum characterised by pervasive apathy. Apartheid state repression was at its height. Then, in the early 1970s, the colonised began to stir. The urban population identified with a call for a new radical political consciousness that was mediated and articulated through Biko's BC, which resonated strongly with Fanon's ideas. Biko noted that the masses were restive and underlying social forces were emerging even when the old order appeared strong, which allowed intellectuals to imagine a radically different society (Keniston 2014). BC began to ask broader questions about power, for instance how power produced particular subject-identities and how to organise against docility from the bottom up. The ANC non-racialists, in contrast, focused on the conquest of state power and constitution of the free legal subject. Biko, like Fanon, began with the lived experience of oppression. It was important to Biko that resistance thought focus on the distinction between how a system of power operates to constitute docile subject identities and the possibilities of agency that same oppression produces in different black experiences. This approach resonates with the double consciousness of Du Bois, Fanon, and more recently Gilroy.

From the standpoint of the predicament of black resistance politics, Biko (2005) analysed the political context facing black politics in his 1972 essay 'White Racism and Black Consciousness'. He discussed the nature of white rule and the means to and goal of liberation, addressing in particular the problem he had with the white liberal influence on black resistance. In Fanon's understanding of the politics of the skin in settler-colonial situations, Biko discovered a set of conceptual tools to apply to South African conditions. He instinctively identified a conceptual apparatus that could answer difficult questions for blacks who wanted to radically change race society. Fanon, they concluded, spoke about 'race' differently and in a language they could identify with, and his emphasis on the multiple manifestations of violence uniquely captured the South African settler-colonial experience. Fanon offered a language to understand and fight against the race society of which South Africa was the paradigmatic illustration.

Fanon called this compartmentalised, divided world and the peculiar ordering of colonial society, which is paradigmatically represented by Apartheid South Africa 'the Manichean World' (1963, 37). In Fanon's 'Manichean society', which is based on the organisation of power according to skin, blacks are left with few choices and (like whites) are born into particular positions in the hierarchy. A free society would have to completely 'overhaul' it. Biko's 'white power structure' is strikingly similar; Apartheid was merely the latest political expression of this complex domination. Completely destroying the white power structure would require that subjects and society be freed from any values attached to discourses of race and racial difference. As 'non-racial' anti-Apartheid practices illustrate, white-black interactions that fall short of this, i.e., are unable to move beyond the value of and association of skin colour with superiority and inferiority, will remain unable to overcome the ghosts of Manichean society. These values mean that blacks deal with festering rage and self-discomfort; whites retain their privileges and have to relate to blacks out of guilt, suspicion and fear. This is a snapshot of the idea of 'relational' or forever incomplete subjects. It is now evident that Biko's white power structure reproduces itself, even if and when key constitutive elements shift. Like Foucault's idea of the interplay and movement of forces within a discourse, the broader configuration changes and yet remains the same.

Biko wrote that the white power structure created and worked comprehensively with 'utter ruthlessness' against the 'Black world'. Not only did the white power structure make violently oppressing blacks a 'tradition forced onto the country', it also divided blacks into ethnic, tribal identities (promoting 'inter-tribal ill-feeling'). With this 'divide and rule', it wanted to reorient black political aspirations towards accepting Bantustan independence and permanently giving up their South African citizenship and identity. While that came from government, liberal whites dominated resistance to the white power structure and determined how blacks responded to oppression. For Biko, this manifested as a totalising white world; its systematic pursuit of black exploitation, creation of black identities (using skin colour as the source of privilege) and assumption of responsibility for fighting this domination forced blacks to question how to conceive of freedom independently of the white frame of reference. Blacks as a start had to ask themselves if they could fight the white power structure, and, if possible, what would this entail.

Biko discussed non-racial groups resisting Apartheid, a topic that stems from the BC South African Students Organisation (SASO) walk out of the National Union of South African Students (NUSAS) conference in 1968, the non-racial, but mainly white dominant student organisation. Under the weight of South African history and at the height of racial segregation, he was aware of the sensitivity of the topic: 'Obviously it is a *cruel* assumption to believe that all Whites are not sincere, yet methods adopted by some groups often do suggest a lack of real commitment' (2005, 70). Or again: 'I am not sneering at the liberals and their involvement' (2005, 71). And lastly: The 'liberal establishment' enjoyed 'the longest confidence from the Black world'. He condemned this normal, spontaneous reaction in colonial situations such as South Africa. Blacks needed to identify appropriate strategies to resist the entire white power structure, and this meant that he was also sceptical about the white left. He even included them in his definition of the white power structure, which played on the title of Fanon's book, *Black Skin, White Masks* (1986), which was then banned in South Africa:

> It is that curious bunch of non-conformists who explain their participation in negative terms: that bunch of do-gooders that goes under all sorts of names—liberals, leftists, etc. These are people who argue that they are not responsible for white racism … who claim that they too feel the oppression just as acutely as the Blacks and therefore should be jointly involved in the Black Man's struggle for a place under the sun; in short, these are the people who say that they have black souls wrapped up in white skins (Biko 2005, 69).

In the past blacks wrongly assumed that 'whoever opposed Apartheid was an ally', and this 'political dogma' influenced them to rely on the liberal establishment for their closest allies. The nationalist struggle made another strategic mistake, focusing almost entirely on the 'governing party and not so much at the whole power structure as the object of their rage' (2005, 68). For Biko, the category of white power structure expands the idea of domination beyond the state and is best understood as the entire systemic structure of domination in which the political field is but one aspect of the economic, social, cultural and psychological oppression of blacks. Biko drew on Fanon's opening chapter of *Black Skin, White Masks* to criticise blacks for relying on a 'political vocabulary' drawn from the liberals: the language of universal rights, law and liberal democracy. These values relate to his criticism of the national struggle's prevailing belief that fighting the status quo of Apartheid 'must necessarily be non-racial in structure' (2005, 69). The weaknesses of such alliances made them a problem for resistance politics because it 'became the occupation of the leadership' to 'calm the masses down' (Biko 2005, 69). The thrust of black resistance thus became an 'art of gentle persuasion'. The resistance approached the white power structure passively. It did not embrace the masses, who sought to establish a counter hegemony, but concentrated on appeasing the liberals to sustain non-racial alliance politics. The resistance believed themselves to having created 'liberated' communities in the process of the struggle. For Biko, the object of liberation was rejecting the white power structure in its totality, in its material manifestations and in the minds of the oppressed. He argued that the white liberal influence 'watered down' black resistance by discouraging this focus on the white power structure.

'We are forced to arrive at this painful conclusion', argued Biko, 'that white activists act out of feelings of guilt rather than 'genuine concern' or 'real commitment', and, in Manichean society benefit from the privilege and protection of the 'natural passport' of their 'white skin' (2005, 71). It was necessary for white activists to engage in deep personal introspection and genuine self-reflection to avoid acting out of guilt. The leadership elites (the black and white middle class) embraced non-racial circles that did not reflect the everyday reality of the masses, who thus felt undermined and confused. The current and dominant approach of the struggle missed its real target, the white power structure, because it was conveniently displaced by an exclusive focus on the government and its policies. This weak strategy paved the way for negotiated solutions, which would legitimise in new ways the entrenched power relations of racialised society and the white power structure.

Until this BC intervention, the non-racial and liberal paradigm of the ANC dominated resistance politics. This tradition considered the politics of the skin irrelevant for political strategy and ideology, although it was a core element in the white power structure and the basis of Manichean society. In the 1970s the consequences of the BC approach, responding to non-racialism with an assertive black solidarity that emphasised the psychological liberation of the black subject from the white power structure, led to a far-reaching resistance practice.

Fanon's colonial situation as domination without hegemony

To understand the contradictions of the mode of politics under liberal democracy in South Africa, in which the middle class focuses its politics on a discourse of rights in the terrain of civil society and subalterns' mass politics demand recognition in political society beyond precarious bare life, the formation of the subject under settler colonialism must be considered. Fanon's contribution to understanding the black subject under settler colonialism is indispensable. This discussion of Fanon's thought emphasises his concept of 'the colonial situation' in four themes: the pervasiveness of violence; the absence of hegemony; the production of racialised subjects; and the questioning of Western knowledge.

Influenced by Marx's analysis of capitalist modernity, Fanon established the 'facticity' of the colonial situation. It seems that his understanding of the 'colonial situation' as a specific analytic category serves the same function as the 'mode of production' does for Marx. It also describes a social force of immense proportions that dramatically reorients all society it encounters. This mode of domination is defined by 'violence … just under the skin' (Fanon 1963, 71), and, because it constitutes a society organised according to racial hierarchy, it is an ongoing terrain of conflict. Moreover, in a colonial situation, power is naturally never complete or stable. The power structure is under permanent threat, expecting the anger and frustration of the colonised to break out at any moment. A system based on radical racial difference, rooted in something as personal as the body and its symbolic identities, cannot but be on permanent guard.

Fanon's analysis examines two inseparable historical processes: the structures of power of the colonial situation and their dismantling in the interests of the colonised (i.e., decolonisation). The immediately noticeable specificity of the colonial situation is the 'cutting of the world into two' and the absence of hegemony. As an organisation and operation of power, settler-colonial modernity's approach to space and institutions and reliance on violence and dominant ideas vandalises, consumes and disorients its subjects. Fanon described this anatomy ('the ordering and geography') of power in a colonial situation exhaustively and microscopically. No topic escapes its ambit, and racialised violence is there for all to see.

It may make sense to separate capitalism, state and identities analytically, but not in a colonial situation. These distinctions would reveal that they overlap differently and significantly in people's everyday lives because power is organised around race. A colonial situation is strongly related to, but not reducible, to capitalist domination and its imperatives for accumulation. We should conceive of the colonial situation as domination without hegemony or domination where violence or the threat of violence is at the fore. The line between the law and violence is indistinguishable, Agamben's (2004) state of exception, although it is the 'normal' and 'permanent' state of affairs for the colonised. The suspension of the law, Agamben's 'Other of the law' and the normalised regulation of citizens may actually serve as relief to the colonised because the law itself is always in a warlike footing towards the colonised subalterns.

Violence as defining element Fanon captured the brutality, the everyday forms, the material effects, the 'fears' of physical violence and the imprints in language and consciousness. These subtle impressions on the consciousness of oppressor and oppressed survived beyond the constitutional changes into a democratic society by assuming new and different manifestations. Violent legacies do not end with the hoisting of a flag announcing a new nation but haunt its formation. The conquest began with violence and the racialised social relations that have been organised for exploitation cannot be maintained and reproduced without violence. The subjects of violence, namely the targets of domination, are distinguished through a discourse of radical difference in which the physical body serves as key signifier. This places the settler-colonial experience apart from the emergence of modernity elsewhere, especially in core capitalist zones; its imprint has a deeper bearing on the unfolding of modernities, where capitalist social relations manifest differently, especially in a country moulded by 'race' like South Africa.

It is known that the concept of violence in Fanon refers to physical and psychological injury, and understanding it along two axes, outside/visible and inside/invisible (and the interaction between them), gives a better sense of its importance in the production of subjects. As stated above, violence pervades the everyday life of the colonised subject, who knows that her cage of skin can be the cause of the multiple forms of violence and thus gradually looks upon herself as a 'thing', an element in an objectified mass of the colonised. Settler-colonial power makes the colonised into an object relying upon the physicality of the skin, the cause of his suffering. The entire structure and organisation of the society, its administrative systems and rules, its systems of exploitation, its cultural values (Biko's white power structure) cannot be divorced from the use of force that defines the relationship between settler and colonised. For the colonised, this environment serves as the personal and collective terrain of struggle against fear, anxiety, death, desire, conquest and forgetting.

Given the uncertainty and vulnerability of the private sphere under colonial conditions, Fanon appreciated that the things that constitute life, like love, family, weddings, birthdays, births and funerals, are just as meaningful in the 'lived reality' of the colonised although violence was never far away. The sustained trauma of a 'lifetime' of living under fear leaves a mark on the consciousness that is indelible unless the national struggle attends to it through creative practices of redress. Here, then, is Fanon's understanding of liberation as the process that fundamentally recreates the universal human from the thing, which had been objectified under settler colonialism; this transformative project had to be a determined process of social and self-questioning with the goal of destroying the idea of 'the skin' and its associated identity values in order to render it meaningless. Fanon distanced himself from Senghor's idea of Negritude. He argued that the Negritude idea remained locked within the physicality and visibility of the skin even if (and precisely because) positive identity values were attached to it, and that this did not render it meaningless. Such knee-jerk reactions of the colonised (especially the elites) troubled Fanon even more because it reinforced a discourse of race and biology, which is the root of the racism defining the settler-colonial order and this kind of modernity. The anti-colonial struggle had no choice but to address the material effects of violence at the psychological level and thus in the realm of consciousness of the subjects of settler colonialism. When it avoided this question, as did the ANC led liberal-democratic tradition in South Africa due to its headstrong focus on control of the state, the historical contradictions and injuries remained even though they express themselves differently over time.

No hegemony, different consequences Fanon understood power broadly and not as limited to the domain of the state; his emphasis is on the microscopic structural ordering and geography of colonial society and the production and constitution of subjects imprisoned by racial discourse. As stated above, material and psychological violence distinguished the colonial situation, which is an important difference from the typical Western trajectory of modernity. Hegemony, following Gramsci, denotes the exercise of power through various ideational mediations between the dominant and the dominated, from which it secures passive consent. This aspect of how power operates is distinctive to Western capitalist formations but not discernable in settler colonialism. The distinctive feature of coercion without consent defines the settler-colonial state, which functions to coordinate and regulate power and produces and monitors the racialised social relations of settler-colonial domination.

The representatives of violence (the police and the army) are the mediators of the ruling order who strive to keep this society of compartments intact because it is not complementary but opposed (Fanon 1963, 38). The black middle class are employed by the colonial state in a subordinate role, and besides this superficial effort at masking the colonial situation, violence holds this society together. In the Western capitalist societies hegemony defines the social formation, thus making resistance more complicated. Under European modernity hegemony or the 'consent' of the governed comes from multiple mechanisms of masking, which is the imposition of 'false' beliefs that make domination more 'believable' and justifiable to the oppressed. In them, the 'aesthetic expressions of respect' taught in the educational system, the 'moral reflexes', 'the exemplary honesty of workers' and the 'affection' that is derived from 'harmonious relations and good behavior' (Fanon 1963, 38), blunt class exploitation in worker consciousness. A dedicated corps of cultural workers function as the effective intermediaries between organised power and subaltern subjects.

Settler-colonial domination is far less subtle and relies on visibility and materiality, which is most immediately evident in the politics of skin colour. In colonial discourse the colour of a person's skin demarcates a 'species' or 'race' and straightforwardly determines status. This immediate visibility can fix the subject in the social hierarchy, depending on where he or she stands in the society as a whole, and that strongly correlates to the person's subjective class position. Fanon best illustrates this instance of 'fixing' when on a street in Paris he hears a child in fear telling its mother, 'Mama, see the Negro', fixing him in his tracks and sending him into a turmoil of inner thought. In the colonial situation the police function as the main corps of intermediaries, and they do not want to soften exploitative relations but make violence and their own power and status more visible in order to reinforce the unequal positions of settler and native.

Relational and incomplete subjects Comparing Fanon's seminal contribution on the construction of the colonial subject in colonial discourse to Homi Bhabha's (1987; 2004) post-structuralist interpretation of the colonial subject will reveal the relational nature of identities in discourse. The settler and the native owe their relational subject identities to the settler-colonial form of modernity. Significantly, for Fanon, the settler 'brought the native into existence and perpetuates his existence' and has a subject identity not only from the property he derives from the colonial system, a direct consequence of global capitalist expansion and imposed Western modernity but a discourse of 'race' (Fanon 1963, 40). The division between settler and native characterise the society. They live apart in isolated 'compartments', yet their identities are directly related to each other and 'live off' this idea of separation:

> The colonial world is a world divided into compartments. It is probably unnecessary to recall the existence of native quarters and European quarters, of schools for natives and schools for Europeans; in the same way we need not recall Apartheid

in South Africa. Yet, if we examine closely this system of compartments, we will at least be able to reveal the lines of force it implies. This approach to the colonial world, its ordering and its geographical lay-out will allow us to mark out the lines on which a decolonized society will be reorganized (Fanon 1963, 37).

Fanon finds it unnecessary to 'recall' South Africa's Apartheid precisely because it is so demonstrative of the paradigmatic case of racial violence and separation. The ordering of the colonial world, especially its spatial organisation, are expressions of power; closely foreshadowing Althusser, they indicate how power interpolates individuals into racialised subjects. Ultimately, the lack of attention paid to this geography of separateness and its impact on the constitution of identities results in superficial postcolonial 'solutions'. It is assumed that merely bringing people together, as in South Africa's 'rainbow nation', can address three centuries of separation and denigration. Or worse, placing blacks or Africans (as it is more racially conceived in existing South African government policy and ANC thinking) before Coloureds, Coloureds before Indians and the three groups before whites in all public positions to 'represent the demographics of the nation'. These mechanical solutions have little bearing on the moral respect they need to garner to socially transform society. They do not move positively towards Biko's and Fanon's higher standard of creating a different and alternative modern society to that of the dominant European model, create conditions enabling subjects to attain what Biko called their 'envisaged self', and move towards rather than away from a society of true humanity.

In the settler-colonial situation, this divided 'world cut into two' (as Fanon repeatedly reminds his readers; 1963, 37), the native and the coloniser are made into particular subjects. This is a world that stamps 'skin difference' at every turn through the organisation, regulation and monitoring of space, institutions and social relations. Fanon explains that settler colonialism's compartmentalised worlds, each so different as to be opposites, creates 'two different species' (1963, 40): The one, the settler fears the loss of privilege. The other, the native enviously wants to take the place of the settler. The geographic separation, differences in material wealth and contrasting features of everyday living have psychological implications although the division does not entail absolute incommensurability. Yet much of the consciousness of each depends on the other. The groups develop particular kinds of 'knowledges' about the other that are used and expanded in the struggle between dominant and oppressed, settler and native. It is a world and a conception of thought that is organised in binaries, one representing 'good', the other 'radical evil.' It dehumanises the native as 'bestial' or 'animal', beyond all values (1963, 32), and 'reason,' 'civil society,' the 'enlightened man' are symbolised and embodied in the coloniser.

Fanon discovered that the psychological 'incompleteness' of the subject is more evident in the colonial situation because the everyday interactions of blacks and whites make it easy to observe that they depend on each other. Du Bois's idea of 'double consciousness', in which the colonised person approaches day-to-day life through the lens of the white and black worlds (Gilroy 1993), captures the incompleteness and mutual dependence of this relational subject. Biko puts this more bluntly in an accurate, beautiful phrase of black experience: this 'powerlessness breeds a race of beggars who smile at the enemy and swear at him in the sanctity of their toilets; who shout 'Baas' (Boss) willingly during the day and call the white man a dog in their buses as they go home. Once again the concept of fear is at the heart of this two-faced behavior ...' (2005, 86).

We could say that Bhabha (1987) pushed Fanon's understanding of the subject to its limits, and by so doing he creatively opened untraveled pathways to understanding the Fanonian subject. Bhabha's interest in Fanon lay in Fanon's split subject, which opened the possibility of a generalised critique of the Enlightenment's modern subject. Towards the end of his essay, 'What Does the Black Man Want?', Bhabha's contribution to a twenty-five-year commemoration of Fanon's death in a special issue of the journal *New Formations*, 'Remembering Fanon', he argues that Fanon remained relevant: 'In order to remind us of that crucial engagement between mask and identity, image and identification, from which comes the lasting tension of our freedom and the lasting impression of ourselves as other' (1987, 123).

We can identify Bhabha's project as more ambitious than merely providing yet another interpretation of Fanon. Though Bhabha interpreted Fanon in relation to Enlightenment thought, he did so in a way that reinterpreted Fanon as an advocate of Bhabha's version of postcolonial theory. He overlooked Fanon's commitment to revolutionary struggle and the resistance praxis of Third World subalterns and the role of this process in identity politics. Bhabha started by complementing Fanon for his devastating critique of the dominant 'discourse of social sovereignty' (1987, 119), a discourse that treats as Other those subjects and practices that do not fit its own criteria and rules. In its European iteration Bhabha's modernist discourse values 'historical rationality', 'cultural cohesion', 'the civil state', 'progress of human nature', 'the autonomy of individual consciousness' and 'the movement from nature to culture' (Bhabha 1987, 119). It holds that law and culture connect the individual to society, an attitude most pronounced in Rousseau's well-known notion of the 'general will' as presented in his classic text, the *Social Contract* (1762).

Rather than asking, 'What does the Black man want?' (which was Fanon's original question), Bhabha asked, 'What does a man want?' to reflect his more ambitious project. Notwithstanding the issues raised for a politics of race that a 'man of reason' develops which is Fanon's focus of critique, here Bhabha interpreted it as about the 'psychoanalytic problem of identification' (1987, 118). His reading of Fanon offers 'a psychoanalytic explanation' for the alienating colonial experience. Colonial discourse constructs the colonised subject as 'the overdetermined (subject) from without', relying on 'image and fantasy', and these figure 'transgressively on the borders of history and the unconscious' (1987, 119).

Bhabha agreed with Fanon that the alienating colonial experience is full of perversions, and that examples including 'collaborations of political and psychic violence within civic virtue, or alienation within identity, drive Fanon to describe the splitting of the colonial space of consciousness and society as a "Manichean delirium"' (1987, 119). Fanon's analysis of the colonial situation allowed Bhabha to inquire into the image and identity of 'post-Enlightenment man', who Bhabha views as a figure haunted by the 'shadow of colonized man'. In reversing Fanon, Bhabha proposed that postmodern European man has a troubled identity that badly copies the figure of the colonised man described by Fanon. In an ironic reversal of fortune, this man has to deal with shadows and fantasies—the Otherness of Self—derived from the colonialised man. The postmodern man's identity turns on *this* image rather than that of the modern, rational subject of the dominant modernist discourse; Bhabha wanted to make this point of slippage or hybridity the centrepiece of his poststructuralist understanding of subject identity.

Bhabha developed Lacan's notion that subject identity is about signification in language because only in the latter can the repressed unconscious be understood. The image of a complete subject put forward by the dominant discourse relies on the conscious-unconscious binary and that which is repressed in the unconscious. Even though identification is never complete, Bhabha wrote, 'it is only ever the problematic process of access to an "image" of totality' (1987, 120). Yet the concept of the image is itself never whole, as 'it marks the site of ambivalence … its representation is always spatially split' (1987, 120). Bhabha relied also on Derrida's floating signifier here, namely, that meaning or the sign can never completely or truly cover the whole of reality and that meaning depends on what is absent and deferred in time but present somewhere else (the Other in the Self). 'Completing' subject identity usually requires radical opposite and repressed meanings. Thus access to identity is always access to an image of identity. This is also how Fanon conceptualised the colonised subject. In other words, settler-colonial discourse objectified the black body by producing multiple forms of cultural alienation. Fanon's answer to 'What Does the Black Man Want?' crucially includes this 'negating activity', recognising that resistance must build upon this self discomfort with imposed identity and target the dominant discourse.

Bhabha criticised Fanon for not being postmodern enough in his analysis of the colonised subject. He admitted that Fanon's discussion of subject and identity contains promising elements of a postmodern recognition of the ambivalence of the Other, but that there are also moments when Fanon falls back on a modernist, dialectic account. Fanon does not rely on a static Self and Other, and he rejects the concept of a 'primordial identity'. Nevertheless, Bhabha warns:

> The place of the Other must not be imaged as Fanon sometimes suggests as a fixed phenomenological point, opposed to the Self, that represents a culturally alien consciousness. The Other must be seen as the necessary negation of a primordial identity—cultural and psychic—that introduces the system of differentiation which enables the 'cultural' to be signified as a linguistic, symbolic, historic reality (1987, 120).

In that point of uncertainty of all identity, that place of ambivalent identification, Bhabha found his source of resistance: 'it is possible … to redeem the pathos of cultural confusion into a strategy of political subversion'. (1987, 123). Herein lies Bhabha's unsatisfactory conception of resistance when compared to Fanon's revolutionary stance.

On resistance, Fanon demanded that the colonised want complete liberation from the colonial situation and, as liberation relates to identity, it is a desire for recognition and 'notice be taken of my negating activity' (Fanon 1986, 218). It is impossible to build a collective movement of mobilisation against a racist colonial order on the basis of 'that moment of ambivalence' that constitutes colonised identities, as Bhabha emphasised. This celebration of ambivalence could not have been the basis of the vast mobilisations that brought the Apartheid regime to its knees. Fanon recognised what Bhabha does not: settler-colonial conflict is about relations between forces. For Bhabha the mere recognition of that moment of ambivalence itself becomes subversion or resistance. However, this narrow, restricted conception rooted at the level of the individual is unhelpful in a settler-colonial situation. In the South African situation, Biko's BC came close to discovering a source of political mobilisation (and the point of ambivalence that Bhabha perceptively recognised as a key contribution of Fanon) in the signifier 'Black'. In the heat of battle, shifting is unavoidable between the politics of questioning the constitution of the subject and constructing a resisting collective subject to enable large-scale mobilisation of the dominated.

Even though Fanon, at least in Bhabha's interpretation, radically questioned the modern subject and its production, it still seems that Bhabha underappreciated that Fanon's colonised subject finds himself caught in the absence of 'grey areas' that defines the settler-colonial situation. Bhabha also weakened Fanon's emphasis on the decolonisation project at the heart of Fanon's concerns. Bhabha's writings seem to resonate more with the metropole than the colony. This overly 'textual Fanon' is not the Fanon who motivated Biko, BC in South Africa and many Third World revolutionary struggles. If Fanon is that student of colonialism who talks frankly about settler colonialism from the standpoint of the colonised and who makes his point of departure the physicality and visibility of the black skin in dominant discourse, his effectiveness lies precisely in demonstrating how colonialism fixes the sign. In short, the black skin (or any skin for that matter) is a signifier that appears rarely to float. Fanon related this physical materiality of the skin, its very visibility, with the organisation of power in a colonial situation. It is what enables a colonial situation, a system of domination in which many differences, some stark but most subtle, are reduced to skin colour. From this very real, visible, immediate 'fact', Fanon presented a critique of the subject under modernity.

When race discourse dominates, this skin 'covering' cannot be hidden, but feelings, emotions, thought—all that constitutes consciousness—can be, at least when the black is in the presence of authority (which means the white). Bhabha wanted to emphasise this idea of excess that power cannot control by using his idea of 'slippage', a point of departure for engaging with Fanon. The difference between Fanon's and Bhabha's interest in the constitution of the subject is now clear. Fanon starts with the 'fact of blackness' (1986) in the colonial relationship, namely one defined by settler domination of a native majority, and the conscious project to resist and overcome colonial society. He then moves to the construction of the subject. His very specific aim follows in the critical tradition of Marx: that project is for the subaltern to take over society and radically transform it based entirely on its lived experience of oppression. Bhabha's project provides a conceptual framework for understanding the limits of dominant discourse in constituting its subject. Its aim is to deconstruct, break open and dismiss the idea of the stable, closed modern subject, a conclusion that Fanon also leaned towards. This 'incompleteness' of the constitution of the subject by dominant discourse, Bhabha claims motivates conceiving of the subject as always hybrid. It is this very incompleteness of the subject, which demonstrates that dominant discourse does not always get its way, that constitutes expressions of resistance or serves as the basis for potential opposition.

Resistance The process of decolonisation is a process of 'complete disorder' (Fanon 1963, 36). Fanon warned that decolonisation should not be reduced to the exclusive domain of the state: 'we could equally well stress the rise of a new nation, the setting up of a new state, its diplomatic relations, and its economic and political trends. But we have precisely chosen to speak of that kind of *tabula rasa* which characterises at the outset all decolonisation' (1963, 35). The disordering process of decolonisation is intricately bound up with the nature of colonialism in a clash of antagonistic forces. Fanon's analysis makes resistance a central value, and from this standpoint he approached the power structure of colonialism. The disordering process of decolonisation emphasises changing consciousness. Decolonisation starts with a change of the consciousness of the colonised, a far-reaching and foundational goal. The changing of the colonial structure entails that all social relations are fundamentally transformed into a new, higher unity, beyond the original opposition, assuming the radical opposite of everything that colonialism was: its violence, its brutality, it suppression, its racism, its unfreedom.

Violent resistance has a 'cathartic effect' on the colonised, assisting those colonised to deal with the accumulated trauma of the lived reality of colonialism. While this outlook may seem to 'romanticise' violence and come across as a reckless and indifferent conclusion, Fanon's years of treating patients suffering from trauma led him to believe that colonialism dramatically interweaved the psychological with the social. In struggling against the colonial Manichean world, the colonised had to confront the day-to-day, unspoken trauma inhabiting the deepest layers of consciousness, which manifested in contradictory ways and 'internal' expressions of violence. If resistance did not confront this psychology of colonialism, it would be easy to predict that the nationalist struggle would face insurmountable pitfalls that would cause untold negative effects.

A Manichean world is likely to produce irrational generalisations. It will lead anything that is not part of the white world to be considered as 'good' and progressive and thus embraced as resistance, as in Njabulo Ndebele's 'uncritical solidarities' discussed in chapter 1. This is Fanon's problem with Negritude. Such 'reactionary' cultural practices of the colonised, which find solace in spirits and fantasy (as in voodoo), can easily be sentimentalised and applauded as 'native culture' (Fanon 1963, 57). He even traced the celebrated association with African dance and rhythm to modern colonialism, not a precolonial nostalgia or essentialism. This is arguably a point of difference between Fanon and Biko. In 'Some African Cultural Concepts' presented in 1971, Biko (2005) speculatively aimed to isolate 'pure' and authentic African cultural practices that survived colonialism, even though African culture has been 'experiencing a process of acculturation' since 1652 and suffered 'severe blows and may have been battered nearly out of shape' (2005, 46). Biko here identified practices of modern African cultural humanism that broke with Western individualist culture, many of which he traced to traditional African culture. Fanon rejected any associations between a 'pure' practice and a racially classified group, believing that such understanding remained locked in a Manichean framework by associating black skin with certain values.

Fanon (like Marx before him and Foucault in the same period) saw resistance to colonialism as reconstituting subjects in resistance practices: 'decolonization never takes place unnoticed, for it influences individuals and modifies them fundamentally' (1963, 36). It must produce 'new men', transforming the objects of exploitation that they were under colonialism into free humans. The goal of decolonisation is bringing the human out of an imprisoned object. The goal has to be an absolute, all-encompassing, complete and radical transformation, as per the Biblical quotation 'The last shall be first and the first last' (Matthew 20:16; Fanon 1963, 37). Anything less is not decolonisation, consequently decolonisation is 'always successful'. Fanon did not appreciate or permit half measures. In his view, reformist measures left the objectified characteristics of the colonised unaffected. Freedom had to be absolute and total or it would not be freedom.

In fighting for the 'last to be first', Fanon, recognised that 'The natives' challenge … is not a rational confrontation …' (1963, 41). The conflict is so straightforwardly about power expressed in everyday brute violence that any talk of values that do not address the principle of 'the last shall be first'—in this context, a common-sense reversal of the colonial situation—are looked upon with suspicion (1963, 46). The dominant discourse represents the colonised as the epitome of evil, beyond all values and reason. But when the stirrings of resistance begin, the colonial order raises the issues of values (normally universal human rights) in hopes of arriving at compromised outcomes. The established nationalist parties and the intellectuals, who are normally cut off from the subaltern masses, are the first to waver in the face of this rising subaltern consciousness, and some of the most radical elements will predictably change course, as will many who will simply use the changing conjuncture to pursue their own self-interests in the new language of change.

Fanon despised the nationalist parties, the intellectuals, and the colonial liberals. He argued that the awakening of resistance among the subalterns gives rise to all such groups, which invariably outmanoeuvre the subalterns. They compromise and sell out the peasantry's radical goals. Despite what the nationalist elites say, their long-term goal is to preserve their own interests. In fact, considering their material conditions, this 'selling out' is unsurprising (1963, 44). As modern classes and products of the colonial educational system, they have been cut off from the mass of peasants, and their subjectivity will inevitably be different. They will thus conceptualise the colonial situation differently than the peasants and the urban marginalised, who easily conclude that force must be met with force and that change must be absolute. The colonised intellectuals necessarily have to confront the question of values. They will agonize over the liberal paradigm of the soft-liners in the colonial power because they owe their identities to those very 'universal values' that are the basis of modern education. For their part, the masses will contradictorily follow the demands of the national parties, demonstrate for the release of imprisoned leaders, and eventually join in the celebrations once the compromised outcomes have been agreed and the new, independent nation has been born. However, they will soon realise that their lives have not changed; they will still be living in the same miserable conditions in which they had always lived under colonialism (Fanon 1963, 75).

It is impossible to ignore that colonial legacies last for a long time. The anti-colonial struggle must therefore address these legacies head-on or the effects will persist and the poor, dehumanised masses, the working class and peasantry, will remain so. Fanon attacked many targets. For the 'wretched of the earth', the obstacles to liberation are many and formidable: the old colonial powers, international capitalism, colonialism as both idea and ideology, the new states, the nationalist bourgeoisie and the ignorance of the masses. The peasants and the urban subalterns serve as the only potential agents of radical change. The emergent nationalist middle class quickly occupies the place of the departing colonialists. They continue to exploit the mass of people and keep them in ignorance, and they will play upon the subaltern's emotions and cultural practices. They pose a dilemma: dance, spirit worship, voodoo and rhythm ought to be understood not as 'givens', but in terms of whether they serve the struggle against colonialism or respond to colonial trauma. He viewed them as cultural coping strategies, which allowed the colonised to create their own world or comfort zone but which may not necessarily constitute progressive elements for popular change.

Fanon consequently became ambiguous about modernity. Like Marx he admired what modernity can achieve by unleashing material resources, yet he located modernity (specifically as the bureaucratic state and capitalism) in the colonial situation with the unfolding of violence, which leads to the decimation of its subjects and wounds them for generations. He does leave open the possibility of an alternative modernity, though. Macey (2000) emphasised Fanon's dedication at the end of *Black Skin, White Masks* (1986), interpreting his plea 'O my body, make me always a man who questions!' as expressing a thoroughly Kantian conception of the Enlightenment. But reason and questioning are not unrelated to the critical project, namely the Marxist commitment towards the exploited and degraded masses seeking to change the world. Fanon wrote in 'The Pitfalls of National Consciousness' (1963) that the masses constitute 'revolutionary capital'. Here he not only identified a different source and path of modernity, but also left the door open for outcomes other than the 'iron cages' that normally constitute subjects in the modern paradigm. Unfortunately, the postcolonial experience, whose character is carved out largely by the national middle class (that unfortunate group produced as intermediaries by settler colonialism), leaves that middle class incapable of embracing the masses. The possibility of real independence (an alternative, radical path to modernity) after colonialism is so bleak that Fanon suggested restarting the decolonisation process. The radical movement in this second effort should prevent the key failings of the nationalist struggle, the rise and consolidation of the nationalist bourgeoisie and guard against any signs of the demobilisation of the masses as active historical agents.

Unsurprisingly, the contemporary malaise in South Africa's political culture is fuelled by the administrative inefficiencies of the nationalist bourgeoisie and its self-seeking activities under the label of Black Economic Empowerment and 'transformation'. At the same time, the ANC's return from decades in exile and reestablishment of its domestic presence in the 1990s demobilised subaltern grassroots structures that had developed to resist Apartheid. They were replaced by a rigid, uncreative and top-down effort that has failed to capture the earlier charismatic politics.

Postcolonial aporias

Fanon's predictions of the failures of the national bourgeoisie are so evident in post-Apartheid South Africa that his essay 'The Pitfalls of National Consciousness' can be readily applied to contemporary politics. Fanon wrote about arresting, and even reversing, the revolutionary process in the new order. Reading the historical process of decolonisation against the grain, he compared the emergence of modernity in Europe with that of the Third World with descriptions resonating strongly with Africa. He identified Marx's argument that the historical development of capital invariably transformed its subject (the capitalist class) into a revolutionary agent until European society was almost completely transformed and the capitalist class had eventually itself become a fetter towards further progress. Fanon saw in the Third World a national bourgeoisie without capital that was hence unable to transform society and behaved like the European bourgeoisie in its decadent phase, i.e., a class having aspirations of transformation but in practice a fetter on progress and an embarrassing burden to the subaltern's project.

The new nationalist bourgeoisie is simply structurally and ideologically incapable of leading the social fragments left by settler colonialism in a revolutionary project and an alternative modernity. The European bourgeoisie had accumulated capital over generations and fought off rivals (the church and the landed-aristocratic estates) (Bendix 1964; Moore 1993), whereas the colonised bourgeoisie has no independent source of power without capital, the moving force of capitalist modernity. The nationalist bourgeoisie is completely dependent on the state or handouts from established colonial capital. It is weak, underdeveloped, and opportunistic, active mainly in small trading, professional activities and education. It remains small and lacks the inventiveness associated with capital in Europe during the period of its emergence. Unlike its European counterpart, the nationalist bourgeoisie has been unable to produce any financiers or industrial magnates. It is concentrated in the capital city and identifies the 'mother country' as the standard against which all values are evaluated.

Due to its weak structural position, the national bourgeoisie in the post-independence period discovered its role to be that of 'intermediary' between the colonial power and the bourgeoisie on the one hand and the popular masses with which it should identify (Fanon 1963, 152) on the other. Lacking capital, it seeks the support of the colonial state and the bourgeoisie, rather than looking to the 'masses' in the colonised country, who could substitute as 'revolutionary capital'. This opportunist class is effectively protecting its own interests by allying itself with the colonial power, the most powerful interests representing it, or, for Biko, the white power structure. The Marikana massacre in 2012 aptly illustrates this thesis. Fanon emphasised the constraints of the institutional structure and its history, aware that settler colonialism produces a weak nationalist bourgeoisie. Yet he also kept open political choice and agency and brought it into his analysis to explain how decolonisation becomes bogged down in a narrow nationalism. The nationalist bourgeoisie's historical characteristics and political choices result in a nationalism that excludes the subalterns from the centre of a critical political practice and culture and thus does not seek to make the nation ever transformative and creative.

The class formation of settler colonialism fosters a superficial nationalist project unless a revolutionary group deeply rooted in workers and peasants takes charge. The progressive elements must be vigilant because the new elite will make every effort to secure their own interests by relying on narrow nationalism to garner the support of the masses; the negative, reactionary expressions of nationalism define the project of the nationalist bourgeoisie. Based primarily on African postcolonial experiences, Fanon's prognosis is dismal. Swathes of people uncritically accept this inward-looking consciousness in which 'the nation is passed over for the race, and the tribe is preferred to the state' (1963, 148) to promote xenophobia, tribalism, and the continued circulation of ideas of 'race' and racism under the cover of transforming and unravelling the legacies of the past.

The working class is also marginal to the social fabric as a whole, because of its small size compared to the developed capitalist formations. It is therefore unable to bring about the revolutionary, radical transformation that Marx predicted (although Fanon's conclusion did not apply to South Africa as at the time he was referring to countries at lower levels of entrenched capitalist social relations compared to South Africa). The weak working class in the urban areas also adopts the narrow nationalism, chauvinism, territorialism and racism of the national bourgeoisie, a racism that is ultimately motivated by 'defence, based on fear' (Fanon 1963, 164) and mostly expressed as a 'vulgar tribalism'. Similar to the national bourgeoisie, it looks for scapegoats for its inability to compete or develop an independent vision. As Fanon wrote (1963, 159), the idea of African unity, 'that vague formula', 'takes off the mask, and crumbles into regionalism inside the hollow shell of nationality itself'. It gives way to violence and demonstrations against other Africans who are viewed as competitors or obstacles in their path towards material upward mobility. 'Old rivalries which were there before colonialism' express themselves (Fanon 1963, 159).

The rise of xenophobic attacks in post-Apartheid South Africa against Africans from other countries, who are the target of mass demonstrations in which struggle songs and slogans are sung, was a surprise development. It went against the dominant ideology's emphasis on Ubuntu and the African Renaissance (but not the everyday state practice of the police and Home Affairs officials who victimise Africans not born in South Africa). Although detailed research of such pogroms reveals that many factors are at work, we cannot ignore Fanon's persuasive point of superficial nationalism and demobilised masses unable to compete and drawn towards easy scapegoating in such xenophobic attacks. Fanon took current examples as he was writing, including attacks of the Dahomian and Voltaic peoples in the Ivory Coast, the breakup of the Senegal-Mali federation with anti-Sudanese demonstrations, and Congolese demands that the Senegalese leave: 'These foreigners are called to leave; their shops are burned, their street stalls are wrecked, and in fact the government of the Ivory Coast commands them to go, thus giving their nationals satisfaction' (1963, 156). The national bourgeoisie identify the former colonisers as their main competition, whereas for the urban mass 'competition is represented principally by Africans of another nation' (1963, 157). However, any hope for a true African unity will require that ordinary people go against their own bourgeoisie (Fanon 1963, 164).

The political dominance of the nationalist bourgeoisie will not produce liberal democracy or socialism: 'This fight for democracy against oppression of mankind will slowly leave the confusion of neo-liberal universalism to emerge, sometimes laboriously, as a claim to nationhood' (Fanon 1963, 148). Instead, it can produce only a mechanical national consciousness that will 'be in any case only an empty shell, a crude and fragile travesty of what might have been' (Fanon 1963, 148). This emerging class lacks confidence, assumes defensive roles and desires to 'mirror' the West, yet it comes across as a pitiful mimicking. Ever fearful of the disgruntled masses, the nationalist party demobilises popular formations and imposes a top-down politics, and previously vibrant branches of the organisation lose popular legitimacy as all power increasingly centres on the national leader. The state becomes a source of rampant corruption amidst rising ethnic identification, regionalism and tribalism. The country remains poor and dependent.

Conclusion

South Africa is the typical case of settler-colonial society. The introduction of the institutions, social relations and practices associated with modernity, such as the state, capitalism and subject identities, came to South Africa with settler colonialism. Modern South Africa 'disrupted' alternative local processes of nation formation, trade, cultural evolution and subject identity. Those alternative paths seem closed and only imaginable. It is no coincidence that Biko was significantly influenced by Fanon's analysis. The turn inward to the consciousness of oppression and the development of a politics surrounding identity inspired mass mobilisations, which culminated in the Soweto revolt and the ruling class's initiatives of de-racialising capitalism. They set in motion what eventually produced a liberal constitutionalist outcome. More significantly, the *aporias* that Fanon identified are uncannily prescient about the pitfalls of the nationalist bourgeoisie in contemporary South Africa.

4| The colonial state and settler-colonial modernism

It seems obvious that modernity produces states, societies and subjects in varied ways, so it is striking that conventional studies of contemporary democracy exclude the driving force in South Africa: the barrel of a gun. Yet, bringing the idea that modernity was imposed through violence into the analysis of South African politics can explain why state-sponsored violence continues and generalised violence permeates society even after the establishment of electoral democracy. The anomalies and contradictions of the bourgeois democratic model in South Africa can be interpreted more persuasively with reference to settler-colonial modernity. As a paradigmatic case of Frantz Fanon's (1963) analysis of settler-colonial modernity, this chapter draws on Fanon, Michel Foucault (1990, 1995) and Giorgio Agamben (1998, 2004) to understand how modernity in South Africa unfolded by the constitution of its subjects through settler-colonial violence. The discussion is organised into four broad themes: the emergence of colonial relations out of slave society; wars of expansion and the consolidation of the state as a source of concentrated power; the relationship between Manichean society and class; and lastly, Apartheid-capitalism and its contradictions that postcolonial democracy cannot resolve. The chapter ends by reiterating that the post-Apartheid experiment with liberal democracy will remain limited if it is framed as a fundamental rupture with its past. That key assumption of recent third wave democratisation literature excludes the history of violence in the processes of the making of modern South Africa and its legacies for the modern state, racialised capitalism and racialised subjects.

Understanding modernity and its questions in South Africa

Guha's observation that the colonial experience consists of three elements, namely violence, exploitation and legality (1997, 156), holds true for South Africa. The violence associated with settler colonialism in South Africa and the subaltern responses to overcome it make the Western-type political modernity that Gilroy describes as 'bourgeois democracy in the genteel metropolitan guise' (1993, 77) improbable. The process by which modernity unfolded in the southern part of Africa introduced colonial states in the wake of the destruction or reordering of local polities that were themselves undergoing processes of political consolidation. Spurred on by an unquenchable thirst for land, labour and eventually mining profits, settler colonialism forced disparate groups into newly imagined 'national' territories (Anderson 1982). The new power racially organised the emerging polity into rigid hierarchies, 'cutting the world into two,' and thereby produced racialised subjects, 'black' and 'white' or native and settler, that were violently 'incomplete' because their identities depended entirely on the Other.

Approaching the state from the perspective of the particularity of settler-colonial-imposed modernity highlights two features: the process of capitalist imperialist expansion imposed this modernity violently from the 'outside' and the state, which once instituted as part of this process, evolved into the primary instrument that managed the system of settler colonialism. The state created the impression of centrally concentrated power; it introduced the crucial distinctiveness, instruments, knowledge and procedures within the new colonial power dynamic while also imposing and maintaining it. A new, distinctive monopoly of violence effectively coordinated the project to produce racialised subjects based on the radical difference in colonial discourse between coloniser and colonised.

In the 1970s, the relationship between modernity and racism attracted much scholarly debate, which demonstrated that South African studies remained within the orbit of Eurocentric habits of thought. On the one hand, in Marxist approaches, the key problem with South Africa is that the majority black workforce was denied political rights, unlike in other industrial capitalist countries; their exclusion from the political system explained the sustained racial policies targeting blacks and essentially discriminating against them (Marks & Trapido 1971). However, this can be identified as a 'problem' or 'anomaly' only if the Western capitalist trajectory is accepted as the universal standard. This distinctive feature in South Africa stems from the relationship between capitalism and racism. How is it that a developed capitalist base relates to an archaic superstructure, which is organised around an ideology promoting deep racial divisions in the society? On the other hand, liberal-modernisation approach identifies it as representing the tension between adaptive modern imperatives, the backward, obstinate traditionalism of African peasant culture, and the Afrikaner ideology shaped by harsh 'frontier experience'. This earlier debate remains influential in the analysis of South African politics.

The key moment of modernity in Marxist scholarship lay in the economics of the mining revolution, namely the emergence of extensive market society and capitalism (Bozzoli & Delius 1990). Liberal discourse considered the positive role of British colonial policies in introducing central administrative structures, legal codes and Enlightenment ideas as fundamental. To explain Apartheid as a political order of state and society, it focused on Afrikaner-influenced racist practice, whereas Marxist thought emphasised the racial organisation of the mining economy and its undermining of class dynamics to accumulate increased surplus value. The differences turned on whether modernity contradicts or complements the racial hierarchies that seemed common-sense in this settler-colonial society. The liberal school had faith that capitalism would eventually overcome the anachronism of systematic racial discrimination after the discovery by South African capitalists that continual dependence on migrant labour would prove unprofitable in the long run (Wilson & Thompson 1971).

An early Marxist critic of the liberal view, Frederick Johnstone (1970), identified what he considered to be the weak premises of the liberal thesis: economic development contradicted white supremacist ideology; capitalist-industrialisation and the market were modernising but segregationist and Apartheid policies were 'backward looking' and expressed rigid ideology; due to the high turnover of unskilled workers, market efficiencies would make migrant labour obsolete and capitalist industrialisation would require skilled and semi-skilled labour; and these contradictions would likely result in the political conflict resolving itself through negotiation and elite accommodation. He disagreed that a contradictory relationship existed between capitalism and white supremacist political ideology. Capitalist-industrialisation and the market were not necessarily liberalising, nor were segregationist and Apartheid policies always 'backward looking' and rigid. He also insisted that the demand for skilled and semi-skilled labour and migrant labour inefficiencies would not be resolved through reforms and elite accommodation (Johnstone 1970).

The discovery of diamonds and gold in the late nineteenth-century ushered in capitalist production, linking South Africa to the developing imperialist global system. The mining sector established coercive labour regulations; political and ideological racist expressions preached black inferiority, white superiority and the super-exploitation of African mineworkers. The state and mining companies established elaborate mechanisms to prevent labour unrest and to secure a constant labour supply. The 'backward' political and ideological policies were necessary for capitalist accumulation, at least at a definite stage of its development. After all, state labour laws enabled the enforcement of extremely low wages to African workers because they prevented African unionisation, disallowed 'racially mixed' trade unions, reserved skilled jobs for whites and restricted the wives, children and extended family of African workers to barren 'homelands'. South African capitalism historically depended on and benefitted from a racial division of labour (Wolpe 1972).

Marxist theory conventionally interprets these state interventions as 'cheapening' the cost of African labour, allowing the capitalist class to rake in super profits from racist policies. Although Marxist writing acknowledges that racism is traceable to the colonial encounter, it draws too strict a separation between that colonial past and the origins of racist labour laws that were designed to address the mining industry's demands (Stadler 1987) and restrictively emphasises the 'role of mining capital in the foundations of modernity and racism. In the formation of the racialised state and the construction of racialised subjects, Marxist analysis tends to ignore the role of pre-capitalist ideas and practices that directly contributed towards and/or prepared the ground for the later capitalist mode to ground itself. Further, white citizens from all classes, including capitalist mine and farm owners, white workers and the middle classes, benefited from Apartheid, colonial laws and the informal privileges that came with white identity. Marxist analysis typically avoided the subjectivity of the colonised (on which Fanon and Biko focused), the humiliations and the politics of skin and of body and mind. Instead, it explored how racism was objectively functional to capitalist accumulation, which it promoted along with the capitalist class. Marxist analysis has been unwilling to adopt Fanon's suggestion:

> The originality of the colonial context is that economic reality, inequality and the immense difference of ways of life never come to mask the human realities ... what parcels out the world is to begin with the fact of belonging to or not belonging to a given race.... In the colonies the economic substructure is also a superstructure. The cause is the consequence; you are rich because you are white, you are white because you are rich. This is why Marxist analysis should always be slightly stretched every time we have to do with the colonial problem (1963, 30).

The conventional and dominant understanding of how capitalism (read: economics or modernity) related to Apartheid (read: political system and/or pre-modernity) echoed Eurocentric and historicist thinking. Although liberal and Marxist approaches were at opposite extremes of this scale, they were joined at the hip about the idea that capitalism (and its agent capital) spreads outwards and 'arises in one part of the world at a particular period and then develops globally over historical time, encountering and negotiating historical differences in the process' (Chakrabarty 2000, 47). The capitalist mode of production promises an end stage or prepares the ground for socialism. In liberal thought it ends with abstract individuals freely contracting with one another in an unbiased market and inhabiting a civil society in which equal citizenship rights apply to all. This template is thought to describe a universal process, so the toolbox of concepts that it generated strongly influenced the social sciences' interest in comparative development. However, it approximates the European and North American experience of capitalism. Fanon made clear that Manichean society fundamentally breaks with this self-image and understanding of capitalism; he wrote that this requires examining how colonising power articulated itself through colonial difference, i.e., the zone of its politics in securing its domination. According to Chakrabarty, writers of subaltern history must 'give up neither Marx nor difference' (2000, 95).

In South Africa and the Third World generally, the 'conquest state' is the main character of the narrative of political modernity. That does not mean that other elements of modernity (capital, its agent/the capitalist class, and discourses that normalise docile bodies) had no or marginal roles to play. Instead, because they function in a theatre defined by the violent relationship of coloniser to colonised, the state is the key driver and mediator. The state's mediation is one impetus for the mode of capitalism's emergence and consolidation; its role in monopolising violence and bureaucratic power to destroy rival sovereigns, control the bodies of the colonised and consider the black mass as *homo sacer* is another. Fanon reversed Marx's famous metaphor when analysing the colonial situation, warning that the elements of the superstructure 'determined' the economic base; it must be accepted that black subjects are moulded by pervasive legal violence and the state of exception was a 'permanent' feature of black life.

The conventional analysis of democracy assumes that, 'as modernity spreads from the Western centres of economic and political power to other parts of the world, it tends to produce societies similar to those of the modern West' and that modernity describes a 'single, homogenous process [that] can be traced to a single causal principle' (Kaviraj 2000, 137). For Marx, that 'single causal principle' is capitalist commodity production, i.e., the commodification of life; for Weber, it is the ever expanding 'iron cage' of rationalisation that suffocates all spheres of social life. Unfolding democracies in Southern Africa are thus disappointing because they hardly mirror the typical Western model. But both assumptions are wrong.

Kaviraj arrived at the prudent conclusion that 'we should expect modernity not to be homogenous' (2000, 138). In the everyday practices of its subjects, modernity introduces a 'radical rupture'; social practices are moulded by the interaction of previous embedded practices, the subjects' willingness and local power dynamics. Consequently, modernity does not operate on a 'clean slate' (2000, 138) but imposes itself as a combination of many different processes that interact but follow their own logic. They do not form a coherent package or necessarily follow an identical sequence. In South Africa, for example, the colonial state rationalised the control of colonised subjects and labour in the productive sphere; the introduction of the Bantu Education Act (1953) allowed the black masses to be educated but aimed to produce subjects with few or no skills. In contrast, India's Macaulay's Minute turned educated Indians into non-white Englishmen and women. Kaviraj (2000) also encouraged the study of modernity's approaches to collective agency and social mobilisation, which normally entails monitoring existing practices and the 'reflexion' of other societies, i.e., their past, present and future. The elites may even intend to achieve their modernising goals differently because they feel alienated from the Western experience of modernity. Hence later modernities will not replicate the experiences of the West.

Kaviraj's reservations are helpful for understanding the unique (read: violent) processes by which modernity produces states, societies and relationally 'incomplete' racialised subjects in Southern Africa (2000). In the previous chapters I have argued that the conventional analysis proposes a historicist notion of political modernity and that, framed ethnocentrically, third wave democracy sets as its goal and standard the 'bourgeois democracy in the genteel metropolitan guise' (Gilroy 1993). It does not account for the way that settler colonialism shaped the emergence of post-Apartheid, postcolonial democracy. The history of violence becomes more significant as it is better understood how the nationalist-modern project became mired in crisis, why elites and masses go off in different directions and how politics is fought in the terrains of civil and political society despite the once-unifying nationalist struggle. It also makes it possible to question and reframe the contradictions of the post-Apartheid bourgeois democratic model.

The colonial situation as violent rupture

From the first days of conquest, the violence meted out to local communities revealed that each member was considered a *homo sacer*, someone without political significance whose killing was neither worthy of juridical evaluation nor religious sacrifice. They were always vulnerable to excessive violence. From the colonisers' perspective, the conquest introduced progress, enlightenment and modernisation to an almost barren and savage land. Racist attitudes are attested from the moment of settlement: Jan Van Riebeeck, the first commander of the Cape of Good Hope, referred to the local Khoi ('Hottentots') as 'the black stinking dogs' who should be killed in 1652 (De Kiewiet 1941, 20). In the initial colonial encounter, the local San and Khoi people faced the dreadful choice of taking up arms and facing death or renouncing their autonomy to participate in the 'political community' as slaves. This situation resonates with Agamben's thinking about bare life as relative to '*zoe*', what remains when the political community that provides significance is destroyed. Yet what remains when local communities are considered valueless and their members 'savages' in situations of colonial conquest is a different question. What remains when the people found in these lands are considered as having no political value or sense of the good life?

According to Wood (2005), the economic imperatives behind capitalist imperialist expansion produced legal principles (*res nullius*, literally 'that which belongs to no one', or ownerless land), racial stereotypes of laziness (indigenous peoples are non-productive and therefore without a right to land), racism (Europeans were superior, therefore conquest was a European right) and the belief that the seizure of indigenous land would eventually benefit the natives. This initial encounter developed into the colonial division of labour along colour hierarchies, with unskilled 'hard work' considered inappropriate for Europeans. Armstrong and Worden discovered that 'by the late 18th century the Cape Colony had become one of the most closed and rigid slave societies so far analysed by historians' (1989, 143). It became normal for masters to be white and slaves black. Once the defeated had been incorporated into colonial relations of domination, those blacks (the San, Khoi, imported slaves and conquered 'tribal' groups) experienced bare life in the sense of that 'zone of indistinction and continuous transition between man and beast' (Agamben 1998, 109) and were always potential targets of violence that did not amount to crime. Their exclusion from the settlement paradoxically included them because it enabled the idea of *bios* and a life of political significance.

What eventually became sovereign power spanning the long, complex and differentiated period from Van Riebeeck's military garrison of the mid-seventeenth-century to the modern-bureaucratic South African state in 1910 thus came with colonial conquest, settlement and slavery. The history of the state starts with the establishment of a fortress settlement of the Dutch East India Company (DEIC), a trading company/military enterprise, on the shores of Cape Town in 1652. The colonial state grew gradually from this halfway station, which supported the DEIC's shipping crews between Holland and its east Asian territories (De Kiewiet 1941). This limited and perhaps temporary administrative base grew gradually as Dutch farmers were allowed to settle farther away. The small convict population and the resistance from Khoi and San communities led the DEIC to import slaves.

In 1658, the DEIC brought 228 slaves from Dahomey and traded 174 slaves from a captured Portuguese slaver bound for Brazil. The slave population grew from these blacks held in bondage in the Cape, although recurring outbreaks of disease, such as the large smallpox epidemic of 1713, killed many. By 1750, almost half the male freeburghers in the colony had at least one slave; when British forces occupied the Cape in 1798, the slave population exceeded that of freeburghers. Slaves' racial background was not distinguished. African, Malagasy, Indian and Indonesian slaves were called interchangeably '*slaaven*' or '*lijfeigenen*' (slaves, literally 'life property'). All persons of colour, whether slave or free, were referred to as '*zwarten*' (black). '*Vrijswarten*' (free blacks) was the label for slaves who had bought their own freedom or who had received their manumission from their masters.

The few farmers with monopoly privileges (through the so-called *pacht* law) to supply the DEIC needed many slaves. Adriaan van der Stel (1699–1707) used them to become the 'biggest landowner, the biggest cattle and wheat farmer, the biggest wine grower and slave owner' (De Kiewiet 1941, 7). But, in the early period of DEIC control, most slave owners had fewer than five slaves. This 'domestic slavery' encouraged the rigid dichotomy between the lifeworlds of the master and slave and reinforced the status and honour of slave ownership. There were significantly fewer manumissions at the Cape than in other slave societies. Local penalties and the Statutes of India of 1642 applied to all slaves, no matter their place of origin. They required slaves to possess a signed letter from their master whenever they ran errands, carry lighted torches at night, observe curfews and not carry firearms or gather in groups of more than three. Bolstered by extreme punishments, they gave masters absolute power. Slaves caught stealing or accused of attacking their masters would be put to death. A *plakkaat* (proclamation) of 1714 allowed settlers to shoot on sight any runaway slaves. Punishment routinely included gruesome torture; the branding of faces was so common that, in 1727, a law was passed to move its usual location to slaves' backs 'out of consideration for the feelings of the Europeans, particularly pregnant women, who might encounter them' (Armstrong and Worden 1989, 156).

The scattering of isolated farms across the Cape peninsula and the small numbers of slaves to each master left slaves vulnerable. Owners were rarely punished for severe violence towards slaves. In contrast to Armstrong and Worden (1989, 161), who counted two slave uprisings involving 'small numbers', Forman wrote about slave revolts in 1707, 1714, 1719 and 1765 (1960, 5). It was more common for slaves to resist less dramatically by running away from farms, converting to and openly practicing Islam, developing their own vernacular (Afrikaans), petitioning the DEIC and even joining the Khoi and San communities.

The demand for land and labour was the common interest of both the Companystate and the freeburghers, and it pitted them against the locals who wanted to protect their land, patterns of subsistence and communities. The steadily growing settler farming population clashed with the DEIC over its restrictive, sovereign-like control. Although it retained a monopoly on the purchase of goods at fixed prices and prevented contacts with local 'Hottentots' by disallowing land grabs beyond the colony's borders, 'at no time was the Company able or willing to ... bring European settlement firmly under its control' (De Kiewiet 1941, 12). It promoted freehold land at first but rented farms annually (£5 for 6,000 acres) from 1717. As long as farmers paid rent, they could use the land as their own. It became common for a *'Boer'* youth leaving his father's farm to walk his horse for half an hour in four directions from a central point to determine the size of his farm (1941, 16). This encouraged larger land grabs and movement into the interior of the country.

Through war and plunder the small, slave-based agricultural Cape colony moved to mass settlement in the eighteenth-century (the trekboers), outward expansion, the intervention of imperial Britain and the eventual drawing up of present-day South Africa. Crucially, the sovereign was externally imposed and created the political community by excluding bare life (i.e., black life), which simultaneously included it by virtue of its absence of political significance and thus left blacks vulnerable to extreme violence. The state remained an entity of violence; its rationale was to obtain compliance in a society divided unequally according to 'race'; even the so-called colour-blind Cape Constitution of 1853 set a £25 property qualification for voting that all but excluded the few non-white voters otherwise treated as citizens. The general laws protected the settlers while targeting colonised blacks and exposing them to sovereign violence. In this settler colonial formation, the state first established sovereign control over the territory and its inhabitants and then, through various systems of forced labour, exploited them for the benefit of the settler population. The wars that started against the Khoi and San in the seventeenth-century ended in the late nineteenth-century with the defeat of the Xhosa. In this period, the state honed its instruments of violence and its war-making capacity. In this process of state and society formation, coercion far outweighed 'market forces' and, as demonstrated by the settlers' dependence upon extra-economic interventions even in the emerging sphere of production, 'free markets' had little meaning outside ideology.

The colonial state and war-making

The modern state is the state as it developed in Europe. Whether the focus is on characteristics, functions or relations within or without, European history provides the standard definition and theories of the state. 'Universal' characteristics gleaned from this regional experience include an administrative structure, association, territory and national claims to represent the polity. Although the European process of state formation came about largely as a result of internal processes that over time produced a central authoritative apparatus, it serves as the yardstick even when it is evidently inapplicable.

States are marked by their particular histories, yet all intend to regulate the behaviour of persons within their territory. In his 1918 lecture 'Politics as a Vocation',

Max Weber highlighted the state's association with violence: the state as an association among many should be defined by its means and not by its ends or tasks, and the 'specific means peculiar to it, as to every political association, namely, is the use of physical force' (1958, 78). Although force is not the only means available to the state, it is unique to the state. In a given territory, many associations historically may have had access to force, but only the state acquired a monopoly and can use it legitimately. In other words, in Weber's view, the state has the 'right' to use violence enshrined in the law. The Weberian state is never isolated from relations of domination because its rationale is to obtain obedience, supported by legitimate violence. Weber attributed the 'inner justifications' for obedience to three ideal types of legitimacy: traditional, charismatic and legal-rational. The legal-rational values dominate the modern state, but all are present.

In Europe, the outcome of the battle to achieve this monopoly of legitimate violence separated the relationship between the executive staff from the means of administration (Weber 1958, 82). Weber defined the state in relation to this monopoly of force and not in the terms of social contract theory:

> The modern state is a compulsory association, which organises domination. It has been successful in seeking to monopolise the legitimate use of physical force as a means of domination within a territory. To this end the state has combined the material means of organization in the hands of its leaders, and it has expropriated all autonomous functionaries of estates who formerly controlled these means in their own right. The state has taken their positions and now stands in the top place (1958, 83).

That states are products of war is relevant to understanding the modern state in South Africa, although its colonial permutation is different from that of Europe. Influenced by Weber, Charles Tilly argued that war-making is inseparable from capital accumulation due to the power-holder's need to extract resources, including capital, by 'outright plunder, regular tribute or bureaucratic taxation' (1985, 181) from a territory's population in return for protection. This extortion of local inhabitants is racketeering; one person or organisation offers protection from their own violence and insecurity. Tilly's metaphor also describes how the state makes inroads into society to eventually become a dominant force of regulation. It participates in the processes of war-making, state-making, protection and extraction, which establish the basis for state legitimacy. The practice of 'war-making' eliminates enemies, i.e., state competition outside the territory, while the 'state-making' activities eliminate enemies and competition within. Each of these interdependent aspects are constitutive of the modern state: war-making with the military, state-making with governing institutions, protection with the courts and representative assemblies and extraction with fiscal structures. In the dominant narrative these internally generated processes and emerging capitalist social relations from the mid-fifteenth century describe the formation of the state in western Europe.

Tilly's analysis is relevant to understanding modern state formation in South Africa because it highlights the differences from the European trajectory. It was a sovereign force and imposed from without, yet, because it was motivated by interests of imperialism, it borrowed knowledge and adapted its learning and techniques of state-building, population control and regulating bodies from Europe. The so-called 'frontier' wars, which incorporated people and territory into the expanding colonial political order, were significant to state-building. Davenport (1977) presented detailed accounts of the ten wars fought against 'the Xhosa' between 1779 and 1879, and Leonard Thompson and Monica Wilson identified the important dates and wars of this colonial expansion:

> During a hundred years the boundary shifted eastward ... In 1772 some Xhosa, mingled with Khoikhoi, were living on the Gamtoos; in 1806 the boundary was the Fish ... in 1811 Ndlambe with 20000 followers were pushed across it. In 1819 the country between the Fish and the Keiskamma was declared neutral; by 1824 it was partly occupied by whites. In 1847 the boundary shifted to the Kei; in 1858 to the Mbashe; in 1878 to the Mthatha; and in 1894 Pondoland between the Mthatha and Mtamvuna, was annexed (1971, 252).

As the frontier moved outwards, the Griqua, Zulu, southern Sotho, Tswana, Swazi, and finally the Mpondo and East Griqua were conquered. The war divided the population of the colony into a political community of significance and a majority defined by its vulnerability to arbitrary violence. In the colonial narrative every victory in war against local communities registered an expansion of civilisation, the 'civilisation mission'.

The discovery of diamond deposits in 1867 and gold in 1886 precipitated a sense of urgency in the British colonial office to stabilise the political community, bring law and order and secure its imperialist control of the region. Whitehall decided that the Cape government should function as its instrument, although it recognised the administration's weakness in the face of formidable challenges: Afrikaner republics were too independent, African polities retained too much control and Germany posed a potential threat to British interests.

The correspondence behind the appointment of Bartle Frere as the new high commissioner of Southern Africa in Cape Town in 1877 reveals this imperialist vision. In 1876 Frere received a letter of invitation from the Secretary of State for the Colonies in London, Henry Herbert, Earl of Carnarvon, setting out Carnarvon's vision for the political reorganisation into a Confederation of the Southern African region under British control. He saw the solution to restructuring an uncivilised, chaotic political landscape into a confederation of federal states governed by London. He chose Frere, he said, because of Frere's skills, colonial wisdom and experience. Carnarvon promised Frere the status of a governor and an even higher position if the confederation succeeded. He warned Frere that his appointment took place at the 'edge of a great native war', so 'the position was one of extreme delicacy from its political as well as its native complications' (Martineau 2009, 187). Carnarvon's reference to 'political' referred to delicate relations between the local 'whites', the British and their relations with the Afrikaner republics. He believed the 'natives' were incapable of practicing or participating in politics. He saw the war between the Transvaal and the natives as an 'opportunity' to increase the role of Britain in the region: a political opening for a spreading imperialism. Frere's task was going to be 'difficult and responsible', but also 'great', as it would 'bring the new machine of government' to this uncivilised land.

Frere's response was, at first sight, strange. He demanded more money to take on this mission, although he acknowledged the responsibility to be 'great' and reiterated his commitment to his country and spreading civilisation. Although Frere contributed to the Boer War after taking up the post, he then believed the British annexation was necessary and beneficial to all (especially after the discovery of diamonds and gold). Imperial intervention would bring civilisation, political community, peace and law. In startling contrast to Giliomee's (2010) sympathetic view of the Afrikaner republics, Frere viewed the Afrikaner republics as corrupt, bankrupt and run by 'uncivilised' Afrikaners from whom the citizens needed to be saved. He envisioned Britain's role as a 'mediator' between Afrikaners and 'natives' but clearly preferred the whites because he feared the natives were uncivilised. He saw the annexation of the Transvaal and war with the Boer republics and Zulu Kingdom as necessary for achieving the larger goal of ordering of the region into a confederation if these groups challenged British authority and remained independent. Yet Martineau, who compiled the correspondence, never mentioned the discovery of diamonds and gold as reasons for the annexation of the Transvaal. Instead, he blamed the breakout of war on Shepstone's hastiness, the delayed correspondence between London and Cape Town and decisions taken in London without reference to local administrators' local knowledge.

Imperialist Britain subordinated African polities through war, settlement, trade, treaties and labour policies. While the outcomes were not inevitable, Lenin identified the structural imperatives behind global expansion. The system of capitalist accumulation needed to move capital, goods and people from Europe and required new markets, raw material and exploitable populations from the colonies. But why the extensive violence and brutal occupation, including the killing of whole populations? In her study of the relationship of capitalism and colonialism to violence, Ellen Wood noted that British colonialism was more penetrating than Spanish or Portuguese; they were extractive, but it wanted to recreate profit-making in the zones themselves. These economic and ideological imperatives were interconnected in legal notions of empty land, dominant ideas that indigenous people were lazy and non-productive and racist beliefs of superior and inferior peoples.

Wood identified that the *res nullius* principle, that the 'civilised' were obliged to take over empty, unproductive land to make it productive, made British colonialism so violent. For British colonialism, it was a moral justification of violent conquest, settlement and the large-scale exploitation of labour. In practice, it allowed the imperial power to demonstrate its power to bring death even to indigenous kings. In 1820–1835 King Hintsa of the Xhosa had made counterclaims to being a sovereign in his own right, based on long tradition. Lieutenant-General Benjamin D'Urban, the governor of the Cape Colony, sent Colonel Harry Smith to lead the frontier war in 1834, and the British fought the Xhosa at Grahamstown. When he was considering a British demand to give up 50,000 of his people's cattle during 'peace talks', he was arrested, held hostage and killed, apparently while trying to escape. While Smith watched, Hintsa's body was mutilated. The severed head was taken to Britain. D'Urban claimed more land from those 'irreclaimable savages' (Keegan 1997, 149), extending as far as the Kei River.

This subjugation by bloodshed enabled the colonial state to stabilise, claim and empirically demonstrate its monopoly of violence; in the colonial situation it did not matter that it lacked the legitimacy Weber considered so central to state domination. Yet, even power expressed largely through violence allows for symbolic ambiguities. Take, for example, the scene of King Solomon KaDinuzulu, leader of the Zulus, at a meeting attended by the British Governor-General of the Union of South Africa Alexander Cambridge, Earl of Athlone in 1930 (Marks 1986). Solomon thought that he should be recognised with the same degree of respect as Athlone, and he openly belittled British rule by criticising it, laughing at its authorities and speaking to his followers rather than addressing the meeting or Athlone. Annoyed British representatives waited for him and his followers to salute Athlone with 'Bayete', a Zulu sign of royal respect. Instead, the crowd shouted 'Bayeza' ('they come'), which was 'vaguely threatening'. Solomon exited the meeting before Athlone, and the people shouted 'Bayete' as he moved through them. Still, he understood his own position as ambiguous in the big power game. He believed that 'only people of Royal Blood are fitted to rule' but was also aware that the chieftain class were in the pay of the colonial authorities and thus required to collect taxes from an impoverished peasantry (Marks 1986, 16–22).

With each victory in the war against local resistance, the state improved its control mechanisms to ensure compliance with new rules of behaviour that served the new ruling order. But this centralised power of the colonial state, and later the Apartheid state, was not exercised on a *tabula rasa* (Kaviraj 2000). Previous indigenous polities had been ruled by minority power-holders who disregarded subalterns; the emerging colonial order built upon these patterns of domination and accommodated and reinforced existing 'traditional' structures of power and their associated normative orders. Its biggest allies were chiefs whose legitimacy came from hierarchies of power rooted in a different cultural order, and the central state exercised its power through these intermediaries whenever possible to regulate the subaltern's behaviour. It manipulated and clashed with the intermediary structures only if the central state's core strategic interests warranted it. Crucially, the colonial (and then Apartheid) state claimed sovereign status from the very beginning but achieved the unwilling subjects' recognition only through coercion.

War-making enhanced the colonial state by extending British imperial domination. As Mitchell (2000) observed, it also taught the British how to defeat its enemies, and this new knowledge of politically subjugating and regulating defeated populations further bolstered its techniques of power in the colonies and Europe. The conflicts and outcomes of the South African colonial encounter followed a pattern: unresolved disputes over land, cattle and ultimately political authority between settlers and natives led to wars; African defeat led to the redrawing of boundaries to extend white control; and defeated Africans became labourers and subjects of colonial sovereignty. Significantly, the labouring class's status defined it outside the political community to *include* it as the Other. Defeated African elites and their subjects lost the power to determine the rules of their everyday modes of subsistence, their historically established cultural repertoire was radically reconfigured, and they had no choice but to accept the new sovereign and its awesome capacity to regulate life and death.

Foucault and the production of docile subjects

The racial hierarchy, Fanon's Manichean society, prevailed in South Africa from the very beginning of colonial rule. The colonial state adopted laws of 'master and servant', which built upon the earlier slave code. Under Apartheid, the restrictive laws applied to blacks followed suit. For example, the 1952 influx control laws adopted by the Nationalist Party government were little different from the restrictions on slave movement in the seventeenth-century, which were revised by the British colonial government in the pass laws of 1896. The laws and everyday social interactions marked the society as racialised, with 'race' as the master signifier.

In Fanon's analysis, these conditions make for unique methods of disciplining and constituting subjects because the rules governing and regulating everyday life are directed at producing racialised subjects, which is another expression of violence. The message to the targeted subjects is, 'You are nothing, you are merely the bearers of bare life, and your only identity is that you are living and vulnerable to death and precarious life'. Blacks were excluded from a form of life with political significance on the basis that they were less than fully human, inferior to whites and therefore unworthy of citizenship.

Whereas accounts of modernisation conceive of the state in relation to an inevitable modernity with little acknowledgement of its past and to Marxism as regards the exploitation of labour and the forceful introduction of capitalism, poststructuralist accounts (Comaroff 2010) follow Foucault's ideas to understand how dominant discourses produce docile subjects. In the South African colonial situation, blacks were constructed as mere bearers of bare life and sources of labour whose value depends on capitalist 'market forces.' In his response to studies of power, Foucault raised suspicions about the exclusive emphasis on repression and examined how power produces positive moral codes and associated behaviours by which subjects eventually police themselves. This equally violent dimension of power is located in discourse and corresponds to Fanon's understanding of the 'geography' of power, its regulation and the production of racialised subjects in the colonial situation.

The colonial conception and later the national elite of subalterns as bearers of bare life, ever vulnerable to violence, cannot be understood without examining Foucault's thinking about how discourses constitute modern subjects, which largely overlaps with that of Fanon. In his article 'Nietzsche, Genealogy, History', Foucault expressed his debt to Nietzsche for the latter's idea of genealogy (Foucault, 1977), which differs from conventional forms of analysing the past. Traditional methods, which Foucault called 'total history', entail composing 'grand' explanatory systems and teleological processes and celebrating great events and individuals. The sought-after prize is the discovery of the single explanatory factor for major historical processes. Genealogy searches for the 'discredited, the neglected, and a whole range of phenomena which have been denied a history (for e.g., reason, punishment, sexuality)' (Smart 1983, 75). Genealogy also rejects the search for 'origins', first and ultimate causes that are embedded in prior discourses and terrains of struggle, difficult if not impossible to identify and contingent on other factors. Foucault instead searched for 'beginnings'. His stand against 'origins' raised questions about timeless 'essences', such as the singular, empirical truths that account for modes of production or foundations of knowledge; his 'beginnings' may be 'numberless' points of departure that may represent different narratives and therefore multiple ways of telling the past (Ferguson 1993, 20–21).

In distinguishing genealogy of descent from emergence, Foucault relates his methodological approach to two aspects of the power-knowledge relationship: the ways powers interact to make subjects and the ways subjects resist and participate in politics. He traced the constitution of the modern subject backwards from the present by using this method to understand how we became like this and also how we came to take these identities for granted. He examines discontinuities, the multiplicity of factors behind an event, and seeks to 'identify the accidents, the minute deviations … the errors … that gave birth to those things that continue to exist and have value for us' (Smart 1984, 76). The genealogy of descent avoids historical constants, essences and uninterrupted continuities, all of which posit a 'stable' past. The genealogy of emergence, in contrast, explores the marginalisation of subjugated knowledges of the Other and considers historical developments as 'transitory manifestations of relationships of domination-subordination, as temporary embodiments of the underlying relationship of forces' (Smart 1984, 76). The attention is on confrontations, conflicts and struggles that constitute subjects differently than (and even in opposition to) the structures and techniques of power. Foucault's earlier structuralist sympathies discouraged him from reducing historical events to individual actor's intentions. Instead, he saw historical events as eruptions of forces. Breaking with traditional analysis, he aimed to foreground 'ahistorical' qualities, such as feelings, sentiment, morality and the physiology, and to draw attention to the local rather than the global, and the particular rather than the general.

Instead of discussing Foucault's studies through the lens of the power/knowledge nexus or his critique of Enlightenment reason from a modern European perspective, it makes sense to follow Rabinow (1984) and focus on Foucault's work on the constitution of the modern subject as it reveals strong similarities to Fanon. Rabinow (1984, 7–11) proposed that Foucault discussed the objectification of the modern subject in three modes.

First, particular Othered groups are targeted, spatially separated and monitored with 'dividing practices'. Foucault illustrated these techniques of power in the isolating of lepers in the Middle Ages; the confinement of the poor, insane and homeless to the Hospital General in 1656; and the practices of punishment, discipline and modern imprisonment. The discourses of power resort to strategic, sophisticated techniques to categorise and classify populations with the intention of developing knowledge about targeted Others and regulating the insiders and the normal. Examples include the definition of 'sexual deviance' in clinical medicine in the nineteenth-century and the rise of psychiatry, which targeted 'the insane' as its subjects. These discourses produce the effects of 'medicalisation, stigmatisation and normalisation' of modern subjects but ultimately concern the regulation of 'life' and the rest of society. Foucault argued that the subject became objectified by the process of division either within him/herself or from others, a point about the splitting of the subject also found in Fanon's thought (see chapter 3). Foucault's historical studies empirically expand on these processes while spelling out their theoretical implications. He researched how individuals are drawn from an undifferentiated mass or specially targeted populations, such as 'delinquents' of working-class communities; the relationship between Othering practices and social science knowledge; the link between the practices of classification, containment and control to a tradition of humanitarian reform; the increased efficiency of techniques in the exercise of power and accumulated knowledge; and, lastly, the application of these procedures to dominated groups whose very identities were the result of such dividing practices.

Second, the subject is objectified through 'scientific classification', which extends the role of knowledge as a form of power. From the gathering of detailed information about individual subjects to whole bodies of knowledge about indigenous societies and their natural habitats, this was characteristic of the colonial project. Foucault did not dwell on knowledge in the colonial situation but concerns himself with its production in the human sciences: how did the human sciences emerge and under what historical conditions of the organisation of power? (Gordon 1980, 230–231). In *The Order of Things* (1973), Foucault examined the discourses of life, labour and language and showed how they became scientific disciplines with a high degree of 'internal autonomy and coherence'. He avoided the typical developmentalist approaches that trace a continuity of ideas in a discipline from lower to higher stages but looked for abrupt changes and significant, drastically discontinuous paradigm shifts. This work is staunchly materialist, because, according to Rabinow (1984, 9), Foucault saw nothing beyond discourse as 'more real' and expressive of an essence. In his earlier studies, Foucault concentrated on discourse (as systems of ideas) and ignored institutions, routinised practices, everyday techniques and strategies of power/knowledge. Later he adopted a wider field of analysis to include 'non-discursive' practices, although the tension between the discursive and non-discursive always remained. Besides accusations of Eurocentrism, Foucault was also criticised for his understanding of resistance to power, a mere assertion that where there is domination, there will be resistance. It has rightly triggered a mountain of critical responses (Anderson 1983; Callinicos 1985; Said 1983).

Third, Foucault was interested in the positive aspects of power and the regulation not of death, but life and moral grounding, which he wrote about in the first volume of *The History of Sexuality* (1978). He recognised intentionality and self-interest here more than in his earlier works, taking as examples the French bourgeoisie of the nineteenth-century, Greek citizens, early Christian ascetics and Church Fathers. This third mode, unlike the first two, focuses on the complex interaction between discourses of power and the role of humans in contributing towards their own subjecthood, in which the individual 'policed' him or herself in relation to an objectified subject. His introduction of power as biopolitics targeting both the regulation of whole populations and the very 'private' domains of the individual again resonates with Fanon, especially on the black persons' subjectivity being trapped in his skin due to racist discourse. Foucault's studies of Europe explore how the exercise of power operates through a broad range of activities to discipline the population, derive knowledge for power and represent the world. But what are its implications for settler-colonial situations, such as that of South Africa?

Although colonial knowledge cannot be discounted in the construction of subjects, the differences between Western modernity and the colonial situation are the role of the colonial state and its reliance on violence to form docile subjects. To accomplish and sustain domination, colonial power required an expansive administrative system that worked through local native structures and relied on local knowledge; after all, the missions were to exploit, educate and produce new, radically different, modern subjects. As Mitchell (2000) noted, these processes of knowledge, institutions and tactical practices of domination had a two-way trajectory and became part of the state-building and productive process in Europe.

The colonial situation and the constitution of class

Fanon's and Foucault's work allows for a specific kind of inquiry into and understanding of the nature of settler colonialism as the racial ordering of social relations dependent on violence and the production of particular types of racial subjects. The imposition of laws on people who did not have the vote and were therefore outside the political community blurred the distinction between law and violence. The state could implement such laws only by violence, intimidation and policing. It also required extensive information gathering to monitor and evaluate the black life and behaviour and the effectiveness of laws, so blacks 'spied' and reported on each other. This situation approximates the 'state of exception', as Agamben argued (1998), but the exceptional features were permanent in settler-colonial conditions. This constituted the subject identities of the targeted people, as did the simultaneous exclusion from and inclusion in the political community. The relationship between law, violence and the production of subjects can be illustrated with just two economic examples: the forced 'recruitment' of black labour to the mines and the privileging of white labour over black labour.

The formative years of capitalist industrialisation (spurred on by the mining industry) established relations grounded in settler colonialism, which followed from the earlier racial division of labour in South Africa. As is typical of settler-colonial forms of modernity (Fanon 1963), capitalist industrialisation consolidated the white working class as a 'labour aristocracy', a comfortable sector of the privileged 'settler community'. The mining industry made labour exploitation and practices of disciplining the subject more detailed and systematic (Legassick 1974; Wolpe 1972), so the black and subaltern population bore the brunt of extra-economic controls.

The deep deposition of gold was the accepted explanation for the extreme exploitation of black mineworkers. The international fixed price compelled mine bosses to keep labour costs low to compete on the world market (Johnstone 1970). The mining industry targeted the vulnerable. It saw in the defeated African kingdoms potentially large supplies of workers, and colonial norms meant that it could pay them subsistence wages, the bare minimum to keep them alive, and control and regulate them through restrictive and repressive policing mechanisms. The economic rationale for coercive labour rules was not too far from the colonial imagination. The political and ideological context of Manichean society had already paved the way, making violent super-exploitation possible and morally justifiable.

Valuing their independence, African small peasant farmers at first refused to work deep underground. The conditions were dangerous, and they would be thousands of miles from their homes and families. So, the Cape parliament and Cecil Rhodes, prime minister of the Cape Colony, passed the Glen Grey Act in 1894, that 'bill for Africa' (Davenport 1977, 106), to force African peasantry into minework. They had to pay taxes (quitrent) for the small patches of land on which they subsisted (only four morgen of land qualified for tax), and those not fortunate enough to have access to land had to pay a tax to discourage squatting. Overnight it created a landless peasantry whose only choice to pay new taxes was to seek work in the mines. Lipton quoted Rhodes's belief that the law was 'a gentle stimulant' to 'remove them from that life of sloth and laziness ... teach them the dignity of labour' (Lipton 1986, 119). The Transvaal Republic added pass laws to state legislation in 1895, further enforcing large-scale labour migrancy (Lipton 1986, 120). The collaboration of chiefs increased the financial pressure by demanding the payment of tributes from minework. To make the African peasantry seek work in the money economy, the colonial state further reduced their land access with the Land Act in 1913. The 'Betterment' schemes of the Native Land and Trust Act in 1936 violently forced the removal of thousands from communal lands and restricted African land ownership to 'reserves' that eventually became Bantustans under Verwoerdian Apartheid. It also expanded the tax regime to include hut and poll taxes (Motlhabi 1984).

But mine-owning capitalists kept complaining about labour shortages and even brought in 50,000 Chinese workers under indenture following the Boer War. They abandoned this scheme after a few years as uneconomical and politically sensitive, as news spread about the terrible working conditions and treatment of the Chinese. The mine owners, whose interests were coordinated through the Chamber of Mines, supplemented the colonial state's regime of laws by establishing their own recruitment mechanisms, such as the Witwatersrand Native Labour Association (WNLA) in 1902 (Webster 1978). Its recruitment was systematic in rural areas. African peasants gave themselves up to WNLA officials, got themselves documented, completed their health inspections, entered into annual six-month 'contracts' for minework in the Vaal region and paid part of their wages for everyday living rations. Like Foucault's reading of the efficiencies of military barracks, the mines housed the men in single-sex hostels called 'compounds'. Gardner Frederick Williams, manager of De Beers at its Kimberley operations and Rhodes's close friend, described the first ones in the Kimberley diamond mines in a way that resonates strongly with Foucault's analysis of the rationalisation of space to produce docile subjects:

> Fully four acres are enclosed by the walls of De Beers' Compound, giving ample space for the housing of its three thousand inmates, with an open central ground for exercise and sports. The fences are of corrugated iron, rising ten feet above the ground, and there is an open space of ten feet between the fence and the buildings ... Iron cabins fringe the inner sides of the enclosure, divided into rooms 25 feet by 30 feet, which are lighted by electricity. In each room twenty to twenty-five natives are lodged. The beds supplied are ordinary wooden bunks, and the bed clothing is usually composed of blankets that the natives bring with them, or buy at the stores in the compound, where there is a supply of articles to meet the simple needs of the natives. Besides these stores there is a hospital and dispensary ... In the centre of the enclosure there is a large concrete swimming bath (1905, 53).

Their living quarters and work were fit for a subject that is half man, half beast. Treating residents like prison inmates, these 'disciplinary institutions' threatened death but systematically regulated the details of migrant workers' lives and monitored their behaviour to warn of the ongoing threat of potential unrest. The internal architecture and spatial arrangement of buildings made for easy and continuous surveillance, discouraging protests and worker absenteeism. In the compound, the arrangement of the living space and organisation of underground work encouraged 'primordial' ethnic identities. The workers were divided along 'tribal' lines by language to prevent a class-conscious identity from taking root. Remarkably, this strategy was successful for decades. Being observed at work by management and by the police and state officials in the broader society taught black subjects how to evade, hide and 'break' the law, which became another element of identity.

The capitalist class's reliance on extra-economic interventions allowed it to enjoy higher profits on the back of lower wages. White workers too had benefitted enormously under racialised rule, with wages eighteen times higher than their black counterparts or almost 40 per cent of the total wage bill (Innes 1984). They defended their privilege using organised politics. The dominant ideology underpinning settler colonialism bolstered their claims. Believing that their class belonged to the dominant 'racial' group, they demanded that black workers' wages not undercut their own and that they perform tasks traditionally reserved for 'civilised' workers. The 1922 strike of thousands of white miners became a civil revolt whose outcome influenced a change of government (Yudelman 1983, 22). The standard Marxist argument of the skilled-unskilled division of labour and the calculating interests of mine owners cannot explain the historic absence of a united working class politics in South Africa without reference to the long tradition of settler colonialism and the mediation of class interest through the lens of 'race'; popular slogans of the strike, such as 'Workers of the World, Unite and Fight for a White South Africa', reveal the strange mix of socialist internationalism and entrenched racism. In comparison to white workers, and due primarily to state restrictions before black union organised, black workers' wages remained low. Black workers may have called the odd strike (1946 was an exception), but they were generally compliant, passive and fearful of the white world for decades. The 1973 strikes of black workers were dramatic because the experience of 'spontaneous' collective action introduced new levels of worker identity, organisation and militancy, ushering in a new era of worker collective action.

The racialised labour system, the backbone and model for the construction of right-less subjects throughout South Africa, influenced all sectors of the economy. Labour tenancy on farms allowed farmers to exploit workers under the extreme conditions of patrimonial familiarity that sustained 'traditional' practices from the Boer farms of the early colonial period. Because the conditions and wages of farm work were unattractive, farmers prevented workers from taking up employment in other sectors, 'locking' whole families into long-term, generational 'contracts'.

From the early settlement, laws regulated the movement of blacks between the territory's white and black zones. This mode of control, which is essential to Manichean society, would have been unthinkable without the tradition of 'race' division that had been established under settler-colonial conditions (Motlhabi 1984). The influx control laws became the modern symbol of blacks' semi-human status, connecting rightlessness, labour exploitation and the absence of human dignity. Crucially, the settler-colonial situation made available a 'race' identity and the 'traditions' of a corresponding ideology of white superiority and a radical civilised/savage dichotomy;

the political community of and for whites provided them with access to the modern bureaucratic state that was used to both exclude and include blacks, leaving blacks in a permanent state of ambiguity in relation to the system of domination.

Apartheid takes Manichaeism to its logical extreme

Settler colonialism had its structural basis in the racialised organisation of labour. In its expression as Apartheid, it imposed a rationalised system of domination that evolved pragmatically as responses to a political field and its competing social forces. Even though the policies regulating relations between whites and blacks were based on violence, the Apartheid project, especially the pernicious policies of land and labour exploitation, gave itself 'the appearance of legality' (Guha 1997, 156). This legalising of white supremacist discourse framed institutions and regulated daily material practices, creating everyday cultures.

Two years after the 1946 black mineworkers' strike, the Afrikaner Nationalist Party (NP) assumed power after campaigning on behalf of Afrikaner nationalism and warnings about the '*swart gevaar*' (black danger) (Davenport 1977). The party revised racist laws, added others and broke with the past by developing the capacity of the state to implement its vision vigorously; Apartheid focused on grand changes to society as a whole, the life of society and the behaviour of individuals in their everyday detail at the micro-individual level. Cillie observed that Apartheid was always a work in progress: 'A system? An ideology? A coherent blueprint? No, rather a pragmatic and tortuous process aimed at consolidating the leadership of a nationalist movement in order to safeguard the self-determination of the Afrikaner' (Giliomee 2003).

Although many laws and social practices of racial separation had been long enough established that Verwoerd could reasonably refer to racial separation as 'tradition', the Apartheid period is best characterised by the systematic manner, explicit ideological grounding and modern-rational approach to Manichean society (Davenport 1977; Wolpe 1972). Three different phases of Apartheid are identifiable. In the 1950s, the NP was unsure about the long-term policy implications of its ideology, so it focused on the systematic classification of 'racial groups' and the establishment of strict residential separation (Giliomee and Schlemmer 1989). In the 1960s, the Verwoerd government faced a more favourable domestic environment with impressive economic growth, weak and ineffective black protest and Verwoerd's confidence in his leadership of the party and government (Lodge 1983). It removed the remaining indirect representation available to blacks, vigorously restricted African movement through the pass laws and embarked on its Bantustan independence strategy. In the period after the Soweto revolt in the late 1970s, the government felt compelled to 'reform' old-style Apartheid and proposed expanding black representation at local government level, recognising black trade unions and loosening restrictions on African movement. It still refused to grant equal citizenship without regard to 'race'.

Conventional conceptions of Apartheid emphasise the racial inclusion/exclusion that defined the political community and its legal implications, assuming that subject identities were 'always already there'. Thus Giliomee and Schlemmer (1989) identified the key areas of Apartheid as labour regulation, communal apartheid and political control. The labour influx controls legislated migrant labour and disallowed African trade unionism; communal apartheid legislated separate access to amenities, education and welfare; and political control defined the political system, giving whites exclusive control of the state and passing laws that differentiated spending and the distribution of resources according to race classifications. Beinart's (2001, 149) summary of Apartheid follows this emphasis on political-legal aspects without much discussion of the politics of subject formation. For him, the main features included the rigid definition of the various races; exclusive white control of central political institutions; the separation of all public institutions, services and territories between whites and blacks and amongst blacks; the spatial separation between urban and rural areas; the control of African movement between rural and urban areas; the rigid hierarchical divisions within the labour market, with jobs assigned on a racial basis; and the social separation and hierarchy of quality of all services and products, from education to park benches.

Immediately after its election victory, and responding to its promises to end the 'poor white problem' and the related fear of miscegenation, the NP government hurriedly legislated the Mixed Marriages Act (1949) to disallow interracial marriage and the Immorality Act (1950) to prohibit inter-acial sex. In 1950, the government also passed the Population Registration Act, whose legacy indelibly marks the South African state, society and generalised consciousness. It mandated that all citizens be classified into racial groups, with their life prospects determined by the group designation (Horrell 1968). The introductory section defined racial subjects relationally; the text placed certainty in the arena of the political. A 'coloured person means a person who is not a white person or a native' (Statutes, 277). A native 'means a person who in fact is or is generally accepted as a member of any aboriginal race or tribe of Africa' (Statutes, 277). And a 'white person means a person who in appearance obviously is, or who is generally accepted as a white person, but does not include a person who, although in appearance obviously a white person, is generally accepted as a coloured person' (Statutes, 277). The Group Areas Act of 1950 forced thousands to relocate, assigning the most valuable areas to whites and moving blacks far from designated white areas. The government's Separate Amenities Act of 1953 provided for separate and unequal services to different race groups. Fanon's compartmentalised Manichean world was thus made into law, implemented and kept in place by state violence (Davenport 1977).

Influenced by its history, South Africa bucked post-World War II trends: when anti-racism and decolonisation gained momentum elsewhere, the South African government stridently announced its white supremacist ideology. When many countries were extending public education to their citizenry, South Africa implemented its Bantu Education policy in 1953 to 'de-educate' blacks and produce subjects believed to be required by its economy and dual market system. It aimed to massify black education, however, the educational content aimed to produce modern yet docile, tribalised, racialised subjects who were expected to tolerate bare life.

Post-World War II the capacities of the state improved dramatically. The NP embarked on the large-scale recruitment of Afrikaners to dismantle the historical English dominance of the police and the military. The new leaders rationalised the surveillance and control of subalterns, focusing on the details of policing and utilising the latest methods. They developed the state's repressive arsenal, creating a vast apparatus of rules and new technologies to observe, monitor and evaluate, starting with implementing the pass laws more effectively. On the ground, policing the vast apparatus of rules under which the subaltern lived entailed 'rewards', threats and punishments (fines and jail terms). The successful processes of state-building and encouraging racialised, ethnic consciousness were well-thought-out machines, leading white and black subjects to find their places in society and believe that they could easily predict the other's behaviour. Only the popular mobilisations from the 1970s made blacks aware of and uncomfortable with their historical docility and their everyday non-disruptive role in the 'success' of Apartheid (Motlhabi 1984).

The combination of powers, which targeted the black population in discourses of health, labour and education and watched over everyday individual racial separation, demanded that they operate on multiple levels. Enforcing and monitoring strict racial separation required subjects who self-policed to laws that segregated playgrounds, water fountains, entrances, lifts, escalators and seating arrangements in cinemas and busses. Strict racial separation in social life, except in the sphere of production, was the Apartheid solution to the long-term settler-colonial issue of a small white minority living amongst a large black majority and having qualitatively different relationships to the European enlightenment and capitalist modernity.

In the 1960s, the government did not focus on the so-called 'petty apartheid' of Jim Crow–like racial separation, i.e., the inconveniences, humiliations and indignities that blacks experienced such as having no access to water fountains on very hot days or toilet facilities and being looked upon and treated with scorn by whites. The government focused on grand apartheid, namely the Bantustan project to create 'independent' ethnic African homelands in a federal system of Southern African states. Treating blacks as radically different, inhuman and of a lower status to whites created deep-seated anger and resentment. Apartheid rule was at its most arrogant in the 1960s, after the Sharpeville massacre, and it is remembered for the layers of humiliation, the absence of dignity and the long silence of any real black resistance.

Verwoerd's policy envisaged that Africans would exercise citizenship in their own states. When the policy was fully implemented, no person classified as African (besides the few exempt from Bantustan residency) could claim South African citizenship. The Transkei, Bophuthatswana, Venda and the Ciskei became independent states in quick succession in the 1970s with lavish ceremonies that mostly mimicked the independence flag raisings in other parts of Africa during the 1950s and 1960s (Davenport 1977). A new elite, which Amilcar Cabral (1979) would call a 'comprador class', and an ethnic middle class benefitted from the new states' budgets and patronage, but the Bantustans were not internationally recognised due to successful campaigns that highlighted their false independence.

The post-1976 Apartheid period witnessed government attempts at political reforms. The reforms were spurred on by pressure from business interests afraid that white supremacy was undermining profits, but other factors also motivated the political class to favour reforms. Typical Marxist analysis of the reform period highlights changes and tensions within the structure of South African capitalism, demonstrating the importance of identifying both contradictions in the capitalist structure and the limitations of ignoring state autonomy and the politics surrounding the constitution of relational subjects. The influence of big capital on the Apartheid state cannot be underestimated. At the same time, the autonomy and institutionalist interests of the Botha led-security state (Innes 1984) was all too evident. Even when it pursued a reform agenda it ultimately showed itself unable to think beyond the parameters of settler colonialism and its identities.

Reading off the needs of the economic structure, the monopoly capital phase accordingly brought with it more mechanisation and the need for skilled labour. Additionally, changes in South African class structure motivated the racial organisation of society represented by Apartheid, functionally needed to be reformed. O'Meara (1982) discovered that the turning point towards a new monopoly phase of capitalist development in South Africa was as early as the 1946 African mineworkers' strike. Monopoly capitalism ended the dual economy of pre-capitalist and capitalist modes of accumulation, which constituted a dominant Marxist reading of pre-war South African society. The growth and influence of finance capital in the 1960s brought Afrikaner and English capital together, creating organic links between state, national and international capital (Murray 1987). Statistical data reveals these economic changes. Between 1963 and 1968, the GDP increased by an average annual rate of 9.3 per cent, compared to 5.2 percent between 1957 and 1962. The manufacturing and construction sectors grew due to mining capital diversifying into these sectors. Additionally, the political restrictions faced by the black working class prevented them from accessing the machinery of labour relations and kept wages low (Innes 1984, 188–89). By emphasising that this monopoly capitalist phase was reached due to marginal growth in secondary industrialisation allows, this analysis can make related claims about necessary societal changes. The decreased profits in mining and agriculture and the loss of South African workers to manufacturing compelled mining capital to employ more workers from Malawi, Zimbabwe, Mozambique, Lesotho, Swaziland and Botswana.

The composition of the capitalist class changed when the concentration of capital increased. By 1981, eight conglomerates and state corporations controlled 70 per cent of the total assets of the largest 138 companies. The Anglo-American Mining Corporation controlled 54.1 per cent of all the companies on the Johannesburg Stock Exchange (JSE), the Afrikaans-owned Sanlam insurance company 11.3 per cent. The white working class was dwindling, and many had moved into the middle class as a consequence of Apartheid policies. Lastly, a black middle class emerged as splits in the black working class between skilled and unskilled workers became increasingly important. Blacks increasingly took up employment at lower wages in jobs formally reserved for whites, and some employers split a skilled job into several unskilled categories jobs. These social changes indicate conflicting class interests that complicated the once-unquestioned racial unities of an earlier period. The mine capitalists wanted migrant labour to continue, the manufacturing capitalist lobbied for government reforms to allow some blacks to have rights to live in the urban areas. The Afrikaner business sector and the enlarged Afrikaner middle class lost uncritical support for Apartheid and had difficulty justifying petty racial separation. Especially by the 1980s, when blacks defined the majority and 'the people', the generalised black exclusion from the political system opened tensions in the previously formidable white consensus.

The government eventually realised it was impossible to maintain social control in this way of representing a small minority in a country inhabited by a large and culturally different majority claiming aboriginal legitimacy. The economic growth of the 1960s spurred on urbanisation. Urban black settlements and townships became the source of mass mobilisation, ushering in a new politics from the 1970s. Large informal black housing settlements formed around the main towns by the 1980s. State authorities and white political parties urgently debated how best to balance the demands for labour with social and political consequences that might threaten white privilege. The democratic regime elected in 1994 has not reversed these politics, as mobilisational politics continues to be evident throughout political society.

Conclusion

After three centuries the systematic consolidation of the racial organisation of civil society produced Manichean society, harbouring many lines of tension: violence or the threat of violence, militarised police functioning as intermediaries between coloniser and subalterns, and enforced 'laws' that mostly operated in a state of exception towards subalterns. The violence, rigorous policing and the ambiguity of law mirror Agamben's concept of the state of exception, or a situation of martial law; it potentially made every black treatable as a criminal. Concepts like Arendt's interwar refugees and Agamben's *homo sacer* resonate in South Africa. In the post-1994 context of rights and of a new assertiveness as citizens, legacies of wounded subjects reveal unresolved internal psychological battles, a point Fanon reiterated, and demonstrate the limitations of procedural democracy compounded by neo-liberal capitalism.

5| Nationalism, ANC and domination without hegemony

In this chapter, I focus on that other modern phenomenon, nationalism. I discuss its organisational expressions, which historically articulate the interests of the intermediary strata of settler-colonial society. When claiming to speak for the nation, it steers subaltern political rationality in directions conducive to its own interests. Unlike in Europe, modernity was introduced in South Africa through external political interventions. The violent colonial conquest and its policies generated the resistance of the colonised, who fought for recognition of their humanity in a struggle for national liberation. The limits of post-Apartheid liberal democracy can be understood only with reference to the equally intense counterforces of settler colonialism and resistance.

In this politics of recognition, the subaltern has two adversaries: the coloniser as enemy and the nationalist elite as class rival. It eventually obtained recognition from colonised elites only though mass mobilisation; together, they were able to wrest substantive concessions from the long-established white power structure. From the 1880s to around 1940, the colonised elite considered the subaltern mass irrelevant to the fight for national recognition and political significance and questioned its right of full admission into the political community. Following dominant colonial discourse, it believed the subaltern was 'backward', 'uncivilised' and in need of tutoring to be ready for civic life. It thus concentrated on rights for the 'civilised', i.e., its members themselves, because their education and property qualified as civilised values in colonial modernity.

When the colonial state began to take popular forms of resistance more seriously than it had taken the colonised elite, the latter realised that the subaltern could not be ignored. It realised its own class weaknesses. Especially after World War II, it made efforts to 'speak' a language of politics with which it believed the subaltern masses would identify. The two major 'struggle' discourses, of rights and identity, spanned rational-legal, and charismatic, idioms. But context is important. For example, Mandela represented rational-legalistic discourse in the 1950s but charismatic in the 1990s. Or, in another register, the discourses of the politics of identity were considered charismatic in the 1950s but irrational in the 1980s.

The relationship between the national elite and the subaltern mass was complicated by differences over ideology, leadership, discipline, control, persuasion and mutual suspicion. From the 1880s to the 1930s, the formative period of nationalist thought, elite and subaltern resisted the colonial order via separate registers. Then, from the end of World War II and leading up to the Marikana massacre in 2012, they became allies despite their wariness of each other and achieved two significant popular national mobilisations. The first and more limited resistance reached a high point at Sharpeville in 1960; it can be seen as a failure because the relationship between the elite and the masses remained somewhat tenuous. The second and more effective established a 'unity' or alliance of elite and subaltern concerns around democratic discourses, mixing a new black political subjectivity with citizen rights, in the 1970s and 1980s; the unexpected, ill-defined combination of the charismatic and rational-legal produced a collective subaltern subject. The mass upsurge created transitory conditions, a battlefield of undecidability that Fanon called the 'decisive moment', before the elites entered and reconstituted the political terrain by negotiating democratic constitutional changes based on a dominant discourse of rights.

The massacre at Marikana in August 2012 serves as a symbolic end to this uneasy alliance, and the next current state of affairs is uncertain. Over the long term, the nationalist elite will be unable to rely on the historical bonds of common identity, as captured in Njabulo Ndebele's notion of 'uncritical solidarities,' and more unashamedly show its true class interests. Also, the legitimacy of the once-popular rights discourse has eroded. The 'social delivery' protests and other forms of mass mobilisation by communities to demand recognition of their political significance by convincing themselves and others that a community member is not a *homo sacer* points to a mode of politics I have labelled 'the subaltern politics of political society', following Chatterjee (2004). Here, subalterns highlight their daily material deprivations, lack of dignity and vulnerability although and because they, too, have rights as legal subjects, as citizens. It also throws into sharp relief their divergence from the project of nationalist modernity, as conceived by the elite. In the last decade, the historically tenuous elite-mass alliances have dissolved. Now the subalterns are left to their own devices, with no clear and independent dominant narrative except remnants of the once-popular mobilisations and 'struggle discourses' of the 1980s. They plea to draw from that moral register, reanimating those mobilisations and drawing upon ethical elements of the liberation narrative. The most important is equality, the idea of 'the people' in democratic citizenship discourse.

In this chapter, I do not pretend to present a detailed historical reading of South African resistance history. I am wary of the conventional focus on the main struggle organisations or their ideologies, although it is easy to fall into that analytical trap. Those paths are well trod. Instead, I draw from the rich history in the literature to trace elite-mass relations in the nationalist struggle against Manichean society and highlight the nationalist middle class's encouragement (in the resistance to Apartheid) and then abandonment (in post-1994 democratic politics) of the mass subaltern subject. Once the nationalist bourgeoisie obtained control of the state, it developed an alliance with the historical white capitalist class (Fanon's 'rapacious bourgeoisie'), abandoning its long-term ally in the subaltern masses. This break-up lead to the development of two terrains and current modes of politics in South Africa, feeble civil society politics and vibrant mass politics, and it can also be identified as part of the pattern of settler-colonial struggles in Southern Africa.

Dilemmas of anti-colonial nationalism

The colonial conquest had important consequences for the state in Europe and the idea of the state for modernising colonised elites in the colonies (Kaviraj 2009). Even though the modern European state may have been largely generated by internal processes, it was not completely insulated from the operation of power in its colonies (Mitchell 2000). The colonial situation provided invaluable knowledge of bureaucratic administration, the efficient use of violence, the development of elevated notions of the nation, the strategic importance of national unity and an 'us versus them' mentality, and the idea of the 'mother country' (Hobsbawm 1987). They became central to dominant state discourse. The modern state 'succeeded' outside Europe, 'first as an instrument, and second, as an idea' (Kaviraj 2009). As an instrument, it was impossible to doubt its capacity to achieve collective action, realise the goals of conquest, and use its military capabilities and resources to build economies and infrastructure. Alternative forms of collective organisation were unable to compete against the modern state. Indigenous kingdoms could not fend off European conquest, and despite the courage of thousands facing bullets and cannons, the traditional, local forms of 'state' were no match against European invasion. Despite many deaths, the relatively easy destruction of local political systems made the first 'modernising' elites acutely averse to being in that position again. This explains dominated elites' envy of and admiration for the effectiveness of the modern state. This is where the state as 'idea' comes in, for it was admired as an instrument for refashioning societies and addressing their communities' vulnerability to outside conquest (Kaviraj 2009).

According to Fanon, the intermediary middle class accommodated itself to work within the colonial order and then set its sights on taking over the colonial state. By then, it had realised the modern state's enormous bureaucratic capacity for organsing the social relations of domination within society (Migdal 1988; Migdal 2001). It also accepted that it could not overthrow the colonial state without significant allies and it could muster sufficient resources to challenge the modern colonial state only 'through a movement that organised the power of entire populations against the colonial state in the form of national mobilizations' (Kaviraj 2009). The small group of educated professionals and small traders thus formed the organisations that eventually produced these national mobilisations, which would overthrow the colonial state or negotiate new terms of power.

The colonial situation, in which nationalist groups believed in the state as instrument and idea, is different to the west European bourgeois revolutions, in which the two major classes of civil society (bourgeoisie and proletariat) saw themselves as the key motivating forces of modernity. In the Third World, these classes had not developed because the dominant mode of production had not reached an equivalent level of maturity, or, in Marx's terms, proletarianisation had not advanced to the level at which peasants lost all access to land and depended on wage labour (Marx 1972). Due to imperialist expansion, the colonies were primarily extractive. Lenin saw them as necessary for the consolidation of monopoly capital in the advanced capitalist states of Europe and North America and for displacing and blunting class conflict in them (Lenin 1999). The structure of colonial capitalism allowed for the modernist impetus to come from the middle strata, which hoped the state would be the midwife of postcolonial modernity.

Fanon built upon Marx's insights to analyse emerging nationalism under settler-colonial conditions. He went beyond the structural limitations of both the lack of mediations in the Manichean world and the intermediary middle class's lack of independent productive access to capital; for him, the revolutionary role taken by the capitalist class during the emergence of capitalism in Europe was taken by the masses, who served as the motivating force for the genesis of modernity in the colonies. Fanon accordingly dismissed the national middle class's political role and identifying its own interests over those of the broader masses and the community as a whole. As the nationalist struggle proceeds, Fanon's nationalist bourgeoisie functions as an untrustworthy ally of the subaltern. Because it is structurally weak as an intermediary class, it uses the masses to unhinge and weaken the colonial state. But once the colonial state agrees to transfer or negotiate political power, it takes over the state and undermines and distances itself from the masses that had helped enable the change (Fanon 1963). He distinguished between the phases of decolonisation and liberation (Fanon 1963); in the Third World and especially in African struggles, the liberation stage is never reached.

Fanon (1963) perceptively discussed how the native intellectual enters the process of struggle in the colonial situation, tracing three stages of consciousness (222–223): having uncritical, assimilative awe towards everything associated with the white and colonial world; adopting the opposite position, becoming alienated from the colonial world; and, finally, expressing the contradictions of active resistance and recognising the complexity of the relationship between the elite and the masses.

The native intellectual at first wholeheartedly embraces the colonial state and colonial institutions (churches, schools, art and culture) and practices, as they signify the modern, the different and the admirable, and single-mindedly aims to participate in them. They leave an indelible mark on his consciousness, and he is proud of them. His admiration for European civilisation knows no limits because he feels that he is learning how to belong to the highest stage of civilisation, or that is how he understands it presented to him. He aspires to be not only closely associated with it, but to become a part of it and its expressive symbol in the colonies.

Then, this engagement with the European imprint and colonial episteme raises reflective questions with unconvincing, contradictory answers. Rejection sets in. Now alienated from the colonial world, the native intellectual feels restless and then angry with himself for having so uncritically embraced the colonial order, which he recognises as the cause of his oppression. He is also embarrassed for betraying himself to friends and family with exaggerated claims about European civilisation and realises that many of them belonged to the poorer parts of the town. Next, his inner activist remembers his childhood. He reclaims his memories, feeling pride rather than shame about events that he reinterprets positively rather than through colonial discourse that condemned everything related to the native as radical Other. After having concluded that the coloniser absolutely lied about native culture, he realises how unfair, wrong, and hurtful the colonising discourse is and how foolish he was to believe those lies about his own culture.

In the third phase, of actual resistance, tensions come to the fore when the native intellectual identifies with the masses. He sees his role as 'raising the people to consciousness' by bringing education and political awareness to the masses. However, yet another disappointment awaits him. In this activist work he finds that he is forever relying on knowledges, methodologies and concepts from the colonial episteme. The more he aims to present a national interpretation and develop a local and indigenous reading on behalf of his people, the more he realises how 'strangely reminiscent of exoticism' it is (223). This grand tussle between the universal (colonial and Western dominant knowledge and narratives) and the particular (everything that is universal Europe's Other) becomes a field of critical recognition and national anxiety. Fanon advised the native intellectual that it was imperative to struggle to see beyond the 'outer garments' of the people and to their 'hidden life, teeming and perpetually in motion … of a much more fundamental substance which itself is continually being renewed' (224). He, however, concludes that the progressive intellectual will nevertheless be resigned to discovering only the 'outer garments' and remain caught between the incommensurable lifeworlds of the colonial episteme and the toiling masses.

Chatterjee (1986), in his study of nationalism, took up a similar theme by arguing that nationalist discourses had an ambiguous relationship with European modernity, both challenging European political domination and conforming to it by implicitly endorsing the modernist premises upon which colonial domination was based. He termed the 'problematic' those dramatic elements of nationalist thought that focus on struggle, practical political action and resistance strategies and tactics for overthrowing colonialism through mobilised campaigns of an oppressed people. He positioned the problematic in opposition to the 'thematic', or normative and epistemological elements of nationalist thought that endorse European modernity rather than challenge its premises. These more perplexing aspects of European thought, which serve 'justificatory' functions and were embraced from the dominant European colonial discourse in order to support its claims (e.g., enlightened reason, the public-private division and the rule of law), are less easily identifiable in nationalist thought. He summarised their differences: 'The thematic … refers to an epistemological as well as ethical system which provides a framework of elements and rules for establishing relations between elements; the problematic, on the other hand, consists of concrete statements about possibilities justified by reference to the thematic' (1986, 38). Anti-colonial discourses are at root troubled 'nativist' responses to European domination. Nationalist discourses problematise some elements of European hegemony, such as double standards in the public sphere, while operating within its general framework to protect a private sphere or indigenous culture, which anti-colonial nationalism claims or is compelled to claim as its own.

Chatterjee (2004), like Fanon, is also suspicious of the colonised middle class, the educated nationalist bourgeoisie and its commitment to a different nationalism than that of the European path. Faced with the colonial situation and its grounding in radical difference, the nationalist response highlights colonial ideology's double standards; colonial liberalism claims to uphold universal values only to expose its own contradictions through its racism and prejudice. The first protests that break out against the colonial order are usually on behalf of the middle classes. Having already accepted the universal values of colonial education, this middle class confidently believes that it qualifies for membership into the colonial order and political community. It is repeatedly rejected, however, and its civilised petitioning for inclusion in the political community as equal members spurned. This rejection leads the middle class to eventually look towards the masses because it assumes the role of representing indigenous society and thereby more strongly authenticating its claims.

In this role it seeks to preserve a 'domain' out of bounds of the dominant colonial ideology: the sphere of traditional and indigenous beliefs. In the nationalist project it seeks to 'appropriate' national popular discourse by mediating between the colonial power and the native majority, seeing itself as a reasoned 'voice' that interprets the popular will for the colonial order. It responds to colonial power by assigning 'equivalent' value to past indigenous knowledge and traditions, giving substance to the claim that 'we, too, have our Golden Age'. The national middle class desires to control the idea of an alternative to colonial modernity. Rather than radically claiming that colonial institutions are 'alien', it proposes that these institutions can be used to complete the idea of modernity, perhaps with an indigenous face (Chatterjee 1999).

The national elite and going it alone

In South African black nationalist thought, 'the struggle' is an all-embracing label for an important idea, idiom, symbol, image, viewpoint and privileged set of values, practices, historical moments and actors. It functions as an autonomous discourse and within other discourses. It represents a dominant narrative of resistance to colonial and Apartheid rule, and it has competed with other such narratives historically and in the contemporary political terrain. The idea of 'the struggle' makes the normative and moral claim of an oppressed 'people' fighting oppression and realising their identity as humans deserving and recognised as having dignity, which is embedded in a unbroken story of resistance over three centuries. Even though the idea of 'the struggle' itself is reducible to many singular goals over varied periods, the generalised demands for rights or material resources and the symbolic and ethical elements expressed in the fight to be acknowledged as humans with dignity animates subaltern politics today.

A problem with examining discourses of 'the struggle' is that it is assumed to be one long effort at something called 'resisting domination'. The subject protesting in the 1980s is thought to be carrying the baton of seventeenth-century resistors, continuing a conversation that connects subjects through time. This is precisely the intention of struggle narratives: to promote the idea of a continuous, unbroken struggle from 1652 that exemplifies the coming into being of the modern nation. By taking this into account and concentrating on the theme of elite and mass relationships, and for heuristic purposes, moments that assume different degrees of prominence in various narrative structures in black nationalist discourse can be identified. At the first arrival, settlement, and Jan van Riebeeck's establishment of a military fort in 1652, the Khoi (Hottentots) and San (Bushmen) fought many battles to protect themselves and their way of life. Then, in the so-called Cape Frontier Wars (1779–1879), African kingdoms were locked in battle with British and Boer armies. Seemingly more organised, they included delegated meetings, declarations of war, decisive battles and 'peace treaties'. The nine wars brought the loss of African land, the imposition of new rules and taxation, and the incorporation of Africans as labourers into the colony. In the next period, 1880–1936, the nationalist elite became an identifiable social group, learned the discourse of civil rights and began to engage with colonial modernity in its broader parameters. Finally, the post-war mobilisations of the 1950s and 1970s expressed elite and mass alliances and announced new forms of social power against the colonial and Apartheid states. The nationalist intermediary class changed the political field by promoting competing discourses to mobilise the subaltern masses. This important development marks the awakening of 'the people' and the beginnings of the formation of the collective mass subject, which is central to South African democratic politics (Fatton 1986; Gerhart 1978; Motlhabi 1984).

When the colonised elite was faced with an intransigent colonial state, it learnt the hard lesson of its own limitations. For many decades it tried to be accommodated within the colonial order. It had demonstrated that it embraced the colonial order by adopting 'civilised' approaches towards the colonial authorities, accepting and preaching liberal values, advocating loyalty to the Empire and converting to Christianity (Lodge 1983). It considered itself different to other colonised classes (Odendaal 1984), displaying indifference and even disdain towards the 'backward' masses. After the political landscape changed between 1880 and 1910, it realised that it needed to think and approach politics differently for its own political interests to be taken seriously. The regular passing of legislation discriminating against blacks from the mid-nineteenth-century made them aware of the 'double standards' of British liberalism (Keegan 1996): the deliberate exclusion of non-whites from the 1910 Union sent a clear signal that they would not be taken seriously and treated with respect unless they organised themselves and lobbied more effectively. The Glen Grey Act in 1894 and the 1913 Land Act caused them much consternation. The latter targeted all Africans (lumping the colonised elite with the colonised masses), had increased impoverishment among the landless peasantry, further squeezed out the land-owning peasantry and made the new middle strata realise that it was an act of pervasive and systematic racism towards all blacks.

The colonised middle strata decided to launch a national organisation even though it was not empirically 'national' and would probably not be for some time. It, however, knew the importance of a national organisation making a modern claim. In the world of imperialism, nationalism and the 'national idea' commanded respect. Especially when talk of Union was rapidly unfolding, making the claim also had strategic significance. The national middle class's claim to represent all Africans was yet another promise and unsubstantiated claim. Boldly, it distinguished the colonised elite and committed it to a form of modern civic politics that broke from rival and past black political approaches to colonial power.

The anti-colonial opposition that it most wanted to distance itself from was the politics of the previous age, which it represented as 'tribal', rural and uncivil. This type of politics was best illustrated by the armed revolt led by Chief Bambatha and his fellow AmaZondi clan 'rebels' in 1906. When the Natal colonial government imposed a poll tax on the African peasantry, Bambatha's community near Greytown refused to pay and resisted. The government's attempt to collect the tax led to the killing of two officers, whereupon it declared martial law (akin to Agamben's state of exception). Bambatha responded with guerrilla-type defence tactics. The colonial government sent troops with machine guns and cannons against Bambatha's supporters, who were armed with *assegais* (spears) and *knobkerries* (clubs). Bambatha was beheaded, three-four thousand resistors were killed and his remaining supporters were flogged (Marks 1986). His politics represented a stand by those as yet mostly outside the colonial order who were resisting incorporation into it. The colonial order considered war with such resistance as a 'state of nature' (Wood 2003); the deaths were its response to a competing authority.

Another kind of oppositional discourse to colonial power and rival of the modern civic politics favoured by the mainstream national middle class was 'Ethiopianism', which developed in the late nineteenth-century. Though its adherents were also 'educated Africans' and therefore very much inside the life of the colonial order, they wanted to retain as much cultural independence as possible. In this way, this discourse of identity politics resonates with later Pan Africanism and Black Consciousness. In this version, nationalist thought held that black peoples' cultural archive allowed for a radically different subject identity than that imposed by colonialism (Gerhart 1978; Lodge 1983). Why Ethiopia? Ethiopia had been one of a handful of countries that had not been colonised (at least not by Europeans) and therefore represented 'freedom' and African independence in African political mythology. Marcus Garvey's agitation for pride in African identity, an emancipatory consciousness and self-reliance expressed an Ethiopianist ideology. Black church leaders in South Africa, who were opposed to the 'white trusteeship' of church denominations, drew on Ethiopian political ideas. In 1884, Nehemiah Tile broke from the Methodist Church to form the Independent Tembu National Church. In 1892, Mangena Makone established an Ethiopian Church of Pretoria. It affiliated to the American church separatist movement in 1896 but withdrew after several years amidst complaints about American dominance (Shepperson 1953).

Modern nationalism is, however, mostly linked to a vocal group of African Christian intellectuals based in the Cape colony. They had enjoyed voting rights in a franchise qualified by 'race', education and property since 1854 (Odendaal 1984; Walshe 1971). They protested against discriminatory legislation and racist discourse using their vote, public platforms and the press. That many were long-time converts to Christianity and established advocates of the British liberal tradition who had studied in Europe or in the United States—all greatly admired virtues in colonial society—gave this group recognisable status. This elite of African society (relative to subalterns of course, but not white society) campaigned for broadening voting rights to Africans who were similarly socially positioned, educated and propertied in the other provinces (Walshe 1971). They were also acutely aware that the possibility of Union meant that their own voting rights would be under threat.

The values of Christianity, voting and civil rights eventually flowed into the politics of the African National Congress, the first national organisation representing all Africans. The combination of the political campaign for rights combined with the legal discourse of the colonial state inspired an embryonic civil rights movement. In a colonial situation, it conveyed legitimacy to the colonial state while accepting the colonial modern as its point of departure. In other words, it was Chatterjee's 'thematic'. After 1850 until the establishment of the Union in 1910, the educated African elite dominated associational black life. In Port Elizabeth the Imbumba Yama Afrika group was formed in 1882 to protest against the Vagrancy Act (1889). The Native Education Association and the Native Electoral Association of 1884 spearheaded the campaign to expand the African vote broadly. With the financial backing from a group of white Cape liberals, John Tengo Jabavu launched the first African newspaper, *Imvo Zabantsundu* (Black Opinion) in 1884. It spoke out against racist laws designed by the colonial state to leverage blacks into a proletariat, without rights or land, including the Voters Registration Bill (1889), the Vagrancy Act (1889), the Ballot Act (1892) and the Glen Grey Act (1894). But these laws also affected the small, educated class by introducing the pattern of steadily raising the property and educational requirements for African voters and prohibiting the sale of alcohol to all blacks (Davenport 1977). Jababu dominated Cape African politics, and in Natal, the Free State and Transvaal, leaders such as Pixley Ka Seme, Mark Radebe, John Dube, Meshach Pelem and Martin Luthuli highlighted the discriminatory policies and practices. Together, these men, who were schooled in the political consciousness of colonial modernity, founded the South African Native National Congress (SANNC) in 1912. It changed its name to the ANC in 1923 (Lodge 1983).

Ideas about politics of the colonised middle class were taking the first hesitant steps towards national consciousness in other forums. The Indian Congresses and the African Peoples Organisation (APO) contributed to the complexity of these initial responses, demonstrating unease and admiration towards the colonial modern. Together with other civil society organisations, they gave a historical foothold to South African liberalism, as it would not otherwise have spread beyond white politics. Through the Natal Indian Congress (NIC), formed in 1894, Mohandas Gandhi promoted an ambiguous political position. He led protests against legal discrimination against Indians, supported the British Empire in its wars against Africans (including the suppression of the Bambatha revolt) and identified with racist distinctions between the elite and subalterns, especially Indian indentured workers and Africans. The NIC defended the rights of the Indian trading and emerging professional groups; it did not take up issues of violence and abuse towards the Indian majority slaving away in the Natal sugar plantations (Bhabha 1987). There, class tensions were evident in the large plantations owned by whites, a few Indians and Africans, all of whom 'employed' indentured Indian and peasant African labour (Marks 1986).

The African Peoples Organisation (APO), launched in 1902 under the inspiring leadership of Dr Abdul Abdurahman (Adhikari 2009), met the British monarch in 1909 to appeal against the proposed national convention that would exclude all blacks. The APO has been historically viewed as a 'Coloured' organisation, yet its name demonstrates a critical attitude towards questions of identity. The Indian Congresses, the APO and other organisations active in African politics could not avoid questions of identity and its relation to politics. This issue was made more complex by a deep colonial concern with the finer divisions of race, language, caste and religion, even of professions and education. These divisive intents made identity politics and 'unity' high in strategic resistance ideologies.

But what did these colonised 'civilised men' want, and how did they plan to achieve their goals? Distancing themselves from Bambatha's violent yet futile response to discriminatory legislation, they concluded that the anti-colonial wars were socially devastating, that the colonial modern was how the real world worked and that it was a more advanced form of society with which they identified (Odendaal 1984). There was no going back to communal forms of social and political organisation; instead, this elite desired assimilation into colonial society in cultural and class terms. Peter Walshe (1971) identified three influences on early Cape liberal black thought: Christianity, Victorian liberalism and the struggle of African Americans. In their understanding of modernity, black liberals espoused universal franchise and citizenship, parliamentary representative government and notions of the rule of law. Through their commitment to constitutional politics, they planned to campaign to extend the Cape franchise to Africans in the other provinces. They wanted to assimilate into colonial modern society in a manner that conformed to the political rationality of the context; in other words, their political strategy would demonstrate that they ought to belong because they exemplified its finest values.

In Seme's Columbia University address of 1902, his message went beyond the South African context to encompass the plight of the African continent. He believed he spoke on behalf of the African 'race' as a whole, and that the continent needed to 'catch up' from its 'darkness' to the rest of the world, especially to those 'enlightened regions'. It was the time for an African renaissance, which embraced the modern world and its knowledge. He did not see a contradiction between an African renaissance and South African conditions, envisaging that African development could work through the colonial political system. The British liberal tradition was a realistic vehicle for realising African aspirations; politically, Africans should identify and work through the imperial office in London and the parliament at Westminster. Accordingly, the emerging nationalist elite viewed the imperial centre as an ally against local white backwardness, parochialism and prejudice.

At first, the Cape black elite remained relatively isolated from those in other provinces. Once talk of Union was in the air and Free State and Transvaal Afrikaner influence in the drawing up of the Union constitution was clear, however, they realised that their own voting rights would come under scrutiny. The ANC brought together existing organisations, including regional bodies, professional groups and 'traditional' chiefs who were very much a part of the elite of colonised society. Their main demand was the extension of the limited African voting rights in the Cape to educated men with property in the other three provinces. The government met their demands with disdain. Still committed to the Empire, they sent three delegations to the Colonial Office and directly appealed to the Queen of England, but to no avail. The last SANNC delegation to the British parliament in 1914 failed to convince Westminster parliamentarians to reverse the South African legislation (Davenport 1977). Yet, it illustrated its commitment to the Crown and the ambiguity in which it found itself by supporting Britain in World War I and encouraging all Africans to join the war effort.

Until the 1930s, the ANC mainly pursued this group's interests and used a politics that could not be considered disruptive by the political system. Between 1936 and 1939 it participated through the Native Representative Councils (NRCs), which were composed of elected white representatives. The strategy of recognising the NRCs stirred much debate in emerging nationalist thought, especially because subalterns had begun to show their frustrations and engage in 'spontaneous' collective protest action. The authorities took these subaltern protests seriously and responded with state repression; indirectly and slowly, the nationalist elite began to recognise the limits of its own social power and need to look beyond itself to realise its class interests.

The struggle and its subjects: the elite embrace mass politics

As a system of domination, settler colonialism responds to forces at play by oscillating between tightening and loosening its grip on the intermediary class, emphasising race over class or class over race. From Union until the early 1970s, it tightened its repressive grip over society, entrenching the idea of the non-humanness of all blacks and squeezing the intermediaries closer to the subalterns. Through various pieces of disenfranchisement legislation and increasing restrictions on black movement, employment and access to public services, the class of educated, Christianised blacks was pushed further into black and subaltern society and away from white social acceptance. The colonised elite was compelled to look towards the 'backward' mass for support, at first reluctantly and then, from the 1940s, desperately. The middle strata was stuck between two social blocs, both of which disliked it and were comfortable in their common-sense places in Manichean society. It thus had to muster the skills and political acumen to adapt quickly to changes in cultural and political space. The elites gradually adapted through their vehicle, the ANC, changing its ideology to embrace a broader notion of democracy and developing the necessary oratorical skills and organisational capacity to mobilise the subaltern population and thereby challenge the modern, colonial state more effectively and be taken more seriously.

In South Africa as in other colonised countries, the nationalist elites assumed it was their natural role to represent the subaltern mass, act as necessary intermediary and eventually control the state to promote modern development. In its African Claims document adopted in 1943, the ANC demanded an unqualified franchise, a one-person-one-vote position, for the first time and projected a larger mandate: 'the primary obligation of any government is to promote the economic advancement of the people under its charge and any obligation, agreement, contract or treaty in conflict with this primary obligation should not be countenanced' (Gerhart 1977, 14). The changing contours of settler-capitalism brought with it changes in social relations. The mines, agriculture and industry constantly demanded more labour, and a class of black proletarians in urban and rural areas began to constitute itself slowly but surely. The increasing bureaucratisation and policing of subaltern life and the intensity of exploitation meant that subalterns' radicalised social awareness was only a matter of time. For a long period, they resisted their conditions of bare life independently of middle-class leadership and organisations such as the SANNC; these regular and 'spontaneous' forms of challenging power had to contend with being appropriated by the discursive histories of nationalist organisations. This 'inner battle' over interpretation never ceased. In its desire to represent the 'indigenous' through its control and leadership of organisations, the intermediary middle class presented their own 'official' struggle narratives, utilising a knowledge reflective of its power. These discourses were in tension with subaltern experiences, occupying the status of subjugated knowledges in Foucault's (1980) sense of the term. In most instances, subaltern protests followed a discourse of the nationalist narrative, but they were were never settled, and subalterns also reinterpreted and appropriated them in their own interests.

In this light, the implicit 'organisational account' below should be read as a contested area between subalterns, who were coming into consciousness of their political status and making social change, and the organisations aiming to win them over, which were mostly controlled by members from the intermediary classes of settler-colonial South Africa. Ever since the first African worker strike in Port Alfred around 1854, mass subaltern politics has been a factor in anti-colonial politics. In 1918, without explicit ties to the SANNC or any other organisation, African women burnt passes and presented themselves for arrest in Bloemfontein and Jagersfontein (Gerhart 1977). When the sanitation workers went on strike in Johannesburg that year (Lodge 1983; Walsh 1971) and African workers downed tools and demonstrated in Bloemfontein the next (Webster 1978), the police suppressed them. These are a few illustrations of spontaneous subaltern protests that dotted the South African subaltern political consciousness in the early post-Union period, from demonstrations that were sufficiently large and significant to make it into the newspapers and attract the attention of the state, employers and police, to the many small acts that James Scott (1985) labelled 'everyday forms' of resistance.

The formal black political organisations gradually began to incorporate strategies of protest as part of their normal praxis, with each call, campaign or event adding to the accumulated knowledge they developed through their actions. In 1906, the Transvaal Indian Congress (TIC) and Natal Indian Congress (NIC) influenced subaltern knowledge with passive resistance by protesting against the 'Black Act', which prevented Indians from moving into the Transvaal. In 1919, the SANNC launched its own anti-pass campaign, wary of its unsuccessful efforts to prevent the passing of the 1913 Land Act. For the duration of World War I, the mainstream in the white South African Labour Party (SALB) suspended 'class conflict', causing the 'left-wing' (principally those opposed to the imperialist war) to organise the 'war on warites' that eventually led to the formation of the Communist Party of South Africa (CPSA, later SACP) in 1921. World War I influenced the colonial situation in South Africa by contributing to the restlessness of the black population, who learnt from every failure and the inconsistent promises of the colonial order. The growth of the armaments industry, white participation in the British forces and resulting increase in black employment increased the urban population and the possibilities of political and class consciousness among subalterns.

The World War I strikes (Webster 1978) drove thousands of workers into the ranks of the Industrial Commercial Union (ICU), teaching the subaltern many important lessons about politics, economics, identity and leadership during this formative phase in its process of becoming a mass subject of politics. Although the government used state repression against the strikers, the ICU could claim to be the first mass-based organisation of black workers. This historic achievement of working-class organisation introduced new issues and questions, placing an awareness about organisation on the agenda. It also made workers conscious of the overlap between politics and economics and taught them to take seriously the relations between race and class by bringing African and Coloured workers together (Gerhart 1978). It is unsurprising that the ICU grew more rapidly than the ANC and CPSA, given that the CPSA was still at pains to resolve its own dilemmas surrounding 'race' and class. Because it believed that white workers constituted the revolutionary subject in South Africa because they were more 'advanced and civilised' than their black counterparts, who were racially restricted to performing unskilled work, it was still concentrating on organising mainly white workers. The surge in ICU membership suggests a stirring of mass consciousness that was increasingly sensitive towards class exploitation and points to a battle over the content of modernity between colonial and nationalist elites and colonial elites and the black working class. This first political unionism of black workers focused on economic and political issues, from whose complex relationship in the colonial situation the nationalist elites shied away. Moreover, the ICU set up structures in rural areas, breaking another entrenched divide that urban-biased elite nationalists regarded as the space of 'tradition'.

It is conventional wisdom to criticise the ICU with regard to its 'general unionism', as opposed to the preferred sectorial unionism (where different unions organise within each sector of the economy) and the 'weak' leadership of the charismatic leader Clements Kadalie (Webster 1978). But both are weak because they ignore the significant political implications of the settler colonial situation. The established white trade unions operated on the craft trade unionism model, which was practiced in Britain and which the South African Labour Party (SALP) naturally supported as the preferred model. The ICU and Kadalie adopted a different, explicitly political approach with a model that was more relevant to the colonial-situation, aiming to stage a general strike of all black workers to bring the government to its knees (Kadalie 1970). The revolutionary potential and the implications of such an understanding were far ahead of that of the nationalist elite, whose political focus was only on voting rights, and the conservative leaders of the established trade unions (mainly of the white working class), who subscribed to a narrow economism. This potentially radical black working-class politics also came under external and internal pressure. The Independent Labour Party in England sent trade unionist William Ballinger to 'advise' the ICU and Kadalie to eschew 'race politics' and concentrate on economic issues (Kadalie 1970). Kadalie refused; he was subsequently criticised for mismanaging records, having a charismatic and personal leadership style and befriending Paul Robeson, an American black Marxist who was in solidarity with the ICU (Boyle & Bunie 2005, 316). Ballinger eventually joined the Liberal Party and abandoned further attempts to direct the ICU away from politics, but factional tensions arose inside the organisation. The ICU's relaxed federal structure was unable to counter them. The organisation's steady decline began when Allison Wessels George Champion, the Natal leader of the ICU, broke away to concentrate on his own regional ICU in 1930 (Webster 1978).

Compared to the growth of the ICU in the 1920s and 1930s, the ANC was largely ineffective as a campaigner for black rights because it was committed to appeals to parliament and sent toothless delegations and petitions to the government. When an All African Convention (AAC) met in 1935 to protest against the 'Hertzog Bills' and the ANC had once again failed in 1936 to prevent it from passing, younger members became frustrated. The AAC, a broad coalition of liberal, nationalist and socialist groups, rivalled the ANC to represent African opinion nationally (Lodge 1983). The ANC declined to participate in the AAC, although individuals could be active in both. Differences in the AAC coalition came to a head when some representatives demanded non-collaboration with government structures and strongly criticised those in the ANC who remained committed to the NRCs. The AAC became the driving force behind the Non-European Unity Movement (NEUM), which was launched in 1943 to promote 'Non-European unity' and socialism, as enunciated in the radical 'Ten Point Program' (Kayser & Adhikari 2004).

The intermediary class dominated debate over conceptual themes of resistance, which divided itself and the undereducated subalterns over political ideology. However, more immediate democratic issues, such as the roles and relationship of leaders and the led, opened up space for subaltern contributions in their own ways. Subaltern debates allowed a broad democratic discourse to develop. It demanded the end of all race-based discrimination, universal franchise and principled non-collaboration in relation to state and civil society; questioned the best form of democratic organisation and different types of resistance strategies; developed a toolkit of appropriate tactics, some of which were more effective than others and the knowledge to analyse tactics in relation to context; increased familiarity with the larger theoretical questions emerging from critiques of capitalism and exploitation; and explored the politics of identity around race, class and gender. Together with the ANC's 1943 African Claims proposals, an open and mixed agenda of democratic discourse began to take shape and filter into subaltern consciousness. As they added to the subjugated knowledges that the subalterns had already accumulated, this phase can be characterised as inchoate political consciousness.

The politics of mobilisation: the 1950s failure

The dialectic between the operation of the settler-colonial power structure and the opposition it generates serves as the political field within which the real actors (the subject positions of whites, intermediaries and subalterns) decide on strategies and tactics in their battles. Two periods stand out in the formation of the collective mass subject of politics in South Africa: the 1950s, which ended with the Sharpeville shootings, and the 1970s, which produced the negotiations in the early 1990s. In both, the competition between discourses of identity politics and civil rights emanated from the middle strata and contributed to the production of the mass struggle subject. Their battles over differing analyses of domination and its major source, the practices of mobilisation and the envisioned 'free society' produced conflict about whose vision of liberated society constituted true 'freedom', which strategies were the most effective in the fight for social justice, whether to enter into negotiations with government and which differences were generated by popular struggle and resistance itself. Concerns about how to 'resolve' crises both became immediate and gave a sense of the radical thrust of each discourse when the national or local state made overtures to negotiate in the midst of these mobilisations.

The post-World War II social and ideological context had significant impacts on the colonial world. The leading powers could no longer justify their empires on the older ideological grounds, which were based on the idea of a hierarchy of races topped with Europeans. Further pressure came from countries like India, the USA and the USSR, which challenged the old colonial order and its status in the post-World War II world system. In many colonies, the colonised elites were also unable to ignore the successes of mass mobilisations in India and radical nationalist- and communist-led struggles in China. In anticipation of social unrest in this new world, the Nationalist Party minister of police threatened repressive legislation in 1950, allowing the government to clampdown on political protests and indicating to the white electorate that government was following through on dealing with the *'swart gevaar'* (black threat) that it had warned about in its election campaign.

Yet, the post-World War II socio-economic and political contexts allowed for new possibilities of resistance. Rapid wartime urbanisation produced 'squatter' settlements around major cities and towns, presenting opportunities for political groups to mobilise people around many social grievances. The desperate demand for housing, combined with the 'urban township policy', contributed to the process whereby black proletarians considered 'politics' as a mass activity rather than a separate or distant 'sphere' of activity restricted to the African intelligentsia. This new township subaltern showed all the signs of becoming a rich and vibrant for social change. At the same time, the intermediary group of nationalists was already showing signs of frustration with pre-World War II strategies and the older guard of leaders. In Johannesburg, thousands of teachers (a crucial mediating and contradictory sector of Manichean society) marched for higher pay, and this black lower-middle class sensitivity to political desire would eventually gravitate towards those political formations, such as the Youth League, the Pan-Africanist Congress (PAC), Non-European Unity Movement (NEUM), and the South African Communist Pary (SACP), which were more leftist than the mainstream.

Frustrated by the older generation's limited and narrowly defined conception of politics, especially its dismissal and fear of subaltern political activity, the ANC Youth League expressed younger people's concerns by demanding a politics that emphasised mobilised protest (Lodge 1983). The 1946 mineworkers strike was a key development in this change in the subaltern political imagination. The Youth League risked questioning the 'old guard' and embraced African nationalism as its 'liberatory creed', an indication of post-war change and modern attitudes, and the continental influence of African political ideologies.

The main influence was that of a young teacher, lawyer and philosopher of ideas, Anton Lembede, who preached African unity derived from the coming into being of the 'African spirit', the social power of Africans when united across differences and the liberation of Africans 'as a race' from foreign domination and leadership. Following Lembede's sudden death at age thirty-three, Ashley Peter Mda, who shared his home and legal offices and knew him as a close comrade and friend, wanted him to be remembered for his towering intellect. Today, we are also able to appreciate the complexity of the black intellectual's critical engagement with modernity as manifested in settler-colonial and Manichean society. Mda wrote:

> There is an old Greek saying that they die young whom the gods love. Young Lembede, one of the most brilliant students that this land has produced, died 'before his prime.' He died at the age of 33, on the threshold of a scholastic, legal and political career that might have been unparalleled in Black Africa. The story of his life reads like a romance.... In June 1945, he submitted his thesis for his Master's Degree on: The Conception of God as Expounded by, and as it Emerges from the

Writings of Philosophers from Descartes to the Present Day ... I read through his thesis before he submitted it. I must confess that I was taken aback by the breadth of learning and profundity of so young a man as Anton. He found no difficulty in compassing the immeasurable regions of thought traversed by such intellectual giants as St. Augustine, St. Thomas Aquinas, Spinoza, Nietzsche, Hegel, Joad, Kant and others. Not only did he summarise their main ideas on the theme, but he drew his own conclusions in a work crammed with closely reasoned hypotheses and marked with great erudition. Mr. Lembede was also a student of languages. He knew Latin, German, Dutch, and was busy at French (1947).

South Africa, Lembede emphasised, must be understood as a case of foreign, settler-colonial domination. As the author of the manifesto of the Youth League, he influenced other young ANC leaders such as Mandela, Walter Sisulu, Mda and Dan Tloome by impressing upon them the needs to conceive of the South African conflict differently and question the dominant liberalism that had held sway in black nationalist thought until then. The following quote from the League manifesto gives a general sense of Lembede's main view but indicates that he was grappling with African identity and the possibility of it being a consequence of settler colonialism:

South Africa has a complex problem. Stated briefly it is: The contact of the White race with the Black has resulted in the emergence of a set of conflicting living conditions and outlooks on life which seriously hamper South Africa's progress to nationhood.... The majority of White men regard it as the destiny of the White race to dominate the man of colour. The harshness of their domination, however, is rousing in the African feelings of hatred of everything that bars his way to full and free citizenship and these feelings can no longer be suppressed.... The African National Congress is the symbol and embodiment of the African's will to present a united national front against all forms of oppression, but this has not enabled the movement to advance the national cause in a manner demanded by prevailing conditions. And this, in turn, has drawn on it criticisms in recent times which cannot be ignored if Congress is to fulfil its mission in Africa.... The formation of the African National Congress Youth League is an answer and assurance to the critics of the national movement that African Youth will not allow the struggles and sacrifices of their fathers to have been in vain. Our fathers fought so that we, better equipped when our time came, should start and continue from where they stopped (1944).

He thought that nationalist resistance was part of the global movement against colonialism. His vision for a united, developed and modern Africa was almost identical to the picture Seme had painted some fifty years earlier (Gerhart 1978; Lodge 1983). In engaging with the questions of modernity and scientific knowledge, Lembede understood the dilemma facing African identity and its complex relationship with power/knowledge. He suggested that Africans had no choice but to develop their own universities because scientific knowledge was a key site of the broader political struggle, part of a crucial life-and-death struggle and a way for the African to 'catch up' to Western standards:

> This grand suggestion ought to receive a country-wide approval and support and it should be translated into action without any further waste of time.... We need science to assist us in our present stage of transition and we shall need it more increasingly thereafter. To the question: What knowledge is of most value—the uniform reply is: science.... It is science that will help us to adapt ourselves to the Western standards of life and to dispel the fogs of ignorance and superstition.... Our Art (including literature) can also receive a great impetus and fillip, from a cultural society or academy of art.... We need artists to interpret to us and to the world our glorious past, our misery, suffering and tribulation of the present time, our hopes, aspirations and our divine destiny and our great future; to inspire us with the message that there is hope for our race and that we ought therefore to draw plans and lay foundations for a longer future than we can imagine by struggling for national freedom so as to save our race from imminent extinction or extermination. In short, we need African Artists to interpret the spirit of Africa (1996).

Lembede's was essentially a discourse of identity. It resonated with Pan-Africanism, which was spreading across the continent (including in South Africa). He identified its main principles: Africa is the land of black peoples; Africans are one; the leadership of Africans will come from the African people; cooperation between Africans and other non-Europeans, while desirable, should only be entered into if Africans act as a united bloc; the divine destiny of the African people is national freedom; and, after national freedom comes socialism (Gerhart 1978). This approach to nationalism emphasises African identity and the belief that 'self-awareness' of an oppressed identity and history, namely of Africans looking at themselves through a positive rather than a negative lens.

As such, it constitutes the beginning of 'mental emancipation'. In settler-colonial formations this inward-looking and positive reinterpretation of precolonial African culture is also, as Fanon reminded, a necessary stage in the consciousness of the intermediary groups. This continuous attempt to eradicate attitudes of inferiority, which were reinforced by colonial institutions and social relations, celebrates that which has been derided, marginalised or simply ignored. To work towards it, Africans had to look within and, at a very minimum, begin to celebrate the uniqueness of the 'African personality'. Group solidarity is important, fostered by a precolonial cultural heritage and reinforced by the material and political conditions of exclusion. Here, Africanism is thus conceived of as a consciousness-raising approach. The unity increases African resources and promotes a better bargaining position by engaging with power from a position of strength rather than weakness. The goal is democratic representation in parliament. Though he was convinced that South Africa was a 'Black man's country', and some have condemned him as a fascist sympathiser, Lembede and Africanist ideology generally emphasise that the nationalist struggle was never against whites but a white system of domination.

This discourse of identity politics undoubtedly has a considerable affinity to Biko's later formulation of Black Consciousness (BC), though some significant differences cannot be overlooked. One is that, following Fanon, BC was more sceptical about cultivating nostalgia for the precolonial past rather than concentrating on and radically critiquing the present. Biko made repeated reference to the 'modern African culture.' BC emphasised the self-understanding of the 'oppressed experience' (the 'lived experience' in Fanon's framing), which examined the ways in which settler-colonial social relations produced relational subjects, including their embeddedness in the material conditions of production. It denied that black subjects had an ahistorical essence outside settler-colonial history and ideology in which the 'settler' brought the 'native' into existence.

This new assertive nationalism encouraged practical interventions, which effectively brought the nationalist elite closer to the subalterns, who, in turn, produced their own tensed dynamic. The 1949 Programme of Action broke with previous ANC programs. It demanded practical and more effective forms of protest, along the lines of mass-based civil disobedience. Dr Alfred Xuma, president-general of the ANC at the time, opposed the program. He lost the confidence of the membership and was replaced by Dr James Moraka in December 1949. The campaign organised three protests to focus attention on the ban on communism, Mayday and worker conditions, the commemoration of those killed in struggle and the pass laws in a National Day of Protest (Lodge 1983). In July 1951, a meeting of the ANC, the Indian Congresses and the Joint Franchise Action Committee prepared an extended Defiance Campaign to defy six Apartheid laws targeted at blacks. It began in June 1952, when volunteers gave themselves up for arrest (Motlhabi 1984), but leadership called it off in October when rioting broke out in Port Elizabeth. A long period of campaigning, often door-to-door, culminated in a large gathering in 1955 in Kliptown, where the ANC approved and adopted the Freedom Charter in 1956. It placed civil rights discourse on a different footing and opened up possibilities of a radical critique of white domination by questioning unregulated capitalism. Its wording split the organisation because those attached to the principles of Pan-Africanism formed a rival national organisation: the PAC.

Pan-Africanists believed the Freedom Charter undermined the colonial question by not mentioning that South Africa was a product of colonial conquest and that it endorsed multiracial alliances in which Africans always assumed the subordinate roles. They criticised the ANC for being too soft and slow and its leadership for failing to guide the Alexandra and Evaton bus boycotts, which it used to claim the ANC was irrelevant to mass protest. The expulsion of Leballo and Josias Madzunya in 1953 further reinforced differences, paving the way for the split in 1958 (Gerhart 1978). The

ANC called for a stay-away during the all-white elections in 1958 but some Africanists considered them irrelevant to Africans, and saw that as the last straw for launching a separate organisation. In response to their breakaway, the ANC condemned the Africanists for alienating white support and for practicing 'racism in reverse'.

A few months after it was launched, the PAC embarked on a 'Status Campaign' to highlight black assertiveness and then the 'Positive Action Campaign' to oppose the pass law. It used its campaigns to popularise itself and to respond to what it assumed was an alienated, angry African population ready for national rebellion, if only the appropriate radical leadership was available. Since then, nationalist elite politics have remained divided between Africanists and non-racialists. The PAC went into exile after the Sharpeville shootings and steadily declined, weakened by continuous factional conflict, poor leadership, the distance and isolation of exile, and the incompatibility of exile with its ideology of mobilisation. Before it was banned, however, the national appetite for popular mobilisation was increasing, and thousands joined protests until the Sharpeville shooting in 1960 created a different political landscape in black politics (Lodge 1983). In 1960–1961, many ANC and PAC activists became attracted to the idea of taking up arms rather than facing state repression, which came with organising popular mobilisation. The military campaigns against the Apartheid state were successfully suppressed for a variety of reasons; besides, the many additional logistical burdens made it a difficult strategy to follow.

Many different, even opposing worldviews, competed within the ANC during its exile of 1961–1990, though it gravitated towards a radical nationalism. Some included African nationalism, Christian liberalism, clandestinity, technocracy, communist popular frontism, Western Marxism, indigenous working-class radicalism, and an incipient BC (Lodge 1987, 24). Despite this diversity, its official positions emphasised its understanding of South African society as captured in the phrase 'colonialism of a special type' (CST), a conception traceable to the SACP (then CPSA) of the early 1950s (Everatt 1992). Drawing on Marxist analysis, the CST is a way to describe the social structure as it developed historically in South Africa and explain national oppression and race dynamics under colonial capitalism. Where it sees the developed 'white' part of the economy as similar to any Western capitalist country where monopoly capitalism holds sway, it identifies the 'black' part as that of a typical colonial society. To quote from the SACP Programme 'Colonialism of a Special Type':

> But on another level, that of 'non-white South Africa', there are all the features of a colony. The indigenous population is subjected to extreme national oppression, poverty and exploitation, lack of all democratic rights and political domination by a group which does everything it can to emphasize and perpetuate its alien 'European' character (1969).

ANC literature holds that these dual features make South Africa unique, but its complexity has another cause:

It is an 'independent' national state, at another level it is a country subjugated by a minority race. What makes the structure unique and adds to its complexity is that the exploiting nation is not, as in the typical imperialist relationship, situated in a geographically distinct mother country, but is settled within its border. What is more, the roots of the dominant nation have been embedded in our country for more than three centuries of presence. It is thus an alien body only in the historical sense (1969).

This analysis of CST motivated a 'two-stage strategy' of social change with socialism following democracy. The first, national democratic revolution, was to be led by the African majority in alliance with all other 'races' that had an interest in overthrowing Apartheid. Although the analysis was primarily grounded in SACP conceptual thinking, the ANC adopted it as its own until differences over the second socialist stage became more evident during the Mbeki years and that goal fell away. CST was a necessary and important contribution to the understanding of South African social formation, but it was inadequate for making sense of political expressions prevalent in post-1994 democracy. Fanon's social-psychological framework presents a more nuanced, complex relationship between ideology, race subject formation and class dynamics.

Is there any relation between the first and second waves of political participation, the mass subjects' coming to political consciousness in the 1950s and the building of mass social power in the 1970s and 1980s? What about the collective subject of the 1970s made its political participation so much more effective, and how is it related to its predecessor in the 1950s? Was it a different relationship of national consciousness to the systematic organisation of power? These are significant questions, but answers are evasive. The adoption and implementation of the Programme of Action in 1949 signified a change in opposition politics (Gerhart 1978), announcing that at least the intermediary middle class wanted to encourage the subalterns to join it against the settler-colonial order. Different discourses were pursued and subalterns began to protest, drawing on democratic rights claims, Africanist identity claims and their own desires for political significance beyond bare life.

The shift from the middle-class politics of persuasion (petitions and deputations) to a defiant position, demanding change through mass action, increased the masses' involvement in protest; subalterns became marginally involved in debates around the goals, strategies and tactics of resistance. In the period prior to the late 1940s, the debate surrounding political protest was centred within the ranks of an educated, articulate, professional elite, who dominated the forums of the ANC and AAC. As the campaigns of the 1950s progressed, subalterns began to see beyond government policies and focus on politics more broadly. While the national elites focused on state power and larger social transformation in terms of modern ideologies, subalterns were infusing the democratic idea of 'the people' with more meaningful substance. These changes brought questions and debates that firmly redefined politics as 'mass politics' and moved it outside the exclusive preserve of the nationalist elites. However, the latter always retained the upper hand (they still composed the leadership) to monitor the masses, and their cultural values were predominant because they conformed to universalist claims.

The second mobilisation: 1970s and 1980s

The next attempt at establishing a nationalist-modern political ideology responding to settler-colonial conditions accompanied the BC mobilisations, which were led by black students (a classic strata of the intermediary nationalist bourgeoisie) before spreading to black townships (Motlhabi 1984). BC answered black oppression under the changed socio-economic and political conditions of the 1960s. The decade following Sharpeville witnessed the intensification of Apartheid social planning, the success of the state in producing docile black subjects and the absence of any noticeable opposition from blacks. Mostly, different white and black liberal groups opposed Apartheid. A lesson of the 1950s was that a discourse of identity/recognition could effectively mobilise the subalterns. The significance of BC lay in retaking this oppositional space, establishing a radical discourse of black oppositional identity, targeting the entire white power structure and introducing a discursive platform that allowed colonised elites and subaltern masses to re-engage in mass protest (Fatton, 1978). BC cannot be traced organisationally or ideologically to the ANC or PAC, although notions like 'nation-building' and 'mental liberation' connect to the earlier PAC. BC's emphases on the totality of the white power structure and independent initiatives of the oppressed resonate the Africanist/Ethiopianist tradition but also break with it.

Struggle discourses had to respond to the Apartheid regime's success in imposing the fear of 'struggle politics', widespread apathy and petty infighting. BC encouraged a new attitude. It encouraged practical activities that did not seem explicitly political at first. Ultimately these interventions made blacks reconsider themselves and question the colonial roles and status they were assigned. This self-assertiveness, confidence and respect for Africanist values and culture helped produce a different political subject wanting to resist the oppressive power structure. Eventually, this discourse filled the political space that had previously been dominated by nationalist liberation politics and then condescending liberalism after the ANC and PAC bans. Its absence caused a 'political vacuum', in Biko's words, that subsumed black politics after the security police had effectively hunted down ANC and PAC activists. The influence of white liberal politics was questioned, then defied and finally rejected (Mzamane 2006).

Robert Fatton's study of BC draws insightfully on a Gramscian approach. He read the key BC ideas as the 'ethico-political' targeting of blacks' mental submission to white cultural hegemony, a radical critique of white liberalism, the demand for solidarity and unity of the oppressed (which was strategically necessary for resistance), and defining 'black' as a political mass subject who questions the whole power structure and self-reflects. 'Black' thus describes changing 'consciousness' as linked to practices, ways of living in a socially and politically oppressive situation and always imagining a different future that is realisable in the present (Fatton 1986). Fatton's words emphasise the present and defend against those who criticised BC for not having openly identified with detailed socialist outcomes:

> Any viewpoint that sets to radically transform society can only offer a vague description of the future revolutionized society and BC was no exception, vaguely describing the future society as majoritarian and socialist.... Black Consciousness was not a theory of the future. Its task was not to describe the classless society of tomorrow, but to ruthlessly criticize the existing white racist order in all its institutional manifestations with the hope of contributing to the rise of black hegemony, and black dignity (Fatton 1986).

The imaginative learning and teaching 'liberation politics', a refashioning exercise of sorts, began with regularly held 'formation schools', where students studied the history of resistance and to teach themselves how to be activists in the oppressive political environment of the late 1960s. At the first 'formation school', held at the Natal University Medical School residence in December 1969, Biko lectured on the significance, role and future of the South African struggle (Fatton 1986). He analysed the recently launched South African Students Organisation (SASO) in relation to the post-Sharpeville failures to resist effectively what he called the 'white power structure'. He identified failures including pervasive ethnic and tribal thinking, the absence of a 'cementing' ideology and weak black leadership. The white National Union of South African Students (NUSAS), as black students had discovered, was unable and unwilling to pursue black students' interests, so they formed their own organisation independently of whites (Stubbs 1978). By establishing an organisation for blacks, the SASO was at pains to distance itself from accusations that it was endorsing government Apartheid policy and promoting racism. It had to defend an independent black organisation as 'a realistic' response to a situation designed to end government policies. In Biko's words:

> What SASO has done is simply to take stock of the present scene in the country and to realize that, not unless the non-white students decide to lift themselves from the doldrums, will they ever hope to get out of them. What we want is not black visibility but real black participation (Stubbs 1978:5).

This new discourse about black identity fell on fertile soil. Initially, university and high school students spread some of its ideas into their working-class, township homes. In a relatively short period, BC ideas that drew from and embedded themselves in charismatic discourse spread SASO's influence from students to communities. The space allowed to independent initiatives of cultural expression (music, arts, theatre, poetry, painting) and community 'building' (education, clubs, churches, welfare), which could not be explicit in its political messages yet still contained political meaning, was ironically enabled by the 'racial' separation of Manichean society. The politicisation of 'skin' and its direct link to oppression were both political and personal. Since any collective activity of blacks had a political bearing and potential in settler-colonial society, these ideas had a larger impact than the government had first assumed. By the mid-1970s, activists were referring to the Black Consciousness 'movement' (Halisi 1999; Motlhabi 1984; Khoapa 1972).

In the communities, all kinds of organisations had taken on a BC mantle and contributed to a black civic and political renaissance. Although the struggle's political focus did not abandon state goals, BC left open the possibility to critique a narrow focus on state power. BC believed that society-centred activity as important, or more important, to resistance politics than capturing the state because it was, after all, realising the goal of making a new subject, a 'new man'. This culture of critical opposition explains the protests over government's imposition of Afrikaans as the language of instruction of scientific subjects in Soweto in 1976 (Kane-Berman 1978; Hirson 1979); a logical realisation of BC discourse promoted this critical opposition to the latest addition to Bantu education. Though the links are indirect and mediated by hundreds of other campaigns, the Soweto revolt laid the groundwork for the more intense mobilisations of the 1980s (Murray 1987).

The reform initiative in the 1980s led the state to loosen its grip and permit civic protests to a degree. In stark contrast to its pre-Biko and Soweto repression, it wanted to 'normalise' black protest within agreeable limits of the law while steering it towards civil rights. This stimulated a wave of mass mobilisation in different discourses. Some were within the confines of the law because they were within the bounds of 'civil rights' discourse or identity politics. Others involved the subaltern mass articulating rebellion and revolution, assuming a militant demeanour agitating for revenge, repossession and the reversal of social relations inspired by Fanon's 'the last to be first' promise in such situations. The momentum developed into a culture of mass protest and mobilisation.

The national elite strata aimed to channel these social forces as much as possible by coordinating the school boycotts in 1980 and the anti–Republican Day celebrations in 1981, campaigning against the President's Council's proposals and the anti-tricameral parliament elections, encouraging trade union–led strikes across sectors from the early 1980s, boycotting schools and targeting local councils with community protests. With the Vaal uprisings in 1984, the community protests in the Eastern Cape and the intensive running battles between Inkatha and United Democratic Front (UDF) and Azanian Peoples Organisation (AZAPO) supporters in Kwa-Zulu Natal, the country was facing what looked like a 'people's revolt' (Murray 1987). The culture of protest, which included 'struggle language', songs, dance, debate, discussion about long-term goals and immediate strategies and tactics, resulted in a complex structure of signs that politically constituted subjects. At the same time, daily threats from the state and rival organisations added to the everyday violence and pathologies of subaltern life under settler-colonial modernity. Ultimately, this gave shape to a mass political subject of enormous capacity that believed it as 'the people', encouraged by the nationalist elites and promised political significance. It had acquired its political consciousness and experience as knowledge. After two states of emergency, thousands jailed and hundreds killed, the state opted to negotiate with the ANC.

Conclusion

This chapter focused on the relationship between the national elite and subaltern mass. It discussed how the politics of nationalism unfolded in settler-colonial situations by examining how Manichean society produces its own subjects of resistance, elites and subalterns, and the initial lines of tension between them. Rather than looking at the main organisations and their ideologies, as per conventional approaches to South African resistance studies, this avoids assuming a singular interest for both the nationalist elites and the masses. Instead, it acknowledges the complicated relationship of ideology, leadership, discipline, control, persuasion and mutual suspicion. It highlighted how the elite at first aimed to 'go it alone' and appeal directly to the colonial state, only to realise its collective weakness. Once having realised the power of the masses, as the colonial order was taking them more seriously, the nationalist elites reluctantly developed ties with the masses. The chapter focused on nationalist elite discourses that competed for subalterns' support: discourses of civil rights and of identity.

Tracing this relationship identified two broad periods in which the elite and subaltern resisted the colonial order via separate registers and then, from the post-war period, became allies despite harbouring mutual suspicion. In the latter, two broad popular national mobilisations were distinguished: a more limited resistance that reached a high point at Sharpeville and the more effective mobilisations of the 1970s to the 1980s. They 'unified' elite and subaltern concerns around complex democratic discourses, which in turn produced a new collective subaltern subject, and succeeded in forcing the settler-colonial order to negotiate new terms of power. The mass upsurge created conditions that Fanon called the 'decisive moment' and, in this crucial period, the elites chose to enter into negotiations about democratic constitutional changes based on a dominant discourse of rights. In the democratic period, the dominant discourse of civic rights is in tension with the material, lived experience of subalterns, who realise that only a politics of mobilisation can help them to achieve their demand for recognition and to move beyond bare life to a life of political significance. This is the moment at which civil society and political society present two domains and modes of politics, and the stage where South Africa finds itself today.

6| Elites, masses and democratic change

From a discussion of the democratic transition emerge two couplets in the dominant narrative: elites/negotiations and masses/violence. These oppositions compete over the content of political rationality. The establishment of a mode of politics that is considered more or less modern assumes central importance for the elites. The nationalist elites wanted to impose a particular political rationality, taking it as self-evident to demonstrate their control over the masses, to discipline the emerging political subject, which however had other ideas about the politics of change, based on centuries of colonial violence. The focus of this chapter is on how elite and subaltern structures of thought—one concerned with political modernity, the other concerned with recognition—relate to each other, where elite discourse translates the latter into its own terms.

The negotiation process of 1990–1994 formally ended Apartheid discriminatory laws and brought the ANC into power in a democratic political system. They also unleashed many other tensions overlooked by the linear narrative of the 'miracle' transition. In fighting against the white power structure, activist organisations applied pressure on the Apartheid state through semi-violent civil protests related to mass social mobilisation, partially supported by international isolation and some acts of sabotage. From the 1970s a broad swath of society mobilised against the Apartheid state, eroding its social control and compelling it to impose martial law. The state of emergency that was declared regionally in 1976/7 and 1985, and country-wide from 1986 to 1989, influenced domestic capital and foreign governments to increasingly call for negotiations. The combination of economic recession, pressure from neighbouring governments, international isolation and civic resistance divided the Apartheid ruling group into *Verligte* ('enlightened'; pro-reform) and *Verkrampte* ('strict'; anti-reform) factions, and caused domestic and international capital to question their support of Apartheid and Nationalist Party rule (Price 1990). In this period of political crisis, obedience to everyday laws by subalterns held little sway. The power dynamics between the state and citizens and between groups of citizens shifted, reaching a stage where some local communities claimed certain areas of social and political life were under 'people's power'.

This chapter interprets how South Africa transitioned to a different mode of politics, with democratic institutions comprehended in the terms of political development, imposing at the same time a vision of the disciplined subaltern subject radically different to that which evolved in oppositional struggle. This chapter focuses on that 'decisive moment' when national elites responded to a 'forward rush of national consciousness', fearful that things—i.e., those subaltern 'excesses the nationalist elite must keep under control and discipline'—might get out of hand (Fanon 1963). The transition displaced a particular type of mass political subject just as it began to emerge, steering it towards conforming to the idea of political rationality as defined by the nationalist elite. In Agamben's (2011) understanding, this marks the movement to, and conception of, politics in which sovereignty about to be constituted by the people becomes sovereignty embedded in government and the law, or the beginning of the shift from the juridico-political to the economic-managerial of the executive government. The end of the democratic transition pushed the subaltern masses from the active centre of political discourse, defining the field of politics, to a passively marginalised role, reducible to democracy as electoral politics.

This chapter examines three areas in the dominant discourse in which the meaning of 'the political' and political rationality—considered acceptable politics—became narrower: the distinction between 'the political' and 'the criminal'; the opposition of negotiations and 'peace' as rational (and as part of elite politics) to 'black-on-black' violence as irrational (and referring to subaltern politics); and the endorsement of an agenda for negotiations which excluded from 'the political' racialised property and related inequality, key elements of the understanding of 'bare life' and the main concern of subalterns. These three themes in the dominant discourse emerged during the transition, and facilitated the shift from a politics of inchoate radical subaltern consciousness to a politics restricted to executive power, elections and the law. The discussion is organised under four separate sections: establishing the political/criminal divide; establishing peace versus violence; elite politics as rational versus 'black-on-black' violence as irrational; and agenda-setting where superficial procedural differences trump racialised property.

Drawing new boundaries between the political and the criminal

Because under Apartheid blacks lived in a permanent state of exception, in which all spheres of life were politicised and all anti-state politics criminalised, the distinction between the political and the criminal was ambiguous and vague. Moreover, for the excluded/included majority, law did not acquire a moral legitimacy and therefore politics and law also had a complex relationship. In struggle discourses, especially from around the Soweto Rebellion of 1976 onwards, the idea that the Apartheid state was illegitimate and criminal was widely expressed. In the eyes of the masses at least, the ruling National Party failed to criminalise resistance, so by the 1980s the resistance had become legitimate and the regime criminal; this political conjuncture had to change. Establishing the political/criminal distinction and regenerating the legitimacy of the state were in the interests both of the Afrikaner Nationalist Party and the nationalist elites, who were leading the struggle and expecting to inherit the old Apartheid state. So, ANC leaders proceeded to negotiate ambiguously, pushing for the release of imprisoned ANC members while wanting to maintain the distinction between political and criminal.

Distinguishing between the proper limits of the political and the confines of the criminal was essential to legal discourse, which laid the foundation for the democratic state. Efforts in this direction can be traced to the very first meetings, which also indicated a desire to displace popular participation and the politics it represented to one more controllable by elites. The meeting at the Groote Schuur mansion in Cape Town on 2–4 May 1990 introduced a tension over law and politics—specifically regarding the definition of 'political prisoners' and the determination of who could qualify for amnesty—that remained throughout the negotiations. Ironically, the government granted immediate temporary indemnity to ANC members attending the meeting who had been convicted under Apartheid security laws; the question of the legitimacy of the Apartheid state and the legal status of its representatives did not come up. Only twice did Mandela publicly raise the issue of the 'illegitimacy' of the Apartheid state, first in his response to De Klerk at the first CODESA conference and just after the Boipatong massacre, when he accused the De Klerk regime of not caring for black life. At the Groote Schuur meeting the ANC delegation demanded the release of all political prisoners, the unconditional return of exiles and amendments to repressive security legislation to allow open political activity, but it never mentioned the illegitimacy of the Apartheid state.

Distinguishing between the political and the criminal is itself fundamentally a political act. The negotiations never entirely resolved this question, as the status of political prisoners twenty years into the democratic period demonstrates. Organisations, such as the IFP and PAC, still complain that they have members who are in prison for political activity. The ANC ambiguously accepted the government's distinction, with the term 'political' setting the parameters for the meaning of 'criminal'. The government defined the meaning of the political based on its negotiating experience during Namibia's transition to democracy. A political act qualified for indemnity on a case-by-case basis, guided by certain criteria. You could distinguish between the 'purely' political and the 'purely' criminal, such as murder or assault in 'ordinary' crimes. However, an 'ordinary' crime could be regarded as a political offence if the motive of the actor was political—as, for example, in the context of a political uprising. To determine this, the law considered 'the nature of the objective as in trying to change the regime or policy'; the 'legal and factual nature of the offence including the gravity'; the relationship between the political objective and the means pursued; and whether the offence had been committed on the order of an organisation (Groote Schuur Minute Report Working Group 1990). Besides these criteria, the two parties agreed that government would have the discretion to 'formulate its own guidelines which it will apply', thus leaving the issue more or less to executive decision (Groote Schuur Minute Report Working Group 1990).

The meetings that followed, such as the Pretoria Minute of 1990, occurred against the background of ghastly violence in many parts of the country. Again the definition of 'political' came up for discussion, and gradually new criteria were added to the list. Now those who had left the country without proper legal papers and who belonged to political organisations could return without prosecution. But the Apartheid government refused to release political prisoners or grant amnesty to those who had been convicted of causing civilian deaths, such as in the Robert McBride case (Waldmeir 1998). The matter was postponed when, at the DF Malan Accord of 1991, a working group was created to continue the discussion on political prisoners.

In rejecting 'violence'—a catchall category—and encouraging 'negotiations', defined as participation in the formal meetings with government politics, 'the political' narrowed to become associated with legal discourse, and participation in negotiations became the only acceptable form of politics. The advocacy of violence for strategic or tactical purposes, or the mention of the 'structural violence' of settler colonialism, were condemned and vilified as being against peace, criminal. By implication, participation in the negotiation process translated into choosing peace over violence. Where did this leave the mass of citizens who for the past fifteen years had been mobilised and supportive of the ANC as active participants in 'the struggle'? Since the negotiations only involved elites, citizens became passive observers of its processes. Even among the elites, and as early as CODESA I, the questionable, grossly undemocratic practice of 'sufficient consensus' was introduced, which meant in effect that only agreement between the ANC and the NP government was necessary. Cyril Ramaphosa, one of the initiators of this practice, defended it on the basis that it was intended to prevent the negotiations from being bogged down and possibly undermined by smaller, ideologically committed parties. Yet it points to the elitist nature of the process, and the determination of the elites to accomplish an end goal of a procedurally democratic constitution as efficiently as possible, even at the enormous political cost of excluding the sovereign people, who were expected to observe largely passively at a distance, reported to on happenings in the negotiations via the press or a managed public participation campaign.

The government consistently demanded that the ANC renounce the armed struggle. This was a strongly emotive issue, because the ANC's mass support base admired and respected the organisation largely due to its taking up arms against the state. The armed struggle was thus an important symbol of ANC identity. The ANC accused the government of supporting 'third force' violence against its members. The ANC also demanded that the government end its support for the IFP's violent campaign. When in July 1990 leading figures of the ANC were arrested for organising an underground ANC network, known as Operation Vula (Butler 2008), Mandela at the Pretoria Minute suspended the armed struggle following an NEC decision. Apparently the Vula structure had been intended to serve as a secondary organisation in case the negotiations failed; those arrested claimed that the government wanted information about the negotiating strategy of the ANC. Mandela demanded that ANC supporters should not endorse violence—what had once been preached and defended as an essential form of self-defence against state violence was now vilified as criminal.

Gradually, the agreements between the government and the nationalist opposition established legal discourse—i.e., the new rules for politics that were considered legitimate. As bystanders to these agreements, the popular forces that had once been active and influential in creating and defining the public sphere found themselves diminished and barely able to decipher the new language of politics. New fields of expertise and education developed—for example, citizen education in democratic processes such as elections, or the dependence on legal experts to educate citizens about the constitutional and political system, which had been worded in a new technical language. The despised black subject was effectively being manufactured into the passive legal subject. The discourse of democratic rights spoke of citizens as individuals harbouring legal rights who were expected to behave in a manner that displayed their obligations to the broader social order being formed. The legal system, which had historically been the face of oppression for three hundred years, was now becoming the dominant medium of interaction, responsible for regulating key social forces of the whole population as well as for disciplining individuals. Yet the new legal discourse ignored the many areas of subaltern life consequential of the structural violence of inequality, and especially of racialised property. The nationalist elite called upon popular forces to demobilise, to leave the addressing of historical struggle demands to the negotiating elites, and at the same time they postponed the issue of the structural bases of inequality. The nationalist elite thus conceived of mass participation instrumentally—i.e., to be used in ways that strengthened the hand of the nationalist elite at the negotiating table.

A 'peace settlement' as opposed to violence

In struggle discourses, the nationalist elite debated the very idea that settler-colonial conditions of rule could be ended through negotiations, and then, after the Sharpeville massacre, the impossibility of a negotiated outcome was taken for granted. For our purposes, it raises the question of the moment of the abandonment of popular demands. Historically, the colonial and Apartheid authorities rejected the proposals of black elites to negotiate, and that the latter were then forced to 'go to the masses' and propose 'mass politics of struggle'. Then, at the decisive moment, when subalterns were close to changing the power dynamic, the subalterns were left abandoned by the nationalist leadership, and told to go back to bodies of docility. It is in the context of this ambiguity that violence, criminality, negotiations and legal discourse have to be analysed. The onset of negotiations problematised the commitments of old struggle discourses, which were based on the mass political subject; instead, the negotiations proposed politics as legal discourse and the docile behaviour that comes with it.

Historically, whether to negotiate with colonial and Apartheid rulers was an issue of much debate. This debate produced strong divisions between anti-Apartheid organisations, which differed ideologically on how they theorised the nature of the white power structure. The Unity Movement rejected the ANC's involvement in the government's Native Representative Councils during the pre-World War II period (Gerhart 1978). After decades of dismissive treatment of their demands by various white governments, and following World War II, the nationalist elite began to recognise the importance of mass mobilisation. To be taken more seriously by the Apartheid state required an emphasis on mass, non-violent forms of resistance to government policies—the younger-generation nationalists frowned upon the pre-war politics of 'working with' the government (Gerhart 1978). In the exile period, from 1960 to the late 1980s, the ANC propagated the idea of a 'people's war' entailing the complete overthrow of the Apartheid state. The ambiguities and ambivalences in its ideology become more evident here, because this thinking followed at one level the revolutionary republican tradition, from the storming of the Bastille to the Bolshevik Revolution in 1917, and also, on another level, the liberal tradition advocating negotiations and compromise.

Amidst the mass popular protest of the 1980s, the dominant ideologies stirring subaltern consciousness spoke about the overthrow of the state and the 'seizure of state power', motivated by aggressive community struggles that demanded equal education, free 'quality of life' state services, and recognition of self-defined subjectivities (Seekings 2000; Murray 1987). Strands of Marxist discourse, mixed with identity politics, became assertive knowledge and, contrary to global trends, even the South African Communist Party (SACP) attracted a resurgence in support among urban youth and organised workers. As widespread civic protests and running battles between the police and township youth became normal events, the suspicion and vehement rejection of negotiations was widespread. Government could not be trusted, 'the system' could not be reformed; 'revolution' was the answer, and this fired the imagination of the subaltern. The possibility of a different modern experience became common sense in Gramscian terms. The negotiated outcomes would not reflect the principles upon which the struggle was waged. First and foremost, struggle discourses viewed the fight against racial supremacy as morally just, and a non-negotiable tenet was that any democratic dispensation had to be based on the will of the majority and the hope that a socialist radical redistribution would ensue, because it was believed that without access to socialised property, individual rights could not have much substance.

The government and the nationalist elite opted to negotiate at the 'decisive moment', which according to Fanon (1963) occurs when the subaltern is first, fleetingly, experiencing its humanity. Rather than allowing the situation to move beyond its control, uncertain and unable to develop confidence in its class capacity (because settler colonialism had made it such), the nationalist elite chose to go with what it knew were the 'universal principles', the globally accepted ways to proceed, which are Fanon's nightmare. The challenge for the nationalist elite was how, within the broad conception of a 'democratic dispensation and the will of the majority', to distinguish and focus on elements that qualified for negotiations, namely the democratic 'rules of the game', as opposed to those elements that were to be excluded in nationalist discourse, namely racialised property.

Elite politics as rational and 'black-on-black' violence as irrational

This section will illustrate how in the dominant discourse during the transition nationalist elite politics gets presented as rational even though differences exist over strategy, whereas through the concept of 'black-on-black' violence subaltern differences are presented as irrational. The politics of representation and how discourses mediate the empirical world is the focus of this section.

Differences over negotiations among the elite

In the 1980s, differences over negotiations in the struggle movement were readily exposed. The Pan-African Congress (PAC), the Azanian People's Organisation (AZAPO) and the Unity Movement (UM) opposed negotiations. Members of the nationalist elite as well, they believed that a change in struggle politics was unnecessary because they felt morally obligated to fight until the realisation of struggle goals (Murray 1987). These activists were committed to principled 'non-collaboration', an idea traceable to the 1930s, when some in the AAC spoke out against black organisations participating in government-created structures such as the NRCs. The followers of Trotskyist Marxism in the UM and BC organisations accused the ANC of unprincipled, instrumentalist politics, citing as examples its support for the NRCs in the pre-war period, its collaboration with Bantustan leaders like Buthelezi in the early 1970s (Gerhart 1978), and its willingness to negotiate with government (Murray 1987).

These groups wanted the liberation movement to form a Patriotic Front, copying the model of the Zimbabwean transition. Together with the ANC, the different groups met to follow up on this proposal in late 1990, but the ANC soon opted out due to insurmountable ideological differences. The PAC and AZAPO rejected the ANC proposal for a multiparty conference to decide on a democratic constitution, demanding instead majority rule without compromises and immediate elections to a constituent assembly to serve as the constitutional writing body representing the sovereign people. Compared to the ANC mainstream and the government, where both were content with an elite-driven process, in this Fanonian 'decisive moment' these organisations with much weaker popular support than the ANC nevertheless (and ironically) saw the role of the collective mass subject differently and preferred a mode of politics that placed the subaltern at the centre. Such differences over how to approach negotiations and the transition reflected deep ideological differences going back decades, and covered radically different points of view on the nature of dominant power relations, strategies of resistance and conceptions of the envisioned 'free' society.

The ANC maintained that negotiations were a question of tactics, not principles, where 'context' should be taken seriously, perhaps even as a determining factor, in characterising them. The organisation reiterated that it was always open to a negotiated settlement, if the government was willing to recognise the 'authentic' black leadership of the liberation struggle and meet certain preconditions. Within the ANC's 'broad church' some were more suspicious towards negotiations than others, and also harboured different views on strategy and expected goals. At the formal organisational level, though, the Harare Declaration of 1989 announced the ANC's commitment to negotiations on condition that the government released, without any restrictions, all political prisoners, that it allowed all exiles to return, that it repealed all discriminatory legislation, and that it prepared for the 'transfer of power to the people as a whole' (OAU 1989).

At the 1991 national conference in Durban, Mandela convinced ANC members to accept negotiations as another terrain of struggle. For the time being, Mandela was still presenting negotiations as one strategy among many, within 'struggle discourses'; but gradually this terrain assumed prominence, allowing the agency of actors to determine outcomes. The conference resolution not only endorsed negotiations, but also gave party leaders negotiating on its behalf 'discretionary powers', which amounted to an open mandate, so long as they remained faithful to ANC policies and reported regularly to the organisation. The ANC did not view a multiparty negotiating forum as an alternative or opposed to the constituent assembly idea, but as a forum preparing the way for the first free elections and the constituent assembly. It expected the multiparty conference to address: establishing a free political climate; reincorporating the Bantustans; deciding on the fundamental principles to frame a democratic constitution; the mechanics of an interim government; the constitution-writing process, the role of the international community and the determination of time frames.

Unsurprisingly, the ANC stance on negotiations shows up the differences between the moderate and radical ideological predispositions, which led to varied internal perspectives on the negotiations (Cronin 1992). Many on the left viewed it strategically as establishing a different basis to continue the struggle. Others saw it as the 'end' of historical conflict. These polar points allowed for wide scope in interpretation, so that reformist and radical nationalists both found comfort, thus forming the basis for an uneasy alliance. Yet the negotiations track increasingly dominated over other complementary forms of resistance, such that eventually most ANC members conceded that elite negotiations had assumed centre stage (Cronin 1992). Moderate reformers argued that negotiations were in fact the only available option for the organisation: from the very beginning, the armed struggle had proven difficult and remained unlikely to succeed—it was more symbolic than realist—and sustaining community protest had its limits. The ANC could not afford to delay, as the momentum would move in favour of the regime. The international campaign of economic sanctions and the sports and cultural isolation of the Apartheid regime was already rapidly subsiding, following De Klerk's February 1990 announcement. However, although armed combat ended and was never a real threat to the repressive apparatus of the Apartheid state, the 'culture' surrounding it persisted, symbolically filtering into and increasing in salience in everyday subaltern political expression.

'Black-on-black violence', criminal elements and obstructionists

In Fanon's 'decisive moment' it is possible to observe how the nationalist elite and the colonial order alike would want to undermine any questioning of a negotiated path to change. One way of accomplishing this is when dominant discourse opposes the political rationality of negotiations and 'peace' (basically amounting to elite politics) against what it sees as the irrationality of 'black-on-black' violence (basically subaltern politics). Establishing this dichotomy of representations amounts to a central shift when the balance of power in the anti-colonial battle reaches a particular stage. And it occurs just when the masses are coming into political consciousness, about to imagine a radically different society.

This shift in nationalist elite discourses—towards thinking about demobilising the emerging mass political subject and imposing the legal discourses of law, rights and obligations to constitute individuated legal subjects—occurred when many signs indicated that the elite was unable to control mass politics and the anger of people whose behaviour, it believed, could easily fall into the 'irrational'. When the National Peace Accord (NPA) conference met in September 1991, political violence had engulfed the country. Between 1990 and 1994, the period of the negotiations, the level of political violence reached unprecedented heights, particularly in Natal and Gauteng (Friedman and Atkinson 1994). Comparing the 1980s, the period of political crisis leading up to the negotiations, with the period of the negotiations themselves, many more people died on account of political causes during the latter. In the dominant understanding of this violence, the limit and latent danger associated with subalternity came to the fore. In dominant discourses the success of the negotiations, and the importance of establishing a rule-based politics, became the limit point because failure would present expressions of subaltern violence, already pervasive, as the alternative—a future 'too ghastly to contemplate' (Kaufman 2012, 29).

Historically, in the dominant discourse of the colonial order, the hidden and latent potential for 'irrational' violence of the colonised was an important element. In a white supremacist state such as South Africa it took on even more prominence, in the *swart gevaar* ('black threat') messages of the ruling party. The belief that black subaltern society always had within it this potential for irrational violence, unless curbed or guided, was a normal feature of state discourses; underlying associations of 'white' with rules and 'black' with violence were incipient as well. But more important than this is its centrality to the discourses of the nationalist middle class as well. This point is easily illustrated in Mandela's painstaking defence during the Rivonia Trial, in which he emphasised the mediating role of the black leadership in wanting to control the unguided violent responses of the increasingly frustrated masses in order to prevent a 'racial bloodbath'.

Features of the violence of the 1990s no doubt lent themselves to this interpretation. Often, random attacks followed revenge attacks. This pattern of seemingly protracted and widespread reprisals—and the grotesque, extreme nature of the violence, where bodies of men, women and children were indiscriminately hacked with crude weapons—saw a stark and desperate counterposing of negotiations and violence. In Natal, supporters of the ANC and the Inkatha Freedom Party (IFP) clashed daily, in a fight over territory, influence and resources (Truluck, 1992). The conventional explanation emphasising turf battles cannot be denied, but in fact more was going on, with different registers characterising the conflict. The violent attacks occurred mainly in the rural and peri-urban areas, where the population faced massive unemployment, large-scale poverty, weak infrastructure and low levels of formal education, all caused by decades of government neglect. Moreover, the political elites of the IFP and the ANC, fuelled by government and the mainstream media, had promoted their political differences and interests—after all, the participants in this conflict came from the same communities and often the same families. The violence was among Zulu-speaking residents, and on each side the poor, unemployed and youth became easy fodder for quick mobilisation.

The unravelling of the ethnic homogeneity assumed and propagated by the IFP, which ruled the Bantustan government of Kwa-Zulu, came from a younger generation attracted to nationalist discourse, identifying with its rejection of the Bantustan policy. Given the fluidity of local context, it was easy for the inter-party political contests to become embroiled in many other sources of conflicts, such as individual jealousies, revenge attacks and long-running local disputes. The youth, either students or unemployed, generally identified with the ANC, while Inkatha supporters more often were older men, who occupied positions of respect in traditional culture. It is plausible that traditional elites feared that democratic changes would threaten their status, power and control over resources.

The economic heartland and home of the mining industry, the Transvaal province, became the other centre of black-on-black violence, though it was somewhat different to the intra-Zulu violence in Natal. Here 'permanent' township residents, referred to as the 'community' and sympathetic towards the ANC (and in smaller numbers the PAC and AZAPO) fought running battles over days in brutal 'mini-wars' against hostel migrants who were closely affiliated to the IFP. The migrants, wielding their traditional weapons of sticks and *pangas* (machetes), confronted large groups of youths throwing stones or petrol bombs. Every so often gunfire was heard, as attackers shot at each other. A spate of random and brutal attacks at various train stations added to the bloody hostilities, with mysterious masked men targeting train passengers or commuters. In a few cases, commuters blamed IFP supporters for the attacks.

The Transvaal violence was attributed to the ANC-IFP rivalry, to the police or to rogue elements in the police and defence forces (the 'Third Force'), and blamed on the hard social conditions that historically made black areas vulnerable to higher rates of violence. Migrant workers made up a section of the urban black working class who were terribly marginalised and insecure compared to other sections of the settled working class, being unable to obtain permanent urban-township residence. This migrant labour policy was a pillar of Apartheid social planning. As a result, migrant labourers lived in unpleasant conditions, housed in single-sex hostels. Urban precariousness promoted a degree of solidarity seeking, thus reaffirming what were problematically called 'traditional' (in this case, rural Zulu) values and practices. Would they lose their meagre foothold in the urban economy in South Africa under an ANC government, as envisioned in IFP propaganda?

The fear surrounding the 'uncontrolled masses', represented by large numbers of blacks shedding blood, prompted numerous calls to address the violence through a parallel initiative to the negotiating process. The National Peace Accord (NPA) was the result. Besides its main aim of immediately ending the spiralling violence, it also functioned as a model of rules and evaluative mechanisms, responsible for monitoring actors' behaviour, which represented key features of the envisioned democratic society. The NPA was far-reaching, a comprehensive pact among the political elites: it formed peace-keeping and monitoring structures, a code of conduct for political parties, special courts to hear contraventions of the code and a commission of inquiry to investigate the causes of the violence. These precedents of elite compromises across the political divide showed that successful constitutional negotiations were possible. At a minimum, it demonstrated that the agreements to end the political violence amongst the elites gave them the impetus to control the subaltern, before the latter assumed a dynamic of its own. While open clashes between political parties declined, the society increasingly became engulfed by a generalised political violence between state and citizens and between citizens; in civil society, however, the dominant discourse now characterised such violence as criminal, even though increasing inequality and unaddressed poverty and subaltern precariousness continued.

Agenda-setting: the disputes were not about the end, but strategy

In Fanon's 'decisive moment', the colonial order and the opposition nationalist elites decide on what issues are 'up for grabs', to be negotiated, while the more important issues close to the subalterns get pushed by the wayside. The agenda for the negotiations excluded from discussion the inherited white accumulation of property, and avoided entirely the relationship between inherited property and democracy. Instead, it focused narrowly on democratic procedures to regulate a society that was framed and characterised as that of a majority and many minorities. In their point of departure, the government and the ANC accepted a narrow definition of Apartheid as a body of racial discriminatory policies against blacks.

The very process of agreeing to negotiate with each other implied an understanding that revolutionary change, which in essence would involve racialised property, was to be avoided. Property relations and Fanon's idea of the 'last shall be first and the first last' were off the agenda, completely removed from the sphere of 'the political'. The nationalist and white elites ring-fenced racialised property, the main source of the social legacies of white rule away from the public sphere, replacing it with issues of superficial—though of significant symbolic value, in the context of South Africa's history—difference. A constitution, crafted in the frame of liberalism, contributed to a discourse that the negotiating elites increasingly took for granted. Their primary aim and hope was to successfully influence the subjectivity of the subalterns by granting equal citizenship as a foundational principle, with the elites ending three hundred years of racial oligarchical rule.

The new political class, emerging from the remnants of the colonised national middle strata, worked within the same discursive structure in which 'modernity' meant political development towards a liberal democratic state and capitalist economic development without the fetters of race. The big picture of struggle politics—imagining a free society that was qualitatively different to settler colonialism, the imagined 'good' society—was not entertained. The focus was on the detailed procedures of formal democracy: deals about power sharing that elites on either side viewed as legitimate to their absent, passive constituencies.

The differences, which took almost four years to resolve, started with the 'talks about talks' phase on the constituent assembly / national convention issue. The ANC preferred a short-lived all-party conference to establish principles, followed by early elections in order to form a constituent assembly that would write the final constitution. The government wanted a drawn-out multiparty conference to determine as much of the final constitution as possible before elections were held (Sisk 1995). The idea of a multiparty conference was an old reform proposal of the National Party, which in the early 1970s suggested bringing together a 'council of leaders' that would make decisions by 'consensus', although at that time it excluded the nationalist liberation movements. This NP proposal favoured the ruling party because all parties would have equal status, despite their substantial differences in legitimacy and popular support. For the National Party, a constituent assembly of members elected on the basis of one person, one vote would leave the ANC with an overwhelming majority of representatives—an unacceptable scenario. The NP strategy was to use the negotiation forums to win as many concessions as possible and secure agreement on as many principles and rules of the final constitution as possible before a democratic election was held. It correctly predicted that a protracted negotiations process would lose the ANC some of its appeal among black citizens.

Buthelezi and the IFP did not attend the national conference at the World Trade Centre on 20 and 21 December 1991, almost two years after the release of Nelson Mandela, when twenty-six political parties gathered at CODESA I. Attending were the ANC and NP and their respective allies, and different black ethnic political parties as well as parties of the Tri-Cameral parliament and the Bantustan system tainted by their collaboration with Apartheid. The IFP protested over having been allowed only one delegation, demanding that it should have been allowed separate delegations for the IFP, the Zulu king and the Kwa-Zulu Bantustan. Over two days, representatives from each party addressed the conference. Each leader justified his party's status in South African society and mostly exaggerated its history and support base. Importantly, when put together, the speeches at CODESA contributed towards the development of a 'consensus' democratic discourse. At the end of the conference a declaration of intent was signed, committing delegates to principles that would inform a new constitution and included: an undivided South Africa; peaceful constitutional change; a multiparty democracy with universal suffrage and separation of powers; a bill of rights (Friedman and Atkinson 1994).

The clash between Mandela and De Klerk at the end of the meeting attracted media attention because of its symbolism. Mandela responded angrily to De Klerk's attack on the ANC for the continued existence of Umkhonto we Sizwe (MK), the ANC's brave, empirically ineffective but still highly symbolic armed wing. When De Klerk accused the ANC of negotiating in bad faith, Mandela took to the podium and responded that the ANC had already agreed, in February 1991, to disband its military wing. He further made mention of the fact that De Klerk represented an illegitimate government, discredited the world over and in no position to be questioning the credentials of other parties. For the South African public, a black man publicly scolding a white leader symbolised in many ways the end of the Apartheid era. In reality, the activity of MK was a non-issue, because at no stage in the three decades of armed struggle had the repressive apparatus of the Apartheid state been seriously threatened. To most intents and purposes, the empirical thrust of the armed struggle, in terms of a realist conception of politics, was long abandoned: a Hobbesian state of nature was hardly likely to come about from it.

Following a victorious all-white referendum supporting De Klerk's reform initiatives, the NP delegation believed its hand to be strengthened. In the Working Committees set up by CODESA I, it demanded veto power for minority parties in a proposed senate representing minorities, and it significantly increased the threshold, to three-quarters of the Constituent Assembly, for making constitutional changes in four areas: the Bill of Rights, the devolution of power, multiparty democracy and minority rights. When CODESA II broke down over this proposal for white veto power, the ANC embarked on 'rolling mass action'. It wanted to demonstrate its power to disrupt normal economic and social activities. Around the same time, the Goldstone Commission released its report implicating the government in the violence. On a visit following a massacre of forty-five people, De Klerk had to flee the Boipatong township. Faced with these pressures, the government reconsidered its intransigent stance. The ANC's campaign of mass action had also experienced unintended setbacks. The campaign decided to march on the small town of Bisho, the administrative capital of the Ciskei Bantustan ruled by Oupa Gqozo. The ANC planned to oust the weak Bantustan leadership there, but Gqozo instructed his troops to shoot into the crowd, killing twenty-eight demonstrators. A series of hurried interventions renewed the negotiations process. Joe Slovo, the leading SACP intellectual, proposed 'sunset clauses' that guaranteed job security for the white civil service, including the police and army, and a government of national unity for the first five years. This was quickly signed into a Record of Understanding between the ANC and the government (Waldmeir 1998).

At the remaining multiparty talks, the government and the ANC rapidly arrived at agreements on universal adult franchise in exchange for a complex system of checks and balances, the protection of private property rights and the cultural recognition of minorities (Welsh 2009). They proposed a coalition government of all parties who had obtained 5 percent of the vote, a party-list proportional representation (PR) electoral system, two houses of parliament, a constitutional court and an independent judiciary. Even when the government and the ANC broke off direct talks, regular conversations between Mandela and De Klerk continued. Leading negotiators Cyril

Ramaphosa and Roelf Meyer met regularly in secret *bosberaads* (out-of-town meetings). This suggested an understanding by the emerging political elite that internal conflicts and key setbacks, such as the Boipotong massacre, the Bisho shootings or the assassination of popular SACP and ANC leader, Chris Hani, would not be allowed to subvert the process (Welsh 2009).

The enthusiasm of the negotiating elites to keep talking to each other, even indirectly when official talks broke down for short periods, indicates the desperate desire of the national struggle leadership to arrive at a palatable resolution that avoided more radical outcomes. They deliberately wanted to avoid third-party diplomacy, frowned upon a peacekeeping force, and largely abandoned popular organisation and protest. This highlights a willingness on the part of the negotiating elites to settle their differences, despite the vast inequalities in their power resources. They also ignored the innumerable questions, issues and obstacles of changing deep-rooted institutions and established social relations of settler colonialism, hoping that these would be somehow resolved under the conditions of electoral democracy.

Negotiations and the problem of the popular: the emergence of legal discourse, the political and outsiders

Retrace the narrative of events produced in third wave transition representations of the 'miracle' transition gives a glimpse of the figure of the mass as silent participant; the displacement of subalterns from the centre of the political field is a necessary element in the 'decisive' moment of change. Though they were the main social force weakening the Apartheid order, popular sectors observed the negotiations from a distance, powerless to influence their process or outcome. The historical and symbolic atmosphere surrounding the events should not be underestimated. Inevitably, they favoured the nationalist elite who could use its media attention and ambiguous language to convey different messages to different constituencies. The negotiations were ending three hundred years of white rule, with enemies and struggle heroes participating, and this presented an unfavourable context to those wanting to question the process or institute a different language. The sense of anticipation surrounding the end of Apartheid meant that to do so could easily be labelled obstructionist—a difficult position to assume when all around seemed to be on board. Thus, once begun, the entire negotiation process favoured elite decision-making (Bond 2000).

It is not surprising that the Apartheid state feared mass mobilisation; what was surprising, though, was the about-turn by the ANC. The Afrikaner leadership constantly accused and reprimanded the nationalist elite for its inability to control the 'transgressions' of popular mobilisation, and the struggle leadership responded apologetically. As the negotiations progressed, the ANC increasingly approached the active participation of the subalterns sceptically (Cronin 1992). Leading up to the negotiations, the ANC had encouraged the popular resistance, often claiming to lead it, as had happened during the UDF upsurge of the 1980s. But once negotiations had begun, it feared that the populist thrust could derail the process. The ANC thus seemed to view mass mobilisation merely as a strategic tool in the negotiations process. At his first major rally in Durban in 1990, Mandela was met with boos from the enthusiastic crowd when he demanded that they throw their makeshift weapons into the sea. The crowd felt that he was unaware of their situation in facing daily attacks from government-sponsored groups like Inkatha.

Central to my reading of the change in South Africa is the displacement, which crucially occurred during the democratic transition, of a particular type of mass political subject into one conducive to the idea of political rationality as defined by the nationalist elite. A collective political subject had been formed during the mass mobilisations from the early 1970s onwards, but during the negotiations this subject began to recede from the centre, together with its role in defining politics. The language of the politics of struggle associated with this earlier period also receded to a subjugated discourse, giving way to a legalist discourse—one of agreements, rights and obligations understood at the individual level—thus instituting a new set of disciplinary behaviours monitored by the elite. This new legal power/knowledge framework was central to bringing about a new mode of politics, albeit one that has not yet established itself firmly. Its highpoint came during the Mbeki years, before factional contestation within the ruling party and Mbeki's structural-adjustment program caused it to flounder.

The question faced by the elites in resolving the 'intractable' conflict of a racially 'deeply divided society' along the lines of Western modernisation was whether the liberal democratic system and its constitution of legal subjects of the law would adequately address the history of objectification of subalterns. The terms by which the masses were included in the different political terrain mattered because the dominant discourse had changed, but not the intensification of their regulation. Undoubtedly, electoral politics contributed to the power dynamics at one level, but it still required active popular mobilisation in the associational life of civil society, which reflected the 'innermost hopes of the whole people' (Fanon 1963, 148) to keep power at a critical distance. Fanon warns that subalterns need to develop the nation *on their terms*, not have it imposed from above. Otherwise a situation prevails in which 'this fight for democracy against the oppression of mankind will slowly leave the confusion of neo-liberal universalism to emerge, sometimes laboriously, as a claim to nationhood' (Fanon 1963a, 148).

The nationalist leadership did not think of popular participation, like Fanon observed, 'as a forward rush of national consciousness' (1963, 72); instead, they regarded it as subaltern practices whose excesses the nationalist elite must keep under control and discipline. In contemporary South Africa, developments in the political field support Fanon's fears. A new national elite, composed of the former white society and the post-Apartheid new black middle class, dominates civil society, while the majority of citizens, with their material deprivations and spiritual alienation, face the choice of electoral politics or a discordant politics of mass mobilisation that is increasingly labelled 'mob rule' and considered a threat to the constitution and the rule of law. This is the terrain, following Chatterjee (2004), of an expanding political society, where subalterns articulate a discourse of rights by drawing on the practices of the nationalist struggle.

The ambiguity and deeply layered influence of the struggle for liberation and the limits of the negotiated transition to liberal democracy, as conceived by the nationalist elites, make possible the present popular mobilisation and intensifying political society. The nationalist leadership forever wanted to modernise the polity along the Western model of liberal democracy. It was compelled to draw upon an ambiguous but mostly instrumentalist 'politics of mobilisation' to wrench concessions from the Apartheid government. The goals for the nationalist leadership were the success of the negotiations, the 'conquest' of the state and, if possible, a 'peaceful resolution' leaving intact the capitalist economic infrastructure. At the same time, it was planning to de-racialise social relations, though without addressing the power dynamics of settler-colonial rule and its legacies for the colonised subject. The popular mobilisation did create necessary conditions for the expression of national identity and raised crucial debates on the national question; it did not, however, go beyond the superficial, because too many questions were left for after legal Apartheid had been removed.

It is also significant that, at the very moment when the subalterns began to recognise themselves as a mass political subject, they became the focus of concern, especially in a society that had politically excluded the majority for three centuries after its emergence as a modern, national state. This is often the ignored story of the South African transition: the anxiety of *both* the ruling and opposition nationalist elites over the constitution of political rationality as it related to mass subaltern politics. The elite representatives of struggle politics worried about control and discipline of the rank and file, a theme that can be traced to the immediate post-war years. In his Rivonia Trial defence, Mandela defined the nationalist leadership's role in overseeing the unfolding constitution of modern politics and imposing control and discipline on disruptive subalterns.

For the subaltern masses, a politics of recognition, going back decades but displaying more determined signs from 1976 onwards, defined its constitution of democratic politics. Even though this evolving social power was the key historical force of change and able to weaken the existing 'colonial order of things' (Fanon 1963, 52) fundamentally, it was unable to celebrate an unquestioned victory. At first uncertain, but still hopeful about the whole field of negotiations and the introduction of new rules defining a democratic political system that was viewed by most as a miracle, the mass subject gradually realised that it had won a severely limited recognition. It was a citizenship that was very narrowly conceived and not involved in quality participation between or beyond elections. In everyday civic life, the mass political subject of electoral democracy has remained confined to the far-flung townships, marginalised to internment camps of squalor, insecurity and hopelessness, as represented by Agamben's *homo sacer* (1998). The politics of 'bare life' (bodily survival, food, sanitation, health, housing) are its preserve, and the quest of the good life—the life of political man, sovereignty and the law—meaningless, because death is so close.

Concluding remarks

In dominant discourses on the negotiations process, popular mass action was approached in a negative way unless it conformed to the passive role assigned to it by the elites, while the middle class was endorsed for its 'reasonable' political behaviour. The nationalist elites' definition of political rationality and ways of disciplining the mass subaltern subject relate to the key outcome of the transition—namely, that the historical and structural bases of inequality remained outside the negotiation agenda. Even before the negotiations began, both sides agreed that accumulated property was non-negotiable and that there was an acceptable role for the mass political subject. While grudgingly allowing for the mass mobilisation of thousands of poor people, the Apartheid state feared the ever-present possibility of increasing social power and popular violence threatening negotiations and, indeed, the whole social order. Interestingly, ANC leaders approached mass mobilisation with similar scepticism.

It is a question, however, that is not reducible to elites and masses. This chapter has highlighted the imposition of key modernist ideas that are constitutive of the dominant discourse during the negotiations (such as progress, order and national identity), and alternatively, the retreat of subaltern conceptions of power as ongoing war and of oppositional active resistance as identity-changing. It is significant how the first structure of thought, which is concerned with modern progress and political development, translates the other, which is the subaltern discourse of change, transformation and liberation, into its own register.

It is significant that at the height of internal civil and popular unrest, and with the promise of revolutionary victories that subalterns believed were at hand, the nationalist elite received overtures from the Apartheid government and resigned itself to ending Apartheid through a protracted process of compromise and negotiation, essentially deciding to postpone the foundational destruction of the previous 'order of things' (Fanon 1963, 52) under the new terrain of liberal constitutionalism. The 'democratic transition' established a new institutional framework. It defined a new political terrain, indicative of the different power holders at the time. A constitutional framework that literally copied the liberal democratic constitutions of the West (and arguably did so with more rights enunciated), defines a modernity that leaves the material inequality of the majority and subject identities unchanged, resulting in their further marginalisation and popular mobilisation. Conflicts over material inequalities along racial lines, employment within key political and economic institutions and the cultural and ideological direction of the state were merely postponed, to be fought under new rules of engagement within a liberal democratic political system. The ANC, perhaps embarrassed that economic power was left in privileged hands, claims to continue its 'historic project' of revolutionary change, at least in discourses directed at the masses; but as the governing party, it espouses conservative policies that are unlikely to change social relations radically.

Since most conflicts that have their source in Apartheid are now fought under the new conditions of electoral democracy, it is not really a matter of debate as to who actually won. Ongoing battles are the order of the day: change often co-mingles with continuity, and sometimes, confusingly, new elites rely on old conservative discourses. The frontal assault on the Apartheid state of the 1980s has been followed by this terrain of trench warfare in the post-Apartheid present, in which the new democratic society unfolds with much reluctance. This is the situation in which South Africa finds itself in the present conjuncture. The main question is whether the differences produced by settler-colonial dynamics can be addressed within the new democratic political system. The strains are evident, as can be seen from increasing mass mobilisations of disgruntled citizens and the near disintegration of the ANC, a party that seems unable to respond to the challenges it faces.

The South African case, with its far-reaching protection of citizen rights and restraints on the reach of government power, has received widespread praise (Koeble 1998). However, once in power, the new nationalist elite faced the massive racial inequalities, legacies of violence and incomplete-relational subjects that are traceable to Manichean settler colonialism. Just as the 'wretched of the earth' had begun to come into national consciousness after a decade of painstaking political mobilisation—Fanon's decisive moment—the nationalist elite decided to enter into pacts with the Apartheid ruling group. This mobilised population was on the move when the political terrain shifted; the negotiated settlement presented a different set of ground rules. In South African politics ever since, nationalist elites have worked with the historically white society to establish the new parameters of domination within a liberal democratic state.

7| Crisis of the national modern: democracy, the state and ANC dominance

Settler-colonial modernity left South Africa with a history of race discourse and associated violence, and it led to a weak nationalist elite unable to establish hegemony as a ruling class. This phenomenon was most evident in the response to racial legacies post 1994 (Fanon 1963a), when, absent key elements needed to secure the 'spontaneous consent' of the national-popular sectors, Mbeki was unable to connect to the mass of subalterns and organise this dormant 'revolutionary capital' to make up for its lack amongst the nationalist bourgeoisie. State racial transformation policies have benefitted only the middle classes. This situation has fostered a politics of the extra-ordinary, with the national-popular sectors wanting their conditions of 'bare life' to be radically altered, resorting to inchoate mobilisation as their solution, yet obtaining (at best) not tangible material improvements but superficial recognition as dominant ideology demarcates them as a 'mob'. In other words, the interventions within the parameters of constitutional liberal democracy and its transitional compromises have proven unable to change the 'ingrained racial habitus that has disfigured both the construction and the perception of reality by the vast majority of South Africans' (Alexander 2007, 101).

Against this backdrop of South Africa's long settler-colonial history, the 2012 Marikana killings dramatically reveal the crisis inherent in South Africa's liberal democratic project and its moral basis, which the black nationalist intermediary class has historically defended and actively supported. The killing by the state of black workers participating in a legal strike marks a turning point in subaltern consciousness: the subalterns have learnt that a black government representing a constitutional democracy, which so far has been considered a 'victory of the nationalist struggle', can and will kill its citizens, even if they have not broken any law. If the killers are not prosecuted—three years later, this seems unlikely—the subaltern will confirm yet again that they conform classically to Agamben's category of *homo sacer*.

The postcolonial conjuncture produces two paradigms of the national middle class once it is in power, with respect to its approach to politics, economics and identity. The first is the discourse of politics associated with charisma and symbolism. This seeks to mediate relations between the colonised elite and subalterns, negotiating and persuading rather than imposing; the attention is as much on 'who says' (i.e., the source of the idea) as it is on what is being said (i.e., the idea itself). It tends to emphasise culture and the past, to be redistributionist towards the economy, and to call on the country to imagine a non-racial nation, presently under construction. The second discourse enthusiastically embraces the idea of modernity. Against challenges marking society it seeks to change and impose its modernist vision onto society, believing this to be its historical mission and moral obligation. In this discourse mediating with the subalterns is avoided; it wants to catch up with the advanced states of Western modernity as quickly as possible, and views the 'backwardness' of the subaltern as the country's major challenge and humiliation, the worst possible legacy of settler colonialism. The key instrument for the nationalist bourgeoisie is to approach politics with the bureaucratic might of the state. It might support neo-liberal economics so that individuals can learn the hard work of succeeding in a Hobbesian international capitalist world. It believes in a future that respects and draws on Africa's rich cultural heritage and that this, at least, infuses the identity of the future nation. We can see that these two discourses are best represented by the figures of Mandela and Mbeki respectively; however, they were not created by them: Mandela and Mbeki are themselves the products of these postcolonial discourses, which we would reasonably expect as responses to settler-colonial violence. Thus South African politics are always likely to move between these two dominant national-modern discourses, of symbolism/charisma and of bureaucratic rationality.

The crisis of the national-modern project in South Africa demonstrates the failings of both the charismatic-symbolic and the rational-bureaucratic discourses to secure ruling-class hegemony over society. These discourses of the national-modern identified the state as the instrument to transform society. Interestingly, this form of statism, which is anchored in the charismatic-symbolic discourse, results in the same demobilisation of subalterns as that effected by discourses of bureaucratic rationality. The control of the state was the goal of the nationalist-modern struggle. In the ANC we can identify four conceptions of the state as the instrument for modernity: neutral, interventionist/developmentalist, cultural/symbolic and patrimonial. These conceptions had implications for party-state relations, corruption, the approaches to transformation, the eroding of the legitimacy of the national-modern project and the undermining of formal political processes—all suggestive of an indecisive and threatened national bourgeoisie. The result has been a subaltern mass that has drawn farther away from nationalist elites by attempting to carve out an independent politics relying on inchoate social mobilisation.

This chapter identifies those factors that have contributed to a crisis of the national-modern. It begins with a debate between Mbeki and Tutu suggestive of the fracturing tensions within the nationalist middle class, which was once united behind the anti-Apartheid democratic project. This debate points to the developing anxiety in the middle class about the increasingly politically alienated subaltern masses. I then discuss the ANC's statism and its different conceptions of the state. This section is followed by an examination of the political discourse that draws inspiration from charisma and symbolism. Mandela's leadership is both characteristic and a product of this political discourse, which resonates as one kind of response to the collective trauma of blacks. It has a long tradition in resistance politics in South Africa: it promoted the 'smooth transition', but also, just as importantly, contributed to the demobilisation of the mass subject and its channelling into a particular conception of politics. The nationalist-modern project is also articulated in another nationalist response, namely that of the rational-bureaucratic discourse exemplified by the Mbeki presidency. It is with the Mbeki presidency that we associate many of the factors explaining the ANC 'squandering its institutional capital' (Sharma 2002, 149) although the project of classic postcolonial state-building operating within a rational-legal register is inevitable (because Western) and will be embarked upon at some stage in post-settler situations. The shift towards neo-liberal economic policies, the entrenching of patronage relations in the ANC, the development of state-party factionalism and the adoption of a bureaucratic approach to politics have all, in their turn, increased subaltern alienation from formal political channels. Subalterns, whose treatment as *homo sacer* remains unchanged despite citizenship rights enshrined in the democratic constitution, have turned towards a politics of mobilisation to seek the recognition they see lacking. These factors have undermined the 'moral basis' that once grounded and cemented the nationalist-modern project behind nationalist elite leadership, indicating the break-up of the link developed in the 1980s between nationalist elites and the mass collective subject and an ongoing contest over the category 'the people.'

The Tutu-Mbeki debate

With Apartheid defined narrowly as a body of racial discriminatory policies, the governing ANC accepted as a point of departure that taking control of the existing state meant that Apartheid could be reformed into a liberal democratic constitutionalism. If the ANC did not genuinely believe in this possibility, at least some in its ranks believed a statist platform was necessary to achieve more radical nationalist goals. The negotiating elites agreed that in post-Apartheid South Africa, having granted equal citizenship as a foundational principle, and having ended legal privileges based on race and racial oligarchical rule, the polity would follow the typical modernist path. The South African case of democratic transition, with its far-reaching liberal democratic constitution protecting citizens' rights and restricting the reach of government power, can be regarded as having passed an important stage on its way to political modernity (Koeble 1998). If, minimally, all democratic transition processes are judged by their institutional outcomes and the absence of violent conflict (in this case for over two decades), then elites can rightfully claim that the regime transition has proven a success.

However, once in power, the nationalist elite faced massive racial inequalities, a dominant-party system prone to factionalism, and a politics driven by state resources and patronage. These factors made the spirit of the liberal democratic constitution and a civic tradition disturbingly elusive. An unexpected mode of politics thus became prominent: one not grounded in the formal institutions of democracy, but involving masses of disgruntled citizens mobilised to realise demands for recognition. This informal terrain of politics directly questioned the political rationality and nationalist-modern conception represented by the elites. It directly challenged their new privileges and comforts. The distinction between formal/elite and informal/mass politics—or, if you prefer, 'normal' and 'extraordinary' politics (Kalyvas 2009)—and a better understanding of these different modes is the focus of this book. Another way to approach the distinction, influenced by Chatterjee (2004), who drew on and adapted Gramsci, is to identify political society as the terrain of subaltern politics and civil society where, through associational life, the nationalist elite defends its privileges and upholds its 'moral leadership'. Often the trend is to fall back on a narrow racial-nationalist discourse as a means of shielding nationalist elites from criticism.

The 2004/5 dispute between Archbishop Tutu and President Mbeki illustrates the growing anxiety of the nationalist middle class and its indecisiveness on what to do with the unravelling of subaltern control. In 2004 the Nelson Mandela Memorial Lecture organisers invited Tutu, a world-famous anti-Apartheid campaigner and Nobel Peace Prize recipient, to be the keynote speaker. Mbeki was then at the height of his power, consolidating his position as president of the country and the ANC, restructuring the state to reflect ANC electoral dominance domestically and implementing his vision for a new course of development and status for the entire African continent.

Tutu's speech, nationally televised on state TV and state-controlled stations and published in leading daily newspapers such as the *Cape Times*, was a kind of friendly intervention taking the form of an evaluation of how far South Africa had progressed—what had been achieved, and what still needed to be addressed—since the election in April 1994. According to Tutu, South Africa was fortunate to have had a series of leaders and events that made the transition from Apartheid relatively peaceful, despite predictions of a 'racial bloodbath'. It was also fortunate to have had a leader like Mandela, who, as a man admired the world over, a statesman of note and a global asset to any society, allowed for white society to accept the democratic transition. Tutu also recognised De Klerk as a key partner of Mandela in the negotiations process. When he announced the release of long-term political prisoners and the unbanning of the nationalist organisations, De Klerk had played an important role in placing negotiations on the political agenda. De Klerk believed that negotiations with the ANC were the only path to end violent conflict and to bring whites on board. South Africans could also be proud of the TRC process. The TRC offered a unique mechanism to address past human rights abuses, without the expectation of retribution from perpetrators and without expecting victims to forget. The process of integrating schools and universities in South Africa occurred with very few racial incidents compared to the ordeals suffered in the United States during its civil rights campaign. Most white schools opened their doors to blacks on a large scale and over a very short period of time—a remarkable achievement, given three centuries of segregation and white supremacy.

On the global front, Tutu equally praised post-1994 developments. South Africa had rapidly established trade and diplomatic agreements with almost all member states of the United Nations, having been viewed as a pariah to most countries while under Apartheid. The country had become a leader on the African continent and a major global player representing Third World interests. Tutu made special mention of Mbeki, praising the president for his leadership role in African continental politics. Mbeki had introduced the vision of the African Renaissance, which encouraged a different relationship between donor countries and Africa, based on partnership rather than inequality, as outlined in the NEPAD policy documents. Mbeki was instrumental in replacing the Organisation of African Unity with the African Union, which placed a stronger emphasis on regional organisation and presented Africa in a new and positive light. For Tutu, South Africa had a stable democracy; it had a firm foundation for developmental improvements, especially compared to Northern Ireland, the Middle East and Russia, where conflict and instability still prevailed and democratic transition had run into longstanding problems.

On the negative side, Tutu criticised the ANC government and specifically Mbeki for his HIV/AIDS policy. He found Mbeki's refusal to acknowledge that HIV caused AIDS unforgivable, and stated that the government was morally obligated to provide free anti-retroviral medication to infected South Africans. Besides these policies being woefully wrong, they made it obvious that the government was also quick to condemn, vilify and marginalise anyone who questioned the president's position, leading to widespread 'kowtowing' to his views. Tutu further said:

> We should not too quickly want to pull rank and to demand an uncritical, sycophantic, obsequious conformity. We need to find ways in which we engage the hoi polloi, the so-called masses, the people, in public discourse through indabas, town-hall forums, so that no one feels marginalized and that their point of view matters, it counts (Tutu 2004).

Tutu raised the problem of the proportional representation electoral system and the party list system as contributing towards the unaccountability of public servants and leaving them out of touch with ordinary people. This echoed a long-standing theme circulating in the media about the lack of accountability surrounding South Africa's electoral system, which undermined voters and made representatives unresponsive to constituencies, alienating mainly the poor. It also placed the ANC in a position where it could abuse its power, because party leaders could pressure lower-ranking members to toe the line or face exclusion from the party list of public office bearers.

Tutu assumed that South Africa's foreign policy would remain firmly committed, after Mandela, to upholding human rights and social justice. However, the country increasingly sided with those who violated human rights, as in the case of Zimbabwe where the 'quiet diplomacy' of Mbeki effectively meant turning a blind eye to ZANU-PF's violence against MDC members and supporters in the 2002, 2005 and 2008 elections. Domestically, the ANC policy of Black Economic Empowerment (BEE), which legislated that companies appoint blacks as part owners and managers, had the effect of producing a wealthy elite, many of whom had close ties to the ruling party. Tutu urged that BEE processes needed to recruit from a broader base of beneficiaries to empower disadvantaged communities. The common ANC defence of comparing

ANC rule to the 'bad old days' under Apartheid, Tutu found unconvincing—the Apartheid regime was hardly a standard to evaluate democratic government against. The 2001 government decision to spend R30 billion on the purchase of military hardware (corvettes and aircraft), the so-called Arms Deal, could not be defended: that money should have been used to address poverty. Moreover, the Arms Deal was embroiled in the large-scale corruption in which many senior members of the government and the ANC were implicated. For Tutu, all of this severely tainted the moral grounding of the ANC, which in its one hundred-year existence had always been associated with a struggle for social justice against a regime that represented the suppression of universally accepted rights.

The ANC's record as South Africa's first democratically elected government expected to offset Apartheid legacies also came in for Tutu's criticism. He referred pointedly to the housing crisis that had continued under the ANC government—a stark, still glaringly visible reminder of an era when separate, vast areas of township housing, with rows of bland and inhospitable houses, were built by the Apartheid government to keep urban blacks under permanent surveillance. Unsurprisingly, blacks had expected the post-Apartheid democratic government to build 'decent' houses as an essential step towards creating viable, secure, community-friendly neighbourhoods. But the houses built by the democratic government were not much better, and in some cases even worse, having been shoddily constructed with poor materials. Residents complained bitterly about houses with leaking roofs and no insulation. Even the minister of housing, Tokyo Sexwale, took the unusual step of demolishing some new homes and rebuilding them, which cost the public purse an additional R150 million. Tutu ended his address by calling for a 'caring, compassionate society'. He was angry that since the advent of democracy, national trends indicated a cheapening of life: rates of violent crime had dramatically increased, cases of rape were among the highest in the world, and the desire to acquire expensive material goods and show these off in public had become ingrained not only among the nationalist elite, but among ordinary citizens too. He appealed for an ethical turn towards the solidarity and the sense of community that had existed under Apartheid.

This lecture should have been a relatively uncontroversial affair—after all, Tutu was renowned for his moral criticism and stance on many controversial issues around the world. However, the government and especially Mbeki turned it into a public fight. Mbeki was in a powerful position, as both president and leader of a party that dominated the political system. Although there were rumours of oppositional forces circulating within and without the ANC, these were as yet not out in the open, and Mbeki was sure, given his knowledge of the politics of exile, to be vigilant for signs of oppositional factional activity. The public only really became aware of far-reaching internal tensions in the ANC with the airing of factional battles in the run-up to the ANC's Polokwane conference in 2007. Hence Mbeki's scathing retort to Tutu, who was an ardent supporter of the ANC (albeit not a member) and the government, indicated his personal sensitivity to this type of criticism and the fracturing of an old nationalist middle-class consensus. The stakes were higher than it might have seemed, at least for Mbeki.

In his 'Weekly Friday Letter' on the ANC's official website, Mbeki (2004) quoted extensively from Tutu's speech. His defensiveness and irritation at Tutu's attack on the lack of democratic debate in the ANC is unusually striking. Mbeki accused Tutu of misunderstanding the ANC's internal democracy and commitment to democratic values and practices with respect to society. Many democratic forums had been established to hear the voices of the people. By ignoring these mechanisms, Tutu was being disingenuous—a liar, even. In response to Tutu's claim that BEE was restricted to a 'small elite that tends to be recycled', Mbeki listed many BEE contracts and the government's procurement practices, to show examples where wealth had spread beyond a small elite. Mbeki drew attention to 'broad-based BEE', the official policy of government that sought to spread and distribute wealth to community organisations and members of trade unions. The Arms Deal was necessary for national security, Mbeki argued, and furthermore included local spin-offs benefiting black businesses and workers. The government's extensive grant programme demonstrated that the ANC had not abandoned poor people. Mbeki concluded by warning Tutu against the spreading of falsehoods and talking to the public gallery. For Mbeki, the debate was really about who set the national agenda. It was about the battle of ideas, an essential part of the historic struggle unfolding in the country.

> The archbishop proposed what our nation needs to do to determine its agenda. But as we have said in this letter, to succeed in this task, all of us must educate ourselves about the reality of South Africa today, internalise the facts about our country, and respect the truth. Together we must avoid the resort to populism and catchy newspaper headlines that have nothing to do with the truth and everything to do with the pursuit of self-serving agendas. Rational discussion also demands that we should take the effort to think, rather than submit to the dictates of a reassuring herd instinct (Mbeki 2004).

The government's reply was less emotional and less robust, acknowledging its respect for Tutu, his role in the liberation struggle and his initiation of a necessary debate. It believed that for each criticism raised by Tutu, a reasonable alternative view was also available: the choice of electoral system was a matter of debate and government welcomed such debate; the Zimbabwean crisis was not as easy to resolve as Tutu made it out to be, and South Africa was playing an important role by being sensitive to all sides of the conflict; the Arms Deal was transparent, the outcome of Defence Review recommendations and a process open to extensive public participation; the government had responded to the AIDS crisis with a comprehensive plan; the few negative outcomes of BEE could not be blamed on government as they were out of its control, involving the actions of private citizens.

This differences between Tutu and Mbeki and the government reflect a mounting anxiety among those in power towards critical opposition. Often the issues of difference are about the 'facts' and their interpretation. For example, what Tutu sees as uncritical following is for Mbeki 'internal ANC' democracy. Mbeki's sensitivity to this kind of criticism suggests that basic democratic values remain uncertain and that everything is contested and contestable; the stakes are considered too high for mere deliberation. Mbeki's jab about Tutu's ignorance regarding internal ANC procedures alludes to who controls the political agenda and political struggle. Both seem to be battling for the moral high ground, wanting to claim to be on the side of 'the people'. Accordingly, Mbeki suggests that it is impossible for the ruling party or the president to step aside and leave 'the people' to be swayed by the archbishop. The subaltern is the targeted audience of both, and this is the new struggle. To quote Mbeki:

> The effort to reach such consensus only means that the struggle continues to define what our country will look like tomorrow and the day after. Time will tell whether this struggle can be engaged without resorting to slanging matches. It is, however, clear that whatever its form and its gentility, politeness or otherwise, this is a struggle about who shall set our national agenda and what that agenda shall be. In this regard, inevitably, the struggle continues—*Aluta continua!* (Mbeki 2004)

The ANC and the idea of 'the state'

Essential to the crisis of the national-modern is the faith and hope the national middle class had in the state and what it could achieve to 'catch up' to the West, to raise the masses from their ignorance and 'backwardness'. As Fanon warned (1963), the national middle class did not see itself as the problem, nor did it regard its lack of connectedness to the masses as an issue, nor, most importantly, did it see the masses as the revolutionary capital that the national bourgeoisie lacked due to settler-colonial modernity. In its eyes, the state, not the masses, was the instrument for national modernisation.

When Manichean society—a society that circumscribes the minute details of social relationships and produces 'incomplete' relational subjects—embraces democratic values, it amounts to a historical event that marks a 'before' and an 'after' in the public life of that society. The break assumes a central place and role in dominant political ideology. The state gives itself a new lease of life. The democratically elected government unavoidably faced the challenge of overcoming centuries of Manichean society and deeply rooted inequalities, in addition to the uncertainties that always accompany any type of political transition (Friedman 1999)—a tall order in itself. Add to this the fact that the negotiated settlement preserved the civil service and retained the National Party, its enemy, in a unity government for the first five years, which worried the ANC sufficiently for it to cautiously consolidate its control of the state apparatus.

However, the ANC did have the national mood on its side. The mass of citizens—the poor, uneducated, historically excluded masses, inhabitants of millions of shacks on the outskirts of cities and the rural poor, constituted in terms of 'tradition' and 'backwardness'—expected radical changes in their lifeworlds. The new ruling elite experienced a sense of exhilaration about occupying state power, coupled with foreboding. The leadership could be confident that South Africa, the most developed state and economy on the African continent, had the resources to address the social and material challenges its supportive constituency faced. The ANC seemed fully aware of the fact that transformation, the desire for which had driven the struggle, was still far from complete. It interpreted the negotiations as 'advances' of the struggle, the control of the state providing a 'platform', in order to further the liberation of the people, and leading to social and economic emancipation (ANC 1998). The ANC government set forth on the road of governing as the new political class, adopting a celebratory attitude as well as reducing expectations and warning people of the challenges ahead (see Sechaba 1994).

The institutional resilience of the ANC helped to oversee and steer the complexities of the compromised transition, legitimating the political system in dominant ideology by conflating ANC rule with the new democratic epoch. In a series of documents, the ANC outlined its understanding of the state and transformation. The imperatives of a liberation movement participating in a broad process that is still unfolding (giving rise to uncertainty) and a ruling party controlling government in a democracy whose mandate is conditioned by regular elections (representing the constraints) was the tension it had to try to balance or work around. In the *State and Transformation*, a paper published in 1996 (ANC 1996), the ANC summarises the transformation process. As is typical of ANC documentation, the language comes from different discourses, sometimes even in the same sentence. Often words are used with different meanings; words associated with the Marxist tradition could, for example, be used to make the case for capitalism. The Marxist tradition drawn upon is itself somewhat obscure involving the application of mechanistic dialectical 'laws of motion' to concrete situations.

The ANC paper sets out the goals and functions of the democratic state. The 'conquest' of the state is part of the broad liberation process; the state is the vital instrument, the 'platform', to effect the 'total liberation' of the black people. The 'primary task is to work for the emancipation of the black majority, the working people, the urban poor, the rural poor, the women, the youth … to champion their course … in such a way that the most basic aspirations of this majority assumes the status of hegemony … of all institutions of government and state' (ANC 1996; ANC 1998). The other goal of the state is to keep democracy stable; to achieve this the ANC has to rule on behalf of 'the people as a whole', including the former oppressors, the whites. The ANC goes on to say:

> To the extent that the democratic state is objectively interested in a stable democracy, so it cannot avoid the responsibility to ensure the establishment of a social order concerned with the genuine interests of the people as a whole, regardless of the racial, national, gender, and class differentiation (ANC 1996).

These two contradictory positions—the desire to realise the goals of national liberation versus the valuing of stability—reflect the uncertainty that is the lot of the nationalist elite, and that Fanon found characteristic of the nationalist bourgeoisie in many other post-settler situations.

The ANC has at different times assumed different conceptions of the state in relation to its liberation and governing projects. Faced with a divided society and wanting supposedly to please all, the ANC understands the state at one level as the mediator of the conflicting interests of society. This understanding is similar to liberal pluralist notions of the 'neutral' state, where the state is conceived as merely a 'black box', acting like a neutral referee without itself playing a role in the conflicts of society. The state functions like a 'cash register': it 'adds up' the different interests, producing compromised preferences that are representative of the whole society (Krasner 1984). Institutionalists believe that the state is an actor in its own right, having its own interests and defining a set of structures that combine to produce preferences in relation to non-state actors. The 'development state' idea (Cosatu 2005; Makgethla 2005; Southall 2006) that the ANC proposed towards the end of Mbeki's presidency conforms to this view. If we take seriously the goals the ANC sets out for itself in the Freedom Charter or the 1969 Strategy and Tactics document, it is the institutionalist conception of the activist state that the ANC has in mind seeking to transform society. And the organisation perhaps could not have ignored the historical examples—European fascism, socialist Eastern Europe, the 'Asian Tigers'—where the state had acted as a rapid economic moderniser. Alexander Gerschenkron's (1962) classic study argued that the late modernisation of Germany, Russia and Japan would not have been possible without the interventionist role of the state. The state was central to national development in these countries and this model remains historically appealing to the ANC.

A third idea of the state, albeit one that the ANC would not readily admit to (but which it has broadly exemplified), comes from anthropologist Clifford Geertz's (1980) notion of the 'theatre state'. Geertz shifts our attention to how the state presents and projects itself to the society, focusing on the symbolic register. Even though Geertz studied the precolonial state of Bali, his idea of the state as theatre seems appropriate to apply to the post-1994 ANC state (Geertz 1980). Consider, for example, the dress, pomp and extraordinary security measures that are used to protect the president and the political class, mimicking rich Western states, even though masses of local citizens cannot even meet the needs of bare life as *homo sacer*. In this idea of 'state theatre', ceremony is central. Geertz suggested that the less the state complies with the rules of the constitutional order or the weaker its capacity in relation to society, the more the state relies on symbols of power to represent itself. The state as theatre reinforces the significance of discourses of charisma in South African politics.

The last notion of the state relevant to the post-1994 democratic South Africa can be gleaned from Clapham's (1985) Weberian conception of the patrimonial state. This is a conception that the ANC as an organisation will not endorse; however, critics and even some in the ANC have seen the state in these terms. When Zwelinzima Vavi, the former secretary general of COSATU, attacked the political elite for behaving like 'political hyenas' intent on turning South Africa into a 'predator state' (Steenkamp 2010), he was referring precisely to this idea of the patrimonial state. Clapham argued that in grossly unequal societies, it is not unusual for the state to undermine civic values and constitutional rules, and to allow 'informal' relations to take precedence. Although at independence a formal changeover takes place, the structure of the state as an instrument of domination continues even under democratic conditions. The state in the new order assumes centrality, and civil society is unable to effectively challenge it; it is strong relative to local society but fragile relative to other states in the international system. The office bearers of the state choose not to distinguish between their positions in public office and their private behaviour and interests. This 'pre-modern cultural disposition' (Weber's terms) remains, and the different roles are either deliberately confused by the elites, or deliberately violated for self-gain.

The alternative to rational-legal values dominating the culture of the state is the attractiveness of charisma. For Clapham, the 'basic problem of the third world state … is its failure in most cases even to approximate to a rational-legal mode of operation' (Clapham 1985, 45). This failure results in 'personal rulership' and exchanges of material rewards for support/loyalty between leaders and followers, re-enforcing similar relations to those entrenched in 'traditional' leadership patterns. According to Clapham, these dependent relations prevail even where modern bureaucracy is in place, thus allowing officers of the state, who regard state assets as their private property, to build networks of patron-client relationships that ultimately undermine the institutions and the rules governing the polity. Clapham labels this 'neo-patrimonialism' (1985).

In the African context, also suggestive of Weber's institutionalist influence of the state as well as on Huntington's thesis on political order, Mamdani (1996) showed how colonial power stamped its mark on African society, only to survive into the post-independence period. Mamdani insisted that this model fits the South African case too, dismissing the long-held South African exceptionalism bias. The form of the state matters: 'To understand the nature of the struggle and of agency, one needs to understand the nature of power.… More than the labour question, the organisation and reorganisation of power turned on the imperative of maintaining political order' (1996, 24). Mamdani agreed with Ake (1991) and warned that the mistake made by the postcolonial African leadership was to retain the structure of the colonial state, as this meant that it inherited the problem of the divided relationship of the state towards the urban and rural peoples, derived from the 'direct-' and 'indirect-rule' strategy of the colonial state. More specifically, the colonial state had treated urban dwellers as citizens endowed with rights; rural dwellers, by contrast, were without rights, falling under the control of traditional authorities and customary law. 'Indirect rule, however, signified a rural tribal authority. It was about incorporating natives into a state-enforced customary order.… Direct and indirect rule are better understood as variants of despotism' (Mamdani 1996, 18). The protracted problem of 'tribal' identity politics can be traced historically to the structuring of relations between state and society; the bifurcated colonial state constituted 'tribal' identities, and the postcolonial state has reproduced them. The relations between the state and the people were not democratised, even in those radical nationalist regimes that made efforts to undermine traditional structures.

The sensitivity of the political class in South Africa, its need to display power and be dismissive towards the 'ordinary citizen', cannot be delinked from colonial history, which supports Fanon and Mamdani's (1996) argument of incomplete subjects and the desire for fullness. The lack of confidence of the 'ordinary citizen' as a historical class partly explains this kind of behaviour of the political elites, who believe the citizens will be accepting of elite privileges and general dismissiveness. In a recent incident, a person was knocked down and killed by a government 'blue light' convoy (IOL 2009); in another, a student, Chumani Maxwele, was arrested for 'showing the finger' at President Zuma's motorcade when the latter almost ran him off the road (Jones & Mtyala 2010). On a regular basis citizens have been bullied by these official brigades and 'blue light' convoys, which have become an ordinary feature of South Africa's daily political landscape, speeding the political class from here to there, disrespecting members of the sovereign body that give government its legitimacy. An all too common phrase used by ANC officials is, 'We are not a banana republic—we have rules here', as if to emphasise South Africa's difference from other Third World and African states. However, this is belied by the ostentatious waste of public resources and the fact that government officials are showering themselves with the paraphernalia of power while local residents starve and basic infrastructure falls apart. Clapham's (1985) classic 'Third World trend' is unfortunately more evident in local municipalities where the ANC is in power and residents are beholden to the local state for grants and resources: patronage relationships and abuse play themselves out not only in state structures like the police and bureaucracy, but also in the classroom and local the trade union office.

Mandela, the figure of modern charisma: a 'smooth' transition?

I have already emphasised how the nationalist middle class leadership placed great value on gaining control of the state and using this as an instrument to project its nationalist, society-transforming goals in order to modernise the society. The leadership used two 'top-down' discourses to engage with and organise the subalterns; each discourse focused on a particular approach to politics (charismatic or rational-legal), economics (redistributionist or neo-liberal), and on the national question (non-racial or Africanist). For heuristic purposes, we can refer to these discourses as the 'symbolic-modern' and the 'rationalist-modern'.

Once in power, the ANC discovered that the instrument of modernity it had admired so much was not as potent a weapon as anticipated. The NP government had passed onto the ANC a bankrupt Apartheid state, having accumulated huge debts to foreign and local banks and a weaker state capacity than it projected to society and the world. Faced with this reality, the ANC embarked upon consolidating its position in relation to its immediate rivals, the NP and IFP and their staunch supporters in the military and police, as well as in the civil service. It is important to remember that what is often described as the 'smooth transition' has much to do with the Afrikaner and African nationalist elite agreeing on how to resolve the crisis in South Africa, with the backing of international and local capital.

In this early phase, Mandela (and the ANC) represented the discourse of the symbolic-modern, relying on the power of symbol, charisma and history to consolidate what they saw as the beginnings of political development. While Mbeki increasingly came to be associated with rationalist-modern discourses, he was at this stage likewise very much a central figure in the symbolic-modern discourse. What are some of the features of this discourse? There is little doubt that the primary aim of the nationalist elite was to bring in the passive 'support' of the masses to the compromised settlement and then go about disciplining them in a definite direction. The first key element was the use of 'the charismatic'. Weber (1958, 79) described charisma as that 'gift of grace, the absolutely personal devotion and personal confidence in revelation, heroism, or other qualities of individual leadership'. The special qualities beyond the 'normal', such as 'heroism' and 'revelation', have always had a significant presence in South African political culture; we need only think about the admiration of 'political sacrifice' in the struggle and its influence in black political culture and morality. This is most aptly encapsulated in a person; accordingly, figures such as Mandela, Biko, First and Fischer richly dot the country's struggle history. The struggle organisations commemorated 21 March, the day of the shootings at Sharpeville, for many years as Heroes Day, until the ANC government renamed it Human Rights Day. Mandela's life experience allowed him to stand above the norm. But Weberians have also extended the concept of charisma-as-in-'heroism' to non-individual units of analysis, such that it can capture what lies beyond the mundane, the extraordinary, the symbolic and all the practices that go beyond the limits of rational-legal and 'traditional' characteristics. We can conceive of the dominant mode of resistance politics in South Africa—because of the need to 'move and motivate' large numbers of people into becoming social forces for change—as a particularly attractive mode of politics of nationalist elite leadership, in addition to fostering numerous cultural idioms that value the charismatic, as in religion, sport and community life. It is often from this group that leadership, particularly charismatic leadership, comes. Mandela, and perhaps Zuma too, are products of such symbolic discourses that engage with the subaltern through this charismatic mode.

Mandela condensed many symbolisms into one person: anti-Apartheid struggle leader, former prisoner of twenty-seven years and post-Apartheid's first black president. He followed in a long tradition of strong individual leadership in South Africa. Adam (1996a), implicitly bringing in colonial conditions, argues that previous white leaders (Botha, Hertzog and Smuts before the war, followed after by Malan, Vorster and Botha) saw themselves as 'protecting' not a normal electoral majority, but the very survival of white domination and 'Western civilisation'. In order to function effectively as a counter discourse, black nationalism had to produce its own strong leaders. As was the case with Mandela, it is also appropriate to apply the concept of charisma to the ANC, because, without appreciating its 'symbolic value', it is difficult, if not impossible, to understand its post-1994 electoral dominance. How else can we make sense of Zuma's oft-repeated message at large ANC electoral rallies that the 'ANC will rule until Jesus Christ returns' (News 24, 8 January 2014).

ANC dominance has encouraged much debate about its broad implications for democratic society (Brooks 2004), but few such debates address how the dominant party steers a normative conception of politics that is aimed at asserting its hegemony over the mass collective subject, something the ANC was particularly successful at in the 1980s. However, Suttner (2006) rightly criticises the notion of the 'dominant party' thesis for its intrinsic conservativeness. This thesis relies on the narrow definition of democracy as the electoral type of democracy, rather than democracy more broadly conceived in its history of the radical tradition, as popular participation and decision-making in everyday life. It is tradition for the ANC to claim to represent the interests of working and poor people, and to define democracy in broader terms to include socio-economic redistribution, believing itself to be a 'people's movement' rather than a conventional political party. Historically the charismatic discourse is essential to its mode of political engagement and strategic thinking. Here is an illustration of how the ANC defines itself:

> It did not see itself in the mould of an orthodox political party, but rather as a broad organization for national liberation. It participated in the 1994 elections on this platform, and even to the present moment adheres to this self-definition. The ANC conceptualises itself as a movement aimed at bringing about the national liberation of the oppressed people and the realisation of a non-racial, non-sexist society in South Africa. While the advent of democracy in 1994 established a critical beachhead, that task is yet to be completed. Accordingly, it also asserts that there is need for maintaining the old ANC/COSATU/SACP alliance. Indeed, in contrast to the general concept of political parties as rivals, the ANC always saw its task to gather together in united mass action as wide a spectrum of forces and organisations as possible, in order to better pursue the goals of the liberation struggle (Mac Maharaj 2008, 25).

Other writings on the 'dominant party thesis' are less concerned about the immediate participatory aspects of democracy or the empowerment and symbolic attachment of subalterns, as would be the case with a people's movement, than about the political stability that a governing party brings (Adam 1999). Hence their argument that dominant-party rule has benefits for all newly democratising societies, where the potential for social instability is high. According to Arian and Barnes (1974, 593), 'the dominant party system suggests a model of how democracy and stability may be combined under difficult conditions'. One-party dominance democratically mobilises citizens to participate in the political system, provides for a stable government, and must be appreciated for providing 'stability in fragmented polities'. Friedman (1999) adds to this mix in the South African context the unique qualities of the ANC, namely its democratic internal structure and historical commitment to a plural democracy. The ANC as a dominant party brings long-term stability, offers short-term safeguards for fearful minorities and it allows democratic institutions to take root, according to Adam (1999). More implicit, yet very significant, is that Adam drew attention to the ANC's role in the 'management' (in our approach, the biopolitical disciplining) of the poor and controlling their political passions and expectations.

Historically and during the transition, Mandela and the ANC's stature, expressions and key elements of symbolic political discourse constituting subjects in particular ways, played a fundamental role in managing fellow elites and subalterns alike. While Mandela was not as well known internationally before his imprisonment in 1961, and while he was not seen for nearly three decades, his release in order to lead an uncertain democratic transition reinforced the power dynamics of his charisma. His was the face of the ANC and the anti-Apartheid struggle. Mandela's power to unify was so enormous that the government asked him to address the nation in the aftermath of the Chris Hani killing, almost suggesting that he was 'above' the politics of the moment. The power of charisma in a fluid political situation helped negate some of the Afrikaner leaders' initial fears. Mandela had regular meetings with the leader of the Freedom Front, Genenerl Constand Viljoen; he publicly celebrated the ninetieth birthday of the wife of Verwoerd (regarded as the architect of Apartheid); and he used South Africa's 1995 Rugby World Cup victory to cement his popularity among Afrikaners, reducing tensions. However, the killing of farmers, a new phenomenon in the post-1994 period, and Afrikaner opposition to Affirmative Action maintained Afrikaner suspicions of ANC rule.

Mandela's charisma helped to undermine the power of Zulu ethnic politics under the IFP and the leadership of Chief Buthulezi, a potential threat to the transition. As president, it was said that Mandela managed cabinet meetings by entertaining all views, until consensus was reached (Schrire 1996). The multiparty composition of the GNU actually required such an approach, but as the consistently radical philosopher of democracy Andrew Nash (1998) observes, this was also in keeping with Mandela's own understanding of democracy, growing up as a child in rural Transkei. Nash quoted from Mandela's autobiography:

> It was democracy in its purest form. There may have been a hierarchy of importance among the speakers, but everyone was heard.... At first I was astonished at the vehemence—and candour with which people criticized the regent. He was not above criticism—in fact, he was often the principal target of it.... The meeting would continue until some kind of consensus was reached. They ended in unanimity or not at all.... As a leader, I have always followed the principles I first saw demonstrated by the regent in the Great Place. I have always endeavoured to listen to what each and every person in a discussion had to say before venturing my own opinion.... Oftentimes, my own opinion will simply represent a consensus of what I heard in the discussion (Mandela 1994).

A second element of symbolic nationalist elite discourse post-1994 approaches what can be called 'identity politics', which is based on the acknowledgement that South Africa comprises different 'racial groups' that must be recognised and brought together as part of nation-building. For Mandela, the approach to the 'national question' mirrored the Congress Alliance of the 1950s, where the Coloured People's Organisation, the white Congress of Democrats, the Indian Congresses and the ANC came together (Lodge 1983). The Freedom Charter endorsed this approach to the 'national question', which was strongly criticised by the ANC's rivals in the liberation movement. This open, inclusive approach to identity meant that existing racial divisions imposed by Apartheid were accepted by the ANC, rather than radically confronted. The NP (by then the New National Party, or NNP) felt so confident that the ANC could be trusted with upholding constitutional provisions that, two years later in 1996, it pulled out of the GNU to function as a 'normal' opposition party. Refusing to take a hands-on approach and allowing line ministries a fair degree of autonomy characterised Mandela's governance style, and this freed him to concentrate on the more important tasks of nation-building and national reconciliation (Schrire 1996). Mandela first and foremost wanted to allay white fears. He also wanted to inspire blacks to bask in a constitutional democracy that recognised their rights as citizens and to use these political 'opportunities' to accomplish modernist personal goals, education being his favourite. In the Mandela administration, the civil service left over from the Apartheid era—with mainly Afrikaners in its employ—committed itself to the new state. Over time, though, Afrikaner bureaucrats took early retirement packages and the ANC filled the state bureaucracy with their own deliberately recruited and 'redeployed' people. The Mbeki years speeded up this redeployment process, with dire consequences for state capacity as well as making ANC membership an attractive option for opportunist elements and personally ambitious people to obtain lucrative and high-status state jobs (Lodge 1999).

The discourse of symbolism, according to Heribert Adam (1996), had the effect of increasing the passivity of citizens, reinforcing trends towards demobilisation, and fostering a cult of personality around Mandela, which meant that citizen autonomy, the very basis of democratic society, suffered. Adam asks how Mandela was so enormously popular when the ANC governance record was so dismal, and when most blacks remained poor. Most importantly, however, the discourse of symbolism prepared the ground for conservative economic policies despite concerns raised by COSATU and the SACP. Mandela, in the popular mind, is still strongly associated with a modest redistributionist approach, called the Reconstruction and Development Programme; but it was during his tenure that the Growth Employment and Redistribution (GEAR) policy was adopted, even though it later became closely tied to Mbeki. Mandela made it clear that the alliance partners had to abide by ANC decisions on economic policy—the change towards GEAR was not up for debate. By devaluing citizen participation in decision-making, such a situation contributes to general apathy.

Citizens withdraw from the public sphere and only participate in politics minimally, at election time.

The figure of rational-legalism: from exile to the bureaucratic approach to politics

It has become popular, even though incorrect, to associate the conservative economic shift exclusively with the Mbeki government. The demobilisation of the main subject, which had brought about the democratic change, began under Mandela's leadership. Though Mandela's charisma imposed a different form of passivity, this was complemented by Mbeki's more prominent statist and technicist approach to politics. Mbeki's more determined implementation of GEAR and especially the 'language' it introduced, emphasised the centrality of the middle classes to the 'revolution'. Lastly, the once coherent image of the ANC was severely dented by factionalist battles, which left the subaltern equally alienated from the political system. The second type of discursive response of the nationalist elite to post-Apartheid rule—neo-liberal in economic policies, rational-bureaucratic in politics and Africanist towards questions of identity—was far more strident in using the state to implement necessary changes in society. In taking statism for granted and assuming the passivity of the subaltern, Mbeki's rationalist-modern discourse ironically contributed towards the crisis of the nationalist-modern project in ways that were perhaps deeper than those of the symbolic-charismatic discourses.

It is unclear why Mbeki became a symbol for the neo-conservative thrust, even more so than Mandela—perhaps because he was more vociferous in defending neo-liberal policies of government and more critical of the SACP and COSATU, 'leftist' opponents in the ANC alliance. The ANC's deinstitutionalisation as a political party is also conveniently traceable to the Mbeki period. The indicators of it becoming a party of patronage and sliding into a crude nativist nationalism were becoming evident during his tenure, although these sit in tension with his state-building, broad Africanist nation-building and ideas about a continental renaissance. Fanon's warnings about the pitfalls of the nationalist bourgeoisie became more apt during Mbeki's period, although we can assume if it were not him, then some other leader would soon enough have represented this nationalist elite discourse in its desire to modernise the polity along the Western paradigm and under the specific conditions of settler-colonial legacies.

One of Mbeki's faces is that of the politics of the 'new left'. His idea of democracy equally values participation but is different to Mandela's invocation of local rural democracy, as we can see in this address to parliamentarians:

> Because you are here by virtue of the will and the sacrifices of the people, you have a special responsibility, over the next five years, actually to serve the people faithfully, honestly and to the best of your abilities. Among other things, this will

require that the necessary measures are taken to enable the honourable members to spend more time with their constituents, as a defining feature of our democracy which we wish to be a participatory system (Mbeki 1999).

It is ironic that, while Mandela made references to communal democracy in his Eastern Cape African village, Mbeki, the Africanist, drew from Western republican theoretical tradition. In practice, the Mbeki period will be remembered for the absence of participatory democracy. The ANC and the government planned citizen participation rather than encouraged spontaneous interaction. This entailed passive listening to stock speeches by politicians—actual questioning, critical participation, holding politicians to account and determining decisions were discouraged. At these stage-managed meetings, organisers approached citizens as objects rather than subjects and sovereign agents. In the Mbeki years, interaction with citizens through the *imbizo* (a gathering, meeting or forum) programmes became instrumental and formulaic, lacking communicative action in the Habermasian sense. How else can we account for protests in exactly those municipalities with a record of *imbizos*, such as Albert Luthuli Municipality and many others? The people were merely 'bussed in' to create a crowd and informed by government officials of state development plans and decisions that had already been taken. The exercise often bordered on electioneering.

The government's conservative shift Following the discourse emphasising charisma, redistribution and non-racialism, the top-down shift to macroeconomic policies under Mbeki presents a classic illustration of the rational-bureaucratic discourse. The broad legitimacy of the ANC—its 'institutional capital', rooted in its long struggle history and overwhelming victories in national elections—was given a sudden shock when Mbeki popularised the language of GEAR. Mbeki made it clear that the priority of his government was to increase the size of the national bourgeoisie, and to develop this black 'patriotic' bourgeoisie as rapidly as possible as the best way to grow the economy and address Apartheid legacies.

When Mbeki assumed power after the 1999 election, the size of ANC dominance enabled a more confident shift and implementation of neo-liberal economic policies. This dominance created conditions to use state resources for patronage and promoting factional conflict that effectively ended the post-1994 'honeymoon' period. In 1994, the ANC embarked on the Reconstruction and Development Program (RDP) as its policy framework to tackle poverty and inequality (Marais 1998), a programme that was the outcome of spirited debates among the Tripartite Alliance. partners. From 1994 to 1996, the ANC defined a more modest and ambiguously social democratic thrust of the RDP, aimed at cautiously redistributing wealth with limited state intervention through the expenditure on community services and infrastructure. However, RDP projects suffered setbacks from funding shortages, problems in effective implementation and widespread campaigning and pressure from local and international capital. The programme failed to attract the genuine popular support it could have had, had the ANC built it within grassroots community structures, such as those that arose in the 1980s. But this approach had hardly been considered, let alone discussed. The technical and state development understanding of the RDP quickly led the ANC leadership to favour more market-oriented solutions, abandoning the RDP for GEAR.

Instead of focusing on redistribution by empowering a large mass of poor people without the basics of bare life to stimulate growth, GEAR was a domestically designed structural adjustment programme. It advocated policies intended to inspire economic growth through increased foreign investment, re-envisaging the role of the state as that of neutral mediator and coordinator. Importantly, the 'language' of GEAR (i.e., its ideological moorings) talked about the 'liberalisation' of the South African economy (its market, tariff policies, wages and monetary policy), and the 'political' imperatives called for the 'withdrawal' of the state from the economic sphere. The mantra was that the market was efficient, public ownership inefficient and wasteful. This justified reducing public expenditure generally. The ANC and government called upon citizens to reduce their expectations of the state, and to follow a new managerial, individualist attitude to themselves and understanding of the public sphere.

The language of GEAR was more potent than its actual policies, because it confirms Althusser's idea of the interpellation of subjects in particular ways by ideology. But the policies were also important. The specific goals of GEAR involved designing the budget to reduce the inherited Apartheid debt as quickly as possible; manipulating interest rates upwards if necessary to lower inflation; allowing the currency and domestic industries to compete globally, without state 'protection', by adopting a floating exchange rate regime; and attracting foreign investment by making domestic conditions and state ideology 'friendly' towards global capitalism (Lundahl 1999; Marais 1998). In keeping with state cutbacks, the privatisation of parastatals was obviously on the cards, but trade union resistance placed this idea, popular idea among economists, on hold. Ministers began to speak more approvingly about 'public-private' partnerships, reducing expectations of the state, now limited to the classical liberal role of infrastructure development. In its public utterances the government had abandoned the struggle demand for a 'living wage', and asked that citizens allow the labour market to settle wage rates, a position that correctly indicated a drastic about turn in the eyes of the organised working class. Capital naturally wanted labour to increase productivity, and defended a more 'flexible' labour market as important to making South Africa more attractive to foreign investment and more competitive globally.

The defence of this policy was simple: Apartheid had made South Africa inefficient and uncompetitive, and GEAR was an instrument to address economic inefficiencies. The supporters of GEAR described the 'bloated state' as a legacy of Apartheid. They spoke about the need to address structural problems of the Apartheid economy, and to reduce tariffs to increase domestic competitiveness (Ramos 1997). These technical economic changes would make the labour force more skilled, because in the long run companies would invest in labour as it was cheaper than spending on capital-intensive goods. GEAR believers argued that foreign direct investments, exports of

South African goods and independent market mechanisms would benefit poor citizens, providing them with more jobs as well as better and more accessible goods and services. GEAR was how the redistribution promises of the RDP would be realised.

Despite these positive assertions about the benefits of the GEAR policy, the outcomes for the poor and working class were devastating. Under Mbeki, in the early years, economic statisticians indeed registered noticeable economic growth and low-enough inflation and interest rates to immediately benefit and contribute to a growing black middle class; however, unemployment also grew and jobs remained scarce. South Africa thus experienced a period of 'jobless growth'. The unhappy combination of lower state budgets, incompetent or under-qualified ANC appointments to the state and widespread corruption at all levels resulted in the poor and working class communities bearing the brunt of the burden.

Micro-management and ambiguous identity politics In keeping with rationalist-modern discourse, Mbeki wanted to redesign and make the state more efficient. After the 1999 elections, the Mbeki government was aware of the declining patience of its constituency. To this end, in official discourse the idea of 'delivery' became central. Mbeki wanted his presidency to be associated with urgency, to be concerned less with deliberative democracy and to be focused more on the practical delivery of resources. He redesigned the office of the presidency, increased its budget—it became much bigger than the budget of Mandela's office, although Zuma's office has since doubled the budget of Mbeki's—and assumed an instrumental political approach. One layer of Mbeki's discourse was organised around 'delivery', 'targets', 'monitoring', evaluation, efficiencies and state effectiveness.

Another layer of his discourse, leaving behind the nitty-gritty of rule, was to outline a grand vision for national reconciliation and Africa's rejuvenation, a form of African nationalism that was as universally open as it was likely to be interpreted as narrow, local and particular. In the South African context, this vision was available for many different uses. Should we consider these as two contradictory poles or should we read them as typical of the dilemma that, according to Fanon, the intermediary class of settler colonialism faces once it is in power, because it keeps one eye looking towards Europe and the other looking to the lost civilisations of the past? It seems to me that Mbeki typifies this love-hate relationship with European modernity and its Enlightenment. We see it in his universalist definition of 'African' and vehement questioning of European drug companies in his analysis of HIV/AIDS as a health problem facing poor Africans in the main; in the latter scenario, he sees himself as protecting the lambs from the beasts.

Mbeki distinguished himself from the 'rainbow nation' idea, so closely bound up with Tutu and Mandela. Subtly, he shifted from a discourse of rights to one grappling with identity politics. When we look at the emphasis he placed on the African Renaissance as an idea and at his two parliamentary speeches on the question of identity, his distancing from the 'rainbow nation' concept allows him to bring it back under a new, Africanist framing. In his first address, in 1996 (Mbeki 2007), he asked 'Who am I?' and proclaimed, 'I am an African!' The second speech deals with reconciliation. It is somewhat more pessimistic, but perhaps more 'realistic' and critical than the former, which is more poetic. The emphasis, besides the history of conflict, is on attachment to the land and on acknowledging great African civilizations of the past. Mbeki defines 'African' in broad terms: 'I owe my being to the hills, valleys, the mountains and the glades … the natural stage on which we act out the foolish deeds of the theatre of our day'. He draws attention to the past and to the particular experiences of each group making up South African society. All of these experiences, the people who experienced them, the victims and perpetrators of conflict, are included in his defining composition of an African: 'I owe my being to the Khoi and San['s] … experience of merciless genocide'; 'I am formed of the migrants who left Europe.… Whatever their actions, they remain still part of me'; 'In my veins … [is] the blood of Malay slaves who came from the East'; 'I am the grandchild of warrior men … Hintsa, Sekhukune … Cetswayo, Mphehu'; 'I am the grandchild … who lay[s] fresh flowers on the Boer graves … [in] concentration camps'; 'I come from those transported … from India and China'. 'Being part of all of these people', he concludes, 'I shall claim that I am an African!' This idea, which is different to the Freedom Charter while not breaking with it, embraces to a degree the rainbow nation too. Mbeki speaks about his own identity, an 'I' constituted by many different elements which combine to make him an African. He is a patriot, a 'member' of the racial and ethnic groups inhabiting South Africa and even beyond. It is a poetic nationalist conception; love of land flows as a central reference point throughout.

Mbeki's approach to the constitution of identity breaks interesting new ground. He recognises and draws upon South Africa's long history of violent struggle and its impact on the constitution of subject identity, consistent with a Fanonian paradigm. This history of violence produced victims who had incorporated into their memories the devastating impacts of these experiences, but who also fought a struggle to overcome. 'I am of a nation' which fought against injustice, he proudly declared. As towards Europe, the modernist intellectual both loves and despises the masses:

> The Great masses … will not permit that the behaviour of the few results in the description of our country and people as barbaric. Patient because history is on their side, these masses do not despair because today the weather is bad. Nor do they turn triumphalist when, tomorrow, the sun shines.… Whatever the circumstances they have lived through—and because of that experience—they are determined to define for themselves who they are and who they should be (Mbeki 1996).

Mbeki speaks of the South African constitution as helping to define that identity too: 'The Constitution whose adoption we celebrate constitutes an unequivocal statement that we refuse to accept that our Africaness shall be defined by our race, colour, gender or historical origins' (1996). The constitution helps to mark an important political beginning with new values, breaking with a South African past when 'African' was defined in racial terms and the society was divided along colour lines. Mbeki does not say the past experiences merely 'influence', or that he 'recognises' or 'embraces' these: he is emphatic that he is a *product* of these experiences and that these different elements are part of his blood. It is an essentialist argument with a twist: these many 'pasts' constitute his identity. Mbeki adopts a political and pragmatic approach to identity, one that recognises the history of racism/inhumanity, the struggle against it, and the commitment to a 'peaceful transition', the new liberal constitution and the future. It is a definition of 'African' that is neither racial nor geographical, but based on our understanding of past experience—what can be learnt, and taken from it. It is also a definition that is not static, but dynamic, being made as we intervene and engage in daily political practice.

This approach to the national question did not, unfortunately, generate widespread deliberation. It was mixed up in the reaction to another of Mbeki's speeches and his stance on HIV/AIDS. Again addressing parliament on receiving the final TRC report in his 'Two Nations' talk (Hadland et al. 1999), Mbeki emphasised that, despite efforts at reconciliation by black South Africans, South African society remained divided between a rich white and a poor black group. This unjust division was not acknowledged by white South Africans; compared to the proactive efforts of West Germans to reconcile with East Germans by investing billions in infrastructure and integration on the East German side, reconciliation in South Africa was disappointing. He believed white South Africans were criticising the ANC government yet were unwilling to transfer wealth to the black poor. The response to Mbeki was harsh. He was accused of racially dividing society and undermining national reconciliation, which had been the hallmark of the Mandela presidency (Chipkin 2007). He had effectively added the white community to his growing list of critics.

Confrontational politics: 'we live on different planets' The unravelling of the Mbeki government was a real dent to the national modern project. An explanation of its ending cannot ignore his controversial HIV/AIDS position as a contributing factor, and here again it was not unrelated to settler-colonial subjectivities and political sensitivity towards African identity politics. Mbeki's increasingly isolated position lost him the popular support he might have called upon when his factional rivals in the ANC, COSATU and the SACP supporting Zuma realised they were strong enough to remove his faction. The HIV/AIDS epidemic spread rapidly among the urban and rural poor; South Africa soon had the highest infection rate in the world. The middle classes had access to antiretroviral drugs through private medical aid schemes and were therefore able to resist the severe symptoms effectively and avoid a premature death. Those who could not afford treatment and were dependent on the public health system, however, faced certain sickness and death. Surprisingly, Mbeki disapproved of the state providing HIV medication. He reasoned that there was no cure and that the drugs were ineffective and even worsened the sickness of patients—Western drug companies conspired to use Africans as guinea pigs, he argued. Instead, he highlighted poverty as the key factor explaining the spread of the virus and the toll it was taking among the South African population.

A series of letters between Mbeki and Tony Leon (Leon & Mbeki 2000), the leader of the opposition DA, reveals how settler-colonial legacies cloud and complicate what in other settings might be straightforward public policy debates. Mbeki read Leon's criticism of government for not buying AZT, even for cases of rape, as employing a number of not-so-subtle racist assumptions about blacks, and felt that Leon's criticism was merely a smokescreen to present himself and the opposition as protectors of democracy against untrustworthy blacks. Mbeki went on:

> I don't believe we should establish a convention where the opposition is an effective opposition while at the same time an active role player in executive decisions. It is obscene to, like Leon, reduce the true question in the country—getting rid of deep-rooted and ongoing racism—to the prevalence of diseases. Your allegation that death and disease do not differentiate between politics, gender or race is completely wrong. Perhaps it is a graphic illustration that we do indeed live on different planets. Contrary to what you say, even a child in the black community knows that our burden of disease correlates with the racial divisions in our country (Leon & Mbeki 2000).

The Mbeki view became known as AIDS denialism, as pitted against Western science. It involved some complex elements, especially since Mbeki understood HIV/AIDS within the frame of colonialism, Western imperialism and the construction of blacks as 'savages' who were unable to control their sexual urges, while the counter argument emphasised medication and the government's moral obligation to help poor citizens, presenting Mbeki's ideological rant about colonialism as a distraction from its failure to do so. Gradually an extremely effective civil opposition, led by the Treatment Action Campaign (TAC), developed, the first truly mass-based post-Apartheid movement. The TAC was a diverse coalition of discourses, many of them traceable to the struggle, such as civil rights adherents, Marxists and new social movement activists inspired by anti-globalisation protests elsewhere in the world.

The TAC demanded that the government provide treatment medicines to those unable to afford them. As thousands of people died of HIV/AIDS, the campaign spread internationally. Mbeki became the target of protesters wherever he travelled, as did Manto Tshabalala-Msimang, his minister of health and close exile struggle comrade. Tshabalala-Msimang became further embroiled in the issue by digging in her heels, defending government policy by attacking her critics and advising HIV-positive citizens to focus on dietary changes. At one point, she suggested the 'African potato' as a remedy.

After four years of effective TAC campaigning and growing international and domestic pressure, divisions in the ANC along many other fronts drew sustenance from

Mbeki's increasing isolation. In a strange twist, the Africanist Western enlightenment man found himself in an anti-modernist position, though he did put together an AIDS-denialist panel of mainly Western scientists to give his position more credibility. Eventually, Mbeki was instructed by his close circle and the NEC to avoid any further communication on the issue, without repudiating his controversial claims. The focus of the campaign then fell exclusively on the minister of health, who fell ill and died shortly after. Only with Mbeki's forced removal from the presidency and after a new health minister, Barbara Hogan, had taken over, did the state provide free anti-retroviral drugs to HIV-positive patients with a high CD-4 count, which indicated an advanced stage of the disease.

Factional opposition In the immediate post-1994 period, the ANC harnessed its formidable capacity to manage internal rivalries, despite taking for granted certain important regional and ideological differences. Even though factional tensions were evident during Mandela's term in office, disputes became more open under Mbeki and in this period we can, following Boucek's classification of factionalist dynamics into cooperative, competitive and degenerative types, identify ANC factionalism as intensely competitive and degenerative (Boucek 2009; Suttner 2009). The shift from mass politics to 'palace politics' and factional battles (ANC 2002; ANC 2011) moved to a higher level when Mbeki mentioned, in 2001, that rivals in his party were plotting a coup. The public announcement by the minister of police, Steve Tshwete, accusing three senior ANC leaders of plotting against the president, was typical of exile politics, but still took many by surprise who were used to the politics of the democratic era. The accused—Cyril Ramaphosa, Mathews Phosa and Tokyo Sexwale—did not represent particular ideologies or strong class constituencies rooted in mass politics (Gevisser 2007). Rather, this was the politics of internal party elites and perhaps the first open sign of ANC weaknesses. All three denied any role in a plot. Likewise Jacob Zuma, Mbeki's deputy president, appeared on national TV emphasising that he too did not harbour any presidential ambitions.

In Mandela's time, Bantu Holomisa was forced to resign from the Mandela cabinet after he refused to apologise for accusing a fellow cabinet minister, Stella Sigcau, of corruption during the Apartheid years (Adam 1996b). Holomisa went on to form his own party, the United Democratic Movement, which, although it did not differ on ideological grounds from the ANC mainstream, could be viewed as a faction from the Transkei region. In the Mbeki years, the fallout from the Arms Deal and the differences over macroeconomic policy with ANC allies, COSATU and the SACP, were complicated by factional identities assuming prominence. The Arms Deal had been signed in 1999 by the government to purchase military equipment from global arms manufacturers costing R30 billion. The tendering process allegedly implicated many high-ranking ANC and government officials, who were accused of receiving kickbacks from the winning bidders.

The roles of Deputy President Zuma and his financial advisor, Schabir Shaik, in the corruption scandal surrounding the Arms Deal motivated the protracted conflict between the Mbeki and Zuma factions. The key structures of the organisation, the National Working Committee (NWC) and the National Executive Committee (NEC), found it difficult to control factional tensions, and eventually these bodies themselves came under the control of one or other faction. Essentially the disputes centred on relations between the party-state leadership, since there were many in the party machinery who felt that the government was bypassing party structures in its decision-making. When Zuma's friend Schabir Shaik was sentenced for corruption because of the financial support he had given to Zuma after Shaik's company won a tender in the Arms Deal, Mbeki fired Zuma as the country's deputy president. However, the party leadership and machinery then supported Zuma, arguing that Mbeki was using the state to fight ANC factional battles (Ceruti 2008).

The factional conflict between Mbeki and Zuma from 2001 onwards took many legal twists and political turns, which were for many years often the main story. Ultimately, this negatively affected judicial, state and civil society institutions. Each faction chose opposing discourses of democracy to interpret the legal charges against, and the investigation of, Zuma. On the one hand, Mbeki and the National Prosecuting Authority (NPA) reiterated the importance of the rule of law and the fight against corruption; on the other, Zuma and his allies focused on Mbeki's abuses of state power and the presumption of innocence before conviction in a court of law.

These factional divisions, while driven in the first instance by access to patronage, are also fuelled in part by ideological differences over approaches to post-Apartheid development. Before the Stellenbosch national conference in 2002, Mbeki attacked what he called the 'ultra-left', referring to COSATU and various organisations and coalitions of the new social movements. Mbeki criticised their anti-capitalist position and their incorrect interpretation of the government's macroeconomic policy as neoliberal, counter-accusing these groups as themselves advancing a neo-liberal agenda in criticising the ANC. Typical of the politics of exile, he condemned critical views as working with the enemy.

The dramatic showdown at the ANC's 2007 national conference in Polokwane, which resulted in victory for the Zuma faction in party elections; the recall of Mbeki in September 2008; and the formation of a splinter party of Mbeki loyalists in November 2008 in the Congress of the People (COPE) together demonstrate the degenerative features of factionalism, as identified in Boucek's classification.

Elites, state and corruption The widespread belief that political corruption is endemic among the political elite is a major contributing factor to subalterns relying on social mobilisation to demand that their concerns are recognised in political society. After all, anti-Apartheid resistance discourses preached a moral register of fairness, equality of treatment and suspicion towards 'double standards'. The statism to which the nationalist elite committed itself fed into the challenge that corruption would pose for the democratic order. Access to state resources (money, posts, influence, status) enhanced patronage linkages and, in a grossly unequal society such as South Africa, these patron-client networks overlapped with factional identities. An IDASA survey as early as 1996 found that 46 per cent of those sampled 'felt that most officials were engaged in corruption'. Only 6 per cent believed that there was clean government, and 41 per cent felt that political corruption was increasing (Lodge 1998). Another survey, cited by Lodge (1998), found that 15 per cent of respondents were certain all public officials were corrupt, and 30 per cent felt that most public officials were corrupt.

Carol Paton, a respected South African journalist, has investigated the negative consequences of corruption for South Africa's democracy. Paton's article (2008) describes the frightening development of a 'black hole in the budget': about 20 per cent of the procurement budgets being lost, amount to about R30 billion annually. Partly this is because public finance regulations do not require adherence to tendering procedures for amounts below R20,000 (Paton 2008). While the big cases, such as the Arms Deal and Zuma's Nkandla private house scandal, were receiving public coverage, small acts of corruption involving local governments, hospitals, schools, clinics and the thousands of daily government purchases or small opportunities opening in larger development projects were going unnoticed. But even where politicians and businesspeople follow tendering procedures, there are ample means for the evaluation committees to be influenced, with the passing of insider information being a key problem. The desire to satisfy private greed even results in the threatening or killing of whistle-blowers, and such cases have often involved different factions in the ANC (Monare 2006).

It is believed that corruption, the 'unsanctioned or unscheduled use of public resources for private ends' (Lodge 1998), is a hangover from the Apartheid state. While this is not entirely inaccurate, it does help to distinguish among different phases of the Apartheid state. The Auditor-General's Report documented 252 cases of 'financial irregularities' in 1967, compared to the period between 2005 and 2010, when the Special Investigating Unit (SIU) investigated 2,524 cases (Paton 2010). In the early, 'ideological' phase of Verwoerd's rule, ideologues used the state to pursue the establishment of Afrikaner hegemony, and corruption was less widespread. During the years of Vorster, Botha and De Klerk, however, corruption increased.

Provincial governments of the democratic political system incorporating former Bantustans have higher rates of corrupt practices, although those provinces such as Gauteng and the Northern and Western Cape, which did not have any Bantustans, are not immune to scandal. Lodge was able to identify many cases of corrupt practices in Gauteng, the most bureaucratised of provincial administrations, with respect to matric exam papers, pensions, housing, appointments of school principals and missing monies in the education department. Mpumalanga, Kwa-Zulu Natal, and the Eastern Cape had the highest number of reported corruption cases. The major problem is at the local, municipal level of government. According to the Auditor-General's Report for 2007–2008, only 2 per cent of all municipalities received a clean audit, and this increased to 17 per cent in 2013–2014. (An audit could not be undertaken of 36 per cent of municipalities because they submitted incomplete data.) In the provinces of Eastern Cape, Northern Cape and Mpumalanga, only 2 per cent of municipalities received a clean audit in 2013–2014; in some provinces, such as the Free State, Limpopo and the North West, municipalities had not received a clean audit since 1994. Most of the corruption came from 'unauthorized, wasteful and irregular expenditure'. The Western Province, run by the opposition DA, came out on top, with seventeen of twenty-four municipalities receiving clean audits (Ndenze et al 2015). At the national level, the tendering for large infrastructural projects, such as the World Cup stadiums and the large projects of parastatals (Eskom, SAA, Petro-South Africa and the SABC), always make the newspapers with allegations of widespread corruption.

Race and transformation The government's response to its frustrated subaltern subject is to rely on a politics of transformation using Affirmative Action and BEE both as policy and, more importantly, ideology. Such redistributive efforts, coupled with neoliberal macroeconomic policies, have so far failed to make a visible dent in the material conditions of the poor, yet also politicised, collective subject. This has left the overarching racial capitalist social structure relatively intact and steadily eroded whatever substantial historical legitimacy the ruling ANC enjoyed in 1994. Under the conditions of electoral democracy, 'race' discourses that are directly traceable to Apartheid and its race classification categories, have become readily available, because citizens are already socialised into them and given South African settler-colonial history, the nationalist elite and the masses can take them for granted. The former aims to retain its mass support and the latter to understand its plight in 'racialised' terms, because the patterns of racial capitalism remain and the black majority continues to experience the daily injustices of marginalisation.

As mentioned earlier, the symbolic modernist discourse of Mandela approached racial issues through the metaphor of building a 'rainbow nation', which promised a multicultural society guided by a constitution enshrining far-reaching individual rights. It was hoped that this would 'cement' a new national identity and unity. The highlight of Mandela holding aloft the Rugby World Cup, surrounded by the victorious Springboks and before thousands of cheering, mainly Afrikaner sports fans, fleetingly symbolised a possible united nationalist consciousness. Meanwhile, however, grinding divisions of the past reared their heads at every opportunity, and the issue of 'race' never left the public domain. Jonathan Jansen, a regular columnist for *The Times* and academic, observed:

> Every now and again something happens that forces South Africa to stare its still unresolved racial troubles in the face. So it was with the death at the weekend of

Eugene Terre Blanche—as it was with the St James Church massacre, the Skierlik shootings and the Reitz incident, to name but a few. At such points, as angry white citizens face off against angry black citizens, the nation has a choice (Jansen 2010).

The opportunities for such outbursts are endless and they consistently help to promote the 'uncritical solidarities' that the nationalist elites thrive upon. All areas in which the society needs to be transformed—economics, politics, education, health, social services—in order to carve out an all-embracing national identity, or to respond to past deprivations and new challenges, such as crime and xenophobia, invariably bring up questions of race.

The selection of national sports teams, appointments to senior government and corporate positions, university admissions policies, the interpretation of matriculation results—basically, wherever disputes are possible, the availability of race discourses promotes their circulation. The ways in which the government has implemented Affirmative Action policies and civil society organisations have understood these policies and practices further divides society and raises questions of race in ugly spats over, for example, 'discrimination against minorities' or questions of excellence, standards and competence. When the state is unable to effectively provide promised social services to poor (black) communities, 'incompetence' is the response of the liberal media, while subaltern groups resign themselves to political alienation or another mass demonstration. The typical, defensive response from government is to evoke the memory of the Apartheid past and the difficulty of overcoming its legacies. In the battle among the middle classes, one pole of society dwells in the present without any reference to a racialised past, while another pole registers only, or primarily, the past to explain their frustrations with the present. The drastic increase in crime, now increasingly targeting middle-class suburbs, is often understood in terms of racial discourse. The debates between the ANC, whose electoral dominance is interpreted to mean the 'black majority', and weak opposition parties, which are reduced to meaning mainly 'white' and 'minority-interest', reinforce this, notwithstanding the metaphors that are constantly invented—'township', 'historically advantaged', 'our people,' 'suburbs', 'model C'—to avoid speaking openly of 'race'.

The ANC has found itself unsure of how to respond to the question of race in a way that offers a radical break from the racial discourses of settler colonialism. One response has been to avoid thinking about it beyond a repeated commitment to 'non-racialism', a term that both denies its existence and deeply embraces it. This confusion is typified by the following example. In 2009, the young leader of the ANC Youth League (and now charismatic leader of key parliamentary party the EFF), Julius Malema, known for his attention-grabbing outbursts in front of the media, openly criticised the composition of the ANC and the Zuma cabinet (Kgosana 2009). He angrily lamented Zuma's appointment of members from 'minority groups' to occupy the key economic departments while 'Africans' were assigned to the departments responsible for security, policing, defence and intelligence. Unrepresentative of the racial makeup of the society, it sent an incorrect message to younger blacks that Africans could not fulfil intellectually demanding areas of governance. Malema's comments stimulated yet another storm of articles and inputs on post-Apartheid racial transformation not notably different from the many previous occasions when race, power, the past and change have become the basis of acrimonious national debate.

Unsurprisingly, the ANC leadership was divided, uncertain as to whether to encourage national debate or reiterate its commitment to a nebulous non-racialism. Dr Pallo Jordan, a leader considered to be on the left in the ANC, believed Malema's criticism did not warrant national debate. The criticism represented a 'marginal' view within the ANC, even though he admitted it might have popular support. Lindiwe Sisulu, a well-known daughter of the Sisulu family, insisted that a national debate was necessary. Gwede Mantashe, the secretary-general, was unhappy with Malema labelling longstanding 'comrades' in the ANC and the liberation struggle as 'minorities'. He saw such language as 'un-ANC', interpreting this as yet another indicator of the need for more political education in ANC traditions among younger members. Jacob Zuma opposed the idea, believing that it would take the country backwards.

Part of the ANC's lack of confidence in handling Malema's criticism was that the question of race was not quite settled in the organisation. For decades, the rules of the ANC did not allow membership of 'non-Africans' (Whites, Coloureds and Indians) who were active in the liberation movement, especially its armed wing, MK. At its Morogoro conference as late as 1969, the ANC changed its rules on race and for the first time opened membership on a non-racial basis, even though afterward for a long time it saw itself as representing the interests of the African majority and only gradually gravitated towards the position where it identified as the party of all the people.

The ANC did not theorise sufficiently enough nor contemplate seriously the distinction between Apartheid race classification and oppositional discourses potentially posing alternative identities. It took the 'racial groups' defined in Apartheid legislation at face value and in its political practice actually reinforced these identities, hence the ongoing Affirmative Action dilemmas. After 1990, Mandela selected his cabinet to deliberately 'reflect' 1980s 'non-racialism', assigning Indians and Whites to head key ministries. The Mbeki administration was a bit more complicated. Mbeki's broad ideology was less deliberate and more circumspect in order to emphasise Africanism, yet even though Mbeki himself did not endorse a narrow racial definition of 'African', the strong association with race and indigeneity prevailing in South Africa made it possible for critics in the ANC to accuse Mbeki of breaking with the non-racialism of the Freedom Charter. In this sense he was accused of standing somewhat outside ANC tradition. Zuma wanted to emphasise his break with Mbeki. He claimed to follow the Mandela approach, and to have returned the ANC to the 'non-racialism' of the Freedom Charter.

Rival liberation organisations approached questions of race differently, making explicit their rejection of the Apartheid racial classification. The Unity Movement and the PAC admitted members regardless of their Apartheid race classification. The PAC expected its members to see themselves as African and to identify with continental African nationalism and African culture and history. Biko and the Black Consciousness (BC) assumed a more provocative position on membership. They considered 'Indian' and 'Coloured' as Apartheid categories that needed to be rejected in favour of a generalised 'black' for all people discriminated against and oppressed under Apartheid laws. Yet it also emphasised that 'black' did not denote skin colour, but rather expressed a political meaning and was about one aspect of a broad consciousness. A 'black' person was one aware of their political oppression and actively standing to oppose it. BC organisations excluded white members, Biko claiming that progressive whites ought to work as activists in white communities because when whites joined black organisations they almost always assumed leadership positions, reinforcing black dependence and inferiority. Blacks needed to learn and practice 'independent' thought. Their resistance should develop black solidarity, and whites needed to learn to participate in the struggle as equals and unencumbered by 'guilt', which Biko believed was historically the problem in South African society. This view has progressed further and retains the moral high ground among the current generation of activists. In recent protests against colonial statues at higher education institutions, such as the University of Cape Town, protesters included black and white students, an outcome following extensive discussion where activists decided that whites should participate as equals so long as they 'check their privilege'.

Programmes of de-racialisation The ANC government adopted neo-liberal, conservative economic policies, expressed the interests of a weak nationalist bourgeoisie and promised to address the racial legacies of settler colonialism, all of which made its approach to 'de-racialising' the polity uncertain. The austere macroeconomic policy favoured business interests, yet the de-racialising program claimed to meet the expectations of subalterns demanding far-reaching redress. How to accomplish this without unsettling the already established material security of whites, a key agreement of the negotiated transition? An intricate and creative juggling act was required. In Affirmative Action and Black Economic Empowerment (BEE) policies, the ANC discovered a solution that allowed for social transformation to be approached less politically and more in technocratic, bureaucratically inspired ways. This effectively undermined the ethical and universalistic foundations of such measures to redress past injustice. Though subalterns' political alienation increased and material life became more desperate, the nationalist elite focused more of its attention on the superficial Africanisation that Affirmative Action and BEE promised. Despite these policies the 2009/10 Organisation of Economic Development (OECD) report stated that:

> While between-race inequality remains high and is falling only slowly, it is the increase in intra-race inequality [that] is preventing the aggregate measures from declining. Therefore policy initiatives [that] address the increase in intra-racial

inequality are recommended, rather than those focused solely on redistribution between inter-racial population groups.

Mbeki promoted the idea that societal transformation required the agency of the black bourgeoisie. So, since the mid-1990s under BEE, high-profile transactions enlisting a small group of beneficiaries in the mining, industrial and agricultural sectors occurred rapidly. Typically a 'black-owned consortium' would buy equity shares in one of South Africa's larger corporations or state enterprises, but with capital provided by the company itself or from substantial loans and borrowings. Sometimes these transactions were combined with appointments of blacks to senior positions in the company management. By means of such transactions, the black-owned consortiums, most often only selected by white capital because of their close ties to the ruling ANC, became instantly and lavishly rich. The underlying basis was political.

In many cases a generalised scepticism accompanied the transparency of the deals, further undermining the legitimacy of and trust towards the nationalist elite. It also exacerbated the cynicism of citizens towards the formal political system that the elites represented. There are important similarities with the label 'crony capitalism' as applied to the Asian countries of Singapore, Malaysia, Indonesia and South Korea, with the exception that South Africa lacks the efficient state bureaucracy characteristic of the Asian Tigers. An important figure in the ANC and in business circles, Saki Macozoma, believed BEE was taking the blame for not 'alleviating poverty' and benefitting an elite—in fact, precisely what it was designed to accomplish:

> Many critics of BEE accept the need to deracialize the economy, but they think that the process has 'elitist consequences'. It is not alleviating poverty, but enriching the few. What did they expect? Where have you ever seen a capitalist system producing socialist results? (Macozoma 2005).

For Macozoma, BEE represented at a minimum the 'de-racialization' of the business class, and by contributing to the creation of a bigger black middle class and more black businesses, it was positively responding to a legacy of Apartheid. In his view, blacks in management make companies more sensitive to black interests and inclined to represent themselves in ways that respond to a broader historically marginalised community. Besides, de-racialization of any sector of South African society is a step forward from a segregated racial monopoly. But many in the nationalist bourgeoisie were not convinced by this limited project. Calls for 'broad-based' BEE were adopted with the aim of 'empowering' communities and workers. When this did not produce the intended results, the government identified a 25 per cent share of company stock to be allocated to 'broad-based' representation. However, given the longstanding separation between management of capitalist enterprises and shareholders, it is debatable whether the new condition will simply benefit a few insiders who will now have access to a bigger bite of the BEE pie or really allow communities to gain access to better-quality lives.

The government passed the Employment Equity Act in 1996 and with it established a legal framework compelling employers to meet affirmative action targets that reflected demographics. This act had to define the targeted group for redress and so decided to see those previously disadvantaged as 'designated groups'—Africans, Coloureds, Indians, women and the disabled, all understood as representing degrees of past oppression. The Department of Labour would impose penalties on employers who failed to meet the requirements of the Act, based on annual reports by enterprises of more than 50 employers submitted to the department.

Although we can think of 'transformation' along a continuum of meanings, from narrow to broad, the focus on 'representivity' is how most civil society organisations and the state understood and implemented this process. This was a transformation in the first instance focused on personnel. According to the former secretary-general of the ANC, Kgalema Motlanthe, speaking on the transformation of Chapter Nine 'democracy enhancing' bodies, transformation so conceived drew a connection between racial representivity and accountability:

> The ANC is firmly of the view that, as with all state organs, those independent institutions tasked with the protection of democracy and clean government must be transformed, if they are to be able to effectively fulfil their responsibility to society. Without being representative of South African society in their composition, and without mechanisms in place for themselves to be held accountable to the people, the capacity of these institutions to serve the interests of democracy will be severely limited (Motlanthe 1998).

While Motlanthe was concerned about representivity in relation to legitimacy, the broader notion of transformation defined by the South African Police Service (SAPS) sits ironically, for that is the one department most notoriously known for its rigid implementation of strict racial quotas, even if doing so drastically undermined its capacity, effectiveness and reputation in the eyes of the public. It does, however, enable us to appreciate the breadth of different meanings within the same government and the difficulty of implementation:

> The overall process of change ... includes rationalisation and amalgamation. It further includes the transformation of policing styles, approaches, priorities, policies, cultures and attitudes whereby the South African Police Service (SAPS) becomes a community service-orientated police service aligned with values and principles such as transparency, accountability, impartiality and professionalism. It thus entails not only the transformation of the nature of the organisation, but of the very essence of policing (Van Kessel 2001).

In 2011 there was a public spat between two senior members of the ANC, Jimmy Manye and Trevor Manuel. In his opening broadside, Manye criticised the 'over-concentration' of Coloureds in the Western Cape and suggested they seek employment in other provinces. This comment had important implications for job hiring, because it dealt with how Affirmative Action ought to be implemented—that is, whether employers ought to consider national or regional demographics when hiring job seekers. Manye's issue was that there was a problem of 'representivity' in the labour force and a problem with racial distribution in the Western Cape. A similar problem presented itself with the over-representation of Indians in the KwaZulu-Natal province. Manye attacked the over-representivity of Indians in Senior Management in that province. In an open letter, Trevor Manuel attacked Manye for not understanding the history of the country or its constitution, and demanded an apology. Manuel wrote that Manye's statements treated Coloureds as 'commodities', that Coloureds were the people who first waged war against colonialism and who had made enormous sacrifices in the struggles of the UDF, which had perhaps its biggest following in the Western Cape, and that in those struggles Manye had been 'conspicuous by his absence'. Manye's behavior was racist, Manuel concluded. Further, Manye did not recognise his identity as black, preferring instead the tribalist label 'Xhosa' (Manuel 2011).

The most unnecessary of tensions is that surrounding the articulation of competing 'rights claims' within communities oppressed under Apartheid. These normally open up historical divisions and hierarchies of settler-colonial conditions, and also raise questions about how adequately these were dealt with during the nationalist struggle by all the different struggle organisations. The regularity of cases about 'unfair' job hiring keeps racial discourses circulating in the air. In one recent case, a man classified as Coloured and appropriately qualified was not given a job in the parastatal company SASOL. Another employee with lesser qualifications, classified African, was appointed instead. On appeal, the Labour Court judge ruled in favour of the company, reasoning that since Africans were the most oppressed under Apartheid, Affirmative Action practices should give preference to Africans. A familiar counter argument is that there was no basis to compare 'degrees of oppression' under Apartheid. Coloureds suffered as much as Africans and could trace their indigeneity to the Khoi and San communities in the Cape before seventeenth-century settler colonialism had enslaved them and driven them to virtual extinction. Similar cases have occurred across the board.

In the many disputed cases over transformation, one side defends its opposition by invoking 'standards' and 'tradition', while the other side complains about continuing white racism as well as new forms of racism that feed on old networks. They argue about double standards in applying institutional rules and procedures and how old institutions have retained established hierarchies by drawing on rights discourses. The areas of sport, education, and city and street name changes bring out the raw emotions around transformation. The selection of national teams in the former white-dominated sports of cricket and rugby remains embroiled in controversy two decades into democracy, because very few black players have been able to make it or have been deliberately excluded from the national teams. In these codes, team selection is highly politicised. The government and the ANC-controlled parliamentary Portfolio Committee on Sport endlessly disapprove of the stark absence of black and African players and have threatened state intervention and penalties. The major problem, everyone recognises, is how to develop young talent from an early age, especially among those who come from deprived communities, and to rebuild and develop these communities so that sport does not have to function as it now does for the working class and unemployed youth, as an 'escape' from the community because of its squalor and poverty. A better approach for the state is to consider sport as a way to uplift the community as part of a broader development of community life in material and psychological aspects.

In a strange sequel of South African Council of Sport (SACOS) arguments in the anti-Apartheid sports debate of the 1980s 'no normal sport in an abnormal society', white-dominated sporting federations, media commentators, and sports fans that oppose ANC policies demand that the ANC 'leave sport out of politics'. They complain about government interference. They lay the blame the at government for underperforming international sports teams. Progressive sports people, on the other hand, demand that instead of fixating on national team composition, the government should upgrade sports facilities at the grassroots level. The ANC's emphasis on representivity—its need to address past discrimination through team selection; its instrumental view of sport only in relation to nation-building—is too limiting an approach, they contend.

In higher education, the national middle class has focused on the number of blacks obtaining entrance into universities, as well as staff composition, while very little attention has been directed at curricula content or working-class and subaltern knowledge. The content of the Western Enlightenment, the sway of instrumental reason, disciplinary boundaries, and the traditional organisation of the academy have remained largely unquestioned and even consolidated on a more confident footing, despite the occasional call (though too often through the neo-liberal lens) to 'Africanise' these institutions. At universities, a new neo-liberal sensibility to the conception and practice of the university has channelled itself deep into the everyday psyche and behaviour. The middle class (both black and white) enclave that traditionally has been the South African university has consolidated itself. And the different universities, given the historically divided nature of higher education along racial lines, have each developed their own unique mix of different discourses—liberalism, Africanism, struggle discourses—in their interaction with ANC higher-education discourse where terms such as 'HE system', 'institutional culture', 'equity', 'quality' and 'effectiveness and efficiency' from ANC-composed neo-liberalism have come to represent the new habitus.

The quest for a continental African renaissance seemed to take the form within South Africa of changing the names of cities, towns and streets. While no doubt culturally important, these exercises became major controversies, as whites and blacks were often divided on the renaming process. Some blacks too felt alienated, as almost all the struggle heroes emanated from the ranks of the ruling party. However, it is noticeable that there is a small lane off the main thoroughfare in the city of Durban, named 'Steve Biko Lane'.

Conclusion

It is a common approach within contemporary South African politics to focus on the personalities of Mandela, Mbeki and Zuma or their policies. But instead, in this chapter I have tried to locate the post-1994 efforts of state-building, macroeconomic policies and identity politics in relation to two nationalist elite discourses of pursuing a national-modern project. I have shown how this project has alienated the subaltern masses, which is indicative of the crisis of nationalist modernism. It suggests a situation where the moral basis of rights and progress is shown to be increasingly hollow, as the subaltern continue to experience very little material improvement in their lives and remain embroiled in the politics of 'bare life'. The double standards in the behaviour of the nationalist elite are prompting this mass collective subject of the 1980s to believe less in formal politics.

Conclusion

As a 'functioning' formal liberal democratic political system, the main feature of contemporary South African politics is two contrasting modes of politics, one concentrated among the elite in civil society, the other of the subaltern mass in political society. I have argued that the failings of post-1994 democracy can be best understood by locating the development of the South African state and society historically in the settler-colonial mode of domination. I interpreted this mode as a particular variant of modernity—it introduced the nation-state, capitalism, and citizen identities based on radical difference and violence. The relationship between settler-colonial modernity and a politics of 'bare life', where vulnerable subalterns demand basic services by relying on extraordinary politics, exposes the limits of the liberal democratic promise. Settler colonialism and the anti-colonial resistance left the nationalist middle class in a crisis, having been unable to secure hegemony over the society. In their study of South African politics, conventional frameworks marginalise this history and rely on uncritical Eurocentric understandings of modernity, thus inadequately interpreting democracy in South Africa.

Let me briefly remind you of my conceptual framework, which drew on an eclectic range of influences to understand the relationship between settler-colonial modernity and the limitations of South Africa's liberal democratic promise. I developed a conceptual toolkit that articulates the critical accounts of modernity of Agamben (*homo sacer* and bare life), Foucault (biopolitics), and Arendt (refugees) on the one hand, and the mainly political analysis of Gramsci and Chatterjee (hegemony/dominance; civil society / political society) on the other. I complemented this with Fanon and Biko's critique of settler-colonial modernity. Last, I drew on Scott, who developed Fanon's analysis of the nationalist elite and wrote about the postcolonial crisis of the national-modernist project in Jamaican politics. Together these different elements allow for a conceptual framework that has helped me analyse the aporias of contemporary South African politics.

In the opening chapter I presented a descriptive mapping of democratic politics in contemporary South Africa. By identifying the important trends in its politics, we can see that politics expresses itself as battles for position, to borrow from Gramsci a concept that denotes masses struggling over moral leadership in 'trench warfare' with other fundamental and auxiliary groups. South Africa is a 'functional' democracy, and the discourses that divide along class and racial lines, with the division between rich and poor largely overlapping with 'race' identity, are expressed in two different modes of politics practised by elites and the masses, concentrated in the terrains of civil society and political society respectively. The whites and the emerging black middle class approach politics in terms of civil-society activity. The mass of poor blacks, the unemployed, the urban and rural poor, rely on mass demonstration. The 'mass demonstration' draws on idioms of struggle politics to articulate and fight for interests or, as in most cases, to obtain recognition as citizens with dignity and to respond to generations of treatment with contempt.

These trends are traceable to many immediate factors such as the inadequate improvement in material conditions and recognition of the poor, the increasing inequality gap as a result of conservative economic policies, and the institutional weaknesses of the ANC as the key unifying organisation of the nationalist struggle. Two assumptions taken for granted at the dawn of democracy, that the negotiated settlement registered a victory of the 'struggle' and that the interests of the elites and masses coincided, have now begun to unravel. This is expressed in the differing modes of politics between elites and masses and indicates the alienation of the masses amounting to a crisis of the nationalist project. The specific factors pointed to above were discussed in Chapter Seven, but these factors are themselves traceable to the subject identities of settler colonialism and the associated subaltern discourses of nationalist struggles.

That settler-colonial modernities are defined primarily by violence contradicts frameworks that are driven by the problematic faith that liberal democracy, again intimately linked to a dominant narrative of Western modernity, is and will be the political end goal of all societies, regardless of their histories. This bias, applied particularly to Africa, functions as the standard against which politics is evaluated—as represented in the modernisation and democratisation literatures associated with comparative politics—and is the target of my critique in Chapter Two. I argued there that Third Wave studies of democracy resurrect the Eurocentric biases of an earlier modernisation literature. This dominant approach simplifies the deeply layered historical processes—the violence embedded in state-building, racialised capitalist social relations of production and subject identities grounded in radical difference—that constitute these societies and also misses the internal contradictions, violence and recurring conflicts that define their politics. In South African studies it ignores the defining feature of settler colonialism as a very specific variant of modern domination, and therefore fails in its analysis to account for democracy's fragility as manifested in weak constitutionalism, dominant-party transgressions and continuing class/race/gender inequalities. Dwelling on a dominant-party thesis or the culture and values of the political elite, the Third Wave paradigm is unable to adequately explain present developments in South Africa. It is unable to see that when nationalist movements become dominant parties or when particular elite politics or elite-mass coalitions rapidly mobilise and mask themselves behind uncritical racial solidarities, these are tensions related to subject identity produced and made possible by the structural conditions born of settler-colonial society.

To establish settler-colonial modernity as a credible and central category of analysis I drew on the work of Eze, Osterhammel and Fanon. The key elements of settler-colonial modernity are violent domination, cultural contempt for native culture and the development of subject identities that are deeply antagonistic, relational and incomplete without the Other. It is impossible to understand the dynamics of settler colonialism, of which South Africa serves as the paradigmatic case, without reference to Fanon. Acknowledging that there are many different interpretations of Fanon's work, I presented my interpretation of settler colonialism as a particular type of modernity, grounded in violence and producing particular subject identities in discourse. I further expanded on the link between Fanon and South Africa, via Steve Biko's Black Consciousness (BC) ideas, showing how Fanon's analysis influenced South Africa's subaltern politics in the 1970s. I concluded that the mass mobilisations that forced the Apartheid regime into negotiations would not have been possible without Biko's BC contributing to the production of a mass political subject. Fanon explained the vulgarities of the politics after independence by referring to colonial legacies, the politics of the nationalist struggle and the damage caused to the psyche of the oppressed and oppressor. This understanding is quite different from mainstream approaches that dismiss the political, economic and psycho-cultural features that were uniquely inherited from the settler-colonial situation and the role of national resistance as it relates to subject formation. Instead it focuses entirely on the culture of the political leadership or its policies.

The historical analysis presented in Chapter Four demonstrates how South Africa is a paradigmatic case of the Manichean world Fanon spoke about—the colonial encounter further entrenched under Apartheid, the imprint on social relations stamped by racialised-capitalist development. The Fanonian framework applied to South African political and social history reveals domination without hegemony. I traced the reliance on physical violence in the historical features of modernity's birth and its organisation of civil society on the basis of race. This allowed me to more deeply grasp the pitfalls of identity that bedevil contemporary democratic politics. It also helped me to reorientate our understanding that emphasises the centrality of settler colonialism and its throwing up of particular conditions that have a bearing on democratic politics.

In Chapter Five I focused on another modern idea, nationalism, and how historically the relationship between the colonised elites and subaltern mass was fraught with tension due to the desire of the nationalist elite to dominate, control and represent 'the struggle' in ways favourable to its interests and values. The nationalist struggle is the focus of this chapter, and the relationship between the colonised elite and subaltern mass is interpreted through the familiar narrative of South African resistance history. At first oriented towards the nationalist elite, I approached the protracted struggle for nationalist liberation with respect to how this modernising class responds to dilemmas imposed, forcefully, by modernity from without, in the form of settler-colonial domination. I identified the ambiguous interests of the colonised elite in the specific settler-colonial context of South Africa, where the ANC historically represented the national bourgeoisie (as in Fanon's professional and educated middle class among the oppressed). However, eventually the nationalist elite realised that without the social power of the subaltern mass it would not be taken seriously by the colonial state, nor would it have enough power to change the balance of forces in the colonial/anti-colonial conflict. It adopted the subaltern mass as a reluctant ally—first the mass mobilisations leading up to Sharpeville, followed by the closer alliance in the 1980s—bringing about Fanon's 'decisive moment' when the nationalist elite opted for democratic transition and negotiations. These contradictions were reflected in the post-1994 period, when the ANC negotiated itself into serving middle-class and privileged interests as well as unconvincingly aiming to retain its traditional mass support through uncritical racial solidarities, repression and contempt of the 'mob', and reformist Affirmative Action and Black Economic Empowerment policies.

In Chapter Six I presented an alternative reading of the 'collapse' of the Apartheid state, the negotiations process and the emerging liberal democratic state expressing compromised majoritarian and consensus features. Instead of approaching this topic conventionally, by emphasising the ideological and tactical differences between the Apartheid government elites and those from the nationalist movement, I asked: what was in their common interest based on the elites abandoning the subalterns in the Fanonian 'decisive moment?' I identified the need of the nationalist elite to control the 'unruly mass', to redirect popular mass mobilisation into a mode of politics that was considered 'normal' and acceptable, and to embrace a particular normative form of political rationality. This form of politics, encouraged by elites from both sides, desired mass demobilisation and the subaltern to uncritically accept a discourse of rights, sovereignty and the law.

In Chapter Seven I drew from elite discourses of transformation in the post-1994 period to focus on the democratic state and its quest to 'de-racialise' state and society and how these efforts manifested in the crisis of the national-modernist project. I discussed the ANC's policies of Affirmative Action and Black Economic Empowerment, key controversies and debates surrounding the politics of identities, and the efforts of Mandela and Mbeki to address the crisis of the nationalist bourgeoisie by representing charismatic and rational-legal discourses respectively.

On a regular basis, South African politics throws up 'events', often at first glance puzzling, that directly relate to the broader arguments presented in this book. The recent, largely middle-class campaign of mainly black students protesting against the lack of transformation in higher education institutions is a case in point. In the midst of these elite protests—which garnered much media coverage, generally supportive of the student campaign to remove statues and change the names of buildings that 'caused them pain'—rapid xenophobic mobilisations in Durban and Johannesburg saw large groups of people attacking 'foreigners' and forcing them out of their homes in many townships and slum areas. Meanwhile, the other 'national stories' were the government's handling of the Marikana Commission report and the public protector's rejection of the police minister's report on Zuma's Nkandla homestead, which concluded that the president did not have to pay back any of the R246 million lavished on upgrades including a swimming pool, amphitheatre and chicken coop.

The students' protests were directly traceable to settler colonialism. At the University of Cape Town, they demanded that the overbearing statue of Rhodes, watching over the campus and thoughtfully looking out into the African continent from his central location, be removed. They emphasised that their campaign against the statue was only the tip of the iceberg. They innovatively demanded 'transformation' defined in broader terms to include not only the more superficial and usual staff-composition component, but also, and more importantly, to stimulate a debate on non-Eurocentric curriculum change. They developed upon the earlier BC viewpoint by demanding that whites 'check their privilege' when joining political campaigns and speaking more openly about white guilt and the politics of activist practices. The xenophobic attacks ended only when police and the army came in large numbers and kept attackers away from immigrant and refugee African residents of South Africa. The army and the police then embarked on an extensive anti-'criminal' campaign targeting 'illegal immigrants'. The Nkandla story has not ended. In June 2015 President Zuma told a World Economic Forum that South Africa was serious about fighting corruption; the day after, Auditor-General Kimi Makwetu pronounced that most municipalities engaged in rampant corruption to the tune of billions of rand wasted in irregular expenditure.

I highlighted the 'obviousness' of the daily life of racial division in South Africa and said that this was traceable to the specificity of settler-colonial modernity. Yet, for less obvious reasons, the term 'settler colonial' has received little attention in the academic study of South African politics. Why? It causes discomfort among whites, and many black South Africans, too. And this is not unrelated to its use in the empirical political world, where it has a certain notoriety, having been associated in the early 1990s with the Pan Africanist Congress (PAC) slogan, 'One settler, one bullet'. There is little doubt that it was used descriptively and analytically in the hands of Mda, Lembede and Sobukwe, all great leaders and intellectuals in the nationalist struggle, and all of whom envisaged a non-racial and democratic post-Apartheid society. However, as used by younger activists and in desperation when the PAC was losing support and terribly factionalised, slogans such as 'one settler, one bullet' contributed towards 'settler colonialism' taking on the connotations of 'hate speech.' It was meant to declare that white South Africans did not belong to the political community of South Africa, hence the discomfort.

The term 'settler colonialism' has thus been used to indicate 'who belongs' and who does not belong to the political community in South Africa. I did not use it in this sense in this book. I believe that political communities, such as the modern nation, are historically constituted in the 'imagination'—they are, as Anderson (1991) persuasively argued, 'imagined communities'. It should be obvious that white South Africans, after three centuries of settlement, played a significant role in the historical constitution of the modern South African political community. It is impossible to imagine a

South African nation without them. Rather, I used 'settler-colonial modernity' to refer to a type or path of modernity. It answers the questions, 'How did the society travel the road to the modern?' or 'How did previous modes of domination end?' In South Africa, the state, the nation and its modern identity came from colonial conquest and the organisation of social relations on the basis of 'native' and 'settler', and it is grounded in violence. The identities of the members who make up the *polis* comes out of this relational experience to the Other.

A study about a particular historical conjuncture of this relatively minor global player may perhaps seem insignificant for our accumulated knowledge. Yet it does have distinctive features that make it meaningful. The South African case offers an important lens through which to observe the global story of modernity. The key questions of modernity—the process Marx describes as 'all that is solid melts into the air'—play themselves out in this part of the world starkly, visibly and violently. The multiple and contradictory manifestations of the modern state, capitalist accumulation and the assertion of dominant identities and values all trouble as well as fascinate. If liberal democracies do not radically confront their histories and legacies—i.e., the historical production of subject identities under conditions of violence—will citizens ever be able to see each other on equal terms and deserving the same rights? The broader question is whether the imperatives of liberal democracy and settler-colonial history can be reconciled. Can South Africans leave behind the historical baggage of race identity, and what kind of political system and political culture best makes this possible?

Rather than avoiding the pathological features of South Africa's modern pathway or its 'beginnings' of modernity, it seems better to confront them head on. And in good Hegelian and Fanonian fashion, it is possible to achieve brightness from darkness, a lotus flower from the mud and true freedom and true humanity from racial and class indignity and oppression. The first step is to be the person who questions.

References

Unpublished sources

Groote Schuur Minute. 1990. *Working Group Established under Paragraph 1 of the Groote Schuur Minute*. Nordic Africa Institute, Uppsala, Pamphlet Collection, South Africa: ANC. (Box No. 30).

Van Kessel, I. 2001. *Transforming the South African Police Service (SAPS): The Changing Meaning of Change*. 1–4 July. Paper presented to the South African Sociological Association Congress Sunnyside Campus, UNISA, Pretoria.

Published sources

Adam, H. 1971. *Modernizing Racial Domination: South Africa's Political Dynamics*, Berkeley: University of California Press.

Adam, H. 1996. 'The Mandela Personality Cult.' *Indicator South Africa* 13(2): 7–12.

Adam, H. 1999. 'Corporatism as Minority Veto Under ANC Hegemony in South Africa.' In Giliomee, H. and Simkins, C., eds. *The Awkward Embrace: One Party Dominance and Democracy*. Cape Town: Tafelberg, pp. 261–280.

Adam, H., et al. 1998. *Comrades in Business: Post-Liberation Politics in South Africa*. Utrecht: International Books.

Adhikari, M. 2009. *Burdened by Race: Coloured Identities in Southern Africa*. Cape Town: Juta and Company Ltd.

African National Congress. 2002. ANC 51st National Conference Secretary General's Report. [Online]. [Accessed 20 March 2012]. Available from: http://www.anc.org.za/show.php?id=2494.

African National Congress. 2011. ANC Report on the State of the Organisation by ANC Secretary General Gwede Mantash. [Online]. [Accessed 20 March 2012]. Available from: http://www.anc.org.za.

African National Congress. 1969. Strategy and Tactics: Morogoro. [Online]. [Accessed 20 March 2012]. Available from: http://www.anc.org.za.

African National Congress. 1996. 'The State and Social Transformation.' [Online]. [Accessed 20 March 2012]. Available from: https://amadlandawonye.wikispaces.com/1998,+ANC,+State,+Property+Relations,+Social+Transformation.

African National Congress. 1998. The State, Property Relations and Social Transformation: A Discussion Paper towards the Alliance Summit. *Umrabulo* 5. [Online]. [Accessed 15 January 2011]. Available from: https://amadlandawonye.wikispaces.com.

African National Congress Youth League. 1944. League Manifesto. [Online]. [Accessed 12 March 2009]. Available from: http://www.anc.org.za/show.php?id=4439.

Agamben, G. 1998. *Homo Sacer: Sovereign Power and Bare Life*. Stanford, CA: Stanford University Press.

Agamben, G. 2005. *State of Exception*. Chicago: University of Chicago Press.

Agamben, G. 2011. 'Introductory Note on the Concept of Democracy.' In Agamben, G. ed. *Democracy in What State?* New York: Columbia University Press, pp. 1–5.

Ake, C. 1991. 'Rethinking African Democracy.' *Journal of Democracy*, 2(1), pp. 32–44.

Alexander, N. 2007. 'Affirmative Action and the Perpetuation of Racial Identities in Post-Apartheid South Africa.' *Transformation* 63, pp. 1–17.

Alexander, N. 2002. *An Ordinary Country: Issues in Transition from Apartheid to Democracy in South Africa*. New York: Berghahn Books.

Alexander, P. et al. 2013. *Marikana: Voices from South Africa's Mining Massacre*. Athens, OH: Ohio University Press.

Alexander, P. 2010. 'Rebellion of the Poor: South Africa's Service Delivery Protests—A Preliminary Analysis.' *Review of African Political Economy* 27(123), pp. 25–40.

Almond, G.A. and Coleman, J.S. 1960. *The Politics of the Developing Areas*. Princeton, NJ: Princeton University Press.

Althusser, L. 1971. *Lenin and Philosophy and Other Essays*, New York: Monthly Review Press.

Arendt, H. 1986. *The Origins of Totalitarianism*. London: Andre Deutsch.

Armstrong, J. C. and Worden, N.A. 1989. 'The Slaves 1652–1834.' In Elphick, R. and Giliomee, H. eds. *The Shaping of South African Society, 1652–1840*. Cape Town: Maskew Miller Longman, pp. 107–183.

Ballard, R. 2005. Globalization, Marginalization and Contemporary Social Movements in South Africa. *African Affairs* 104(417), pp. 615–634.

BBC. 2008. *Death Toll Climbs in SA Violence*. [Online]. 27 May. [Accessed 31 January 2012]. Available from: http://news.bbc.co.uk/2/hi/africa/7420708.stm.

BBC. 2008. *Thousands Flee S Africa Attacks*. [Online]. 19 May. [Accessed 19 May 2008]. Available from: News.bbc.co.uk/1/hi/7407914.stm.

Beinart, W. 2001. *Twentieth-Century South Africa*. Cape Town: Oxford University Press.

Bendix, R. 1964. *Nation Building and Citizenship*. New York: Wiley.

Berlin, I. 2000. *The Proper Study of Mankind: An Anthology of Essays*. Hardy, H. and Hausheer, R. eds. New York: Farrar, Straus and Giroux.

Berman, M. 1988. *All That is Solid Melts into Air: The Experience of Modernity*. London: Penguin.

Bhabha, H. 1987. 'What Does the Black Man Want?' *New Formations* 1, pp. 118–124.

Bhabha, H. 2004. *The Location of Culture*. New York: Routledge.

Biko, S. 2005. *I Write What I Like*. Johannesburg: Picador.

Bill, J.A. and Hardgrave, R.L. 1981. 'The Quest for Theory.' *Comparative Politics: The Quest for Theory* 36(1), pp. 262–263.

Bond, P. 2001. *Against Global Apartheid: South Africa Meets the World Bank, IMF and International Finance*. Cape Town: UCT Press.

Bond, P. 2000. *Elite Transition: From Apartheid to Neoliberalism in South Africa*. London: Pluto Press and University of Natal Press.

Bond, P. 2009. 'Power in Pretoria?' Reply to R.W. Johnson. *New Left Review* 58, pp. 77–88.

Bond, P. 2010. 'South Africa's Bubble Meets Boiling Urban Social Protest.' *Monthly Review* 62(2), pp. 17–28.

Bond, P. 2011. 'South African Splinters: From "Elite Transition" to "Small-a Alliances".' *Review of African Political Economy* 38(127), pp. 113–121.

Boucek, F. 2009. 'Rethinking Factionalism: Typologies, Intra-Party Dynamics and Three Faces of Factionalism.' *Party Politics* 15(4), pp. 455–485.

Boyle, S.T. and Bunie, A. 2005. *Paul Robeson: The Years of Promise and Achievement*. Amherst, MA: University of Massachusetts Press.

Bozzoli, B. and Delius, P. 1990. 'Radical History and South African Society.' In Bozzoli, B. and Delius, P. eds. *History from South Africa*. East Haven, CT: The Radical Historians' Organization, pp. 13–45.

Brooks, H. 2004. *The Dominant Party System: Challenges for South Africa's Second Decade of Democracy*. Johannesburg: EISA.

Butler, A. 2008. *Cyril Ramaphosa*. Oxford: James Currey.

Butler, A. 2010. 'What May Hide in ANC "Factionalism" Crackdown.' *Business Day*. [Online]. 8 February. [Accessed 21 March 2011]. Available from: http://www.bdlive.co.za.

Cabral, A. 1979. *Unity and Struggle: Speeches and Writings of Amilcar Cabral*. New York: Monthly Review Press.

Camus, A. 2013. *Algerian Chronicles*. Boston, MA: Belknap Press.

Chakrabarty, D. 2000. *Provincializing Europe: Postcolonial Thought and Historical Difference*. Princeton, NJ: Princeton University Press.

Chatterjee, P. 1999. *The Partha Chatterjee Omnibus: The Nation and its Fragments*. New Delhi: Oxford University Press.

Chatterjee, P. 2004. *The Politics of the Governed: Reflections on Popular Politics in Most of the World*. New York: Columbia University Press.

Chilcote, R.H. 1994. In *Theories of Comparative Politics: The Search for a Paradigm Reconsidered*. Boulder: Westview Press, pp. 81–126.

Chipkin, I. 2007. *Do South Africans Exist? Nationalism, Democracy and the Identity of 'The People'*. Johannesburg: Wits University Press.

Clapham, C. 1985. *Third World Politics: An Introduction*. London: Croom Helm.

Cohen, J.L. and Arato, A. 1994. *Civil Society and Political Theory*. Cambridge, MA: MIT Press.

Comaroff, J.L. 2010. 'Reflections on the Colonial State, in South Africa and Elsewhere: Factions, Fragments, Facts and Fictions.' *Social Identities: Journal for the Study of Race, Nation and Culture* 4(3), pp. 321–361.

Cosatu. 2005. A Developmental State for South Africa? [Online]. [Accessed 15 June 2012]. Available from: https://amadlandawonye.wikispaces.com/SA+development al+state+query,+COSATU+CC,+2005.

Cronin, J. 1992. 'The Boat, the Tap and the Leipzig Way.' *African Communist*. Third Quarter 130. [Online]. [Accessed 27 July 2015]. Available from: https://www.nelsonmandela.org/omalley/index.php/site/q/03lv02424/04lv02730/05lv03005/06lv03006/07lv03030/08lv03039.htm.

Crush, J. 2000. 'The Dark Side of Democracy: Migration, Xenophobia and Human Rights in South Africa.' *International Migration* 38(6), pp. 103–133.

Crush, J. 2008. *The Perfect Storm: the Realities of Xenophobia in Contemporary South Africa*. Cape Town: IDASA.

Davenport, T.R.H. 1977. *South Africa: a Modern History*. Toronto: University of Toronto Press.

De Jager, N. and Du Toit, P. 2013. *Friend or Foe? Dominant Party Systems in Southern Africa: Insights from the Developing World*. Cape Town: UCT Press.

De Kiewiet, C. 1941. *A History of South Africa*. London: Oxford University Press.

Du Bois, W.E.B. 2008. *The Souls of Black Folk*. Rockville, MD: Arc Manor LLC.

Du Plessis, C. 2013. *Zuma: Don't Think Like Africans in Africa*. Citizen Alert ZA. [Online]. 22 October. [Accessed 27 July 2015]. Available from: http://citizenalertzablogspotcom-tango.blogspot.co.uk/2013/10/zuma-dont-think-like-africans-in-africa.html.

Dussel, E. 1998. *The Underside of Modernity: Apel, Ricoeur, Rorty, Taylor and the Phi-*

losophy of Liberation. New York: Humanity Books.

Easton, D. 1957. 'An Approach to the Study of Political Systems. *World Politics* 9(3), pp. 383–400.'

Easton, D. 1965. *A Systems Analysis of Political Life*. New York: Wiley

Eckstein, H. 1963. 'A Perspective on Comparative Politics: Past and Present.' In Eckstein, H. and Apter, D. eds. *Comparative Politics: A Reader*, Glencoe: Free Press of Glencoe, pp. 3–32.

Ekeh, P. 1975. 'Colonialism and the Two Publics in Africa: a Theoretical Statement.' *Comparative Studies in Society and History* 17(1), pp. 91–112.

Everatt, D. 1992. 'Alliance Politics of a Special Type: The Roots of the ANC/SACP Alliance, 1950–1954.' *Journal of Southern African Studies*, 18(1), pp. 19–39.

Eze, E.C. ed. 1997. *Postcolonial African Philosophy: A Critical Reader*. Oxford: Blackwell.

Fabricius, P. 2013. 'A Gaffe of Continental Proportions. IOL.' [Online]. 29 October. [Accessed 14 August 2015]. Available from: http://www.iol.co.za/news/a-gaffe-of-continental-proportions-1.1598989#.Vc8aV7cxXuQ.

Fanon, F. 1963. *The Wretched of the Earth*. New York: Grove Press.

Fanon, F. 1986. *Black Skin, White Masks*. London: Pluto Press.

Fatton Jnr. R. 1986. *Black Consciousness in South Africa: The Dialectic of Ideological Resistance to White Supremacy*. New York: SUNY Press.

Ferguson, K. 1993. *The Man Question: Visions of Subjectivity in Feminist Theory*. Berkeley CA: University of California Press.

Forman, L. 1960. *From the Notebooks of Lionel Forman: Black and White in S.A. History*. Cape Town: Real Print and Publishing.

Foucault, M. 1980. *Power/Knowledge: Selected Interviews and Other Writings, 1972–1977*. New York: Pantheon Books.

Foucault, M. and Rabinow, P. 1984. *The Foucault Reader*. New York: Pantheon.

Foucault, M. 1990. *The History of Sexuality, Vol. 1: An Introduction*. Reissue edition. New York: Vintage.

Foucault, M. 1994. *The Order of Things: An Archeology of the Human Sciences*. Reissue edition. New York: Vintage.

Foucault, M. 1995. *Discipline and Punish: The Birth of the Prison*. 2nd ed. New York: Vintage.

Friedman, S. 1999. 'No Easy Stroll to Dominance: Party Dominance, Opposition and Civil Society in South Africa.' In Giliomee, H. and Simkins, C. eds. *The Awkward Embrace One Party Dominance and Democracy*. Cape Town: Tafelberg, pp. 97–126.

Friedman, S. and Atkinson, D. 1994. *The Small Miracle: South Africa's Negotiated Settlement*. Johannesburg: Ravan Press.

Fukuyama, F. 1989. 'The End of History?' *The National Interest*. Summer 1989, pp. 3–18.

Geertz, C. 1980. *Negara: The Theatre State in Nineteenth-Century Bali*. Princeton, NJ: Princeton University Press.

Gerhart, G. 1978. *Black Power in South Africa: The Evolution of an Ideology*. Berkeley, CA: University of California Press.

Karis, T.G. and Carter, G.M. eds. 1977. *From Protest to Challenge: A Documentary History of African Politics in South Africa, 1882–1964*. Vol. IV. Stanford, CA: Hoover Institution Press.

Gerschenkron, A. 1962. *Economic Backwardness in Historical Perspective*. Cambridge, MA: Harvard University Press.

Gevisser, M. 2007. *Thabo Mbeki: The Dream Deferred*. Johannesburg: Jonathan Ball.

Gibson, N.C. 2011. *Fanonian Practices in South Africa*. Durban: University of KwaZulu Natal Press.

Giliomee, H. 1995. 'Democratization in South Africa.' *Political Science Quarterly* 110(1), pp. 83–104.

Giliomee, H.B. 2003. 'The Making of the Apartheid Plan: 1929–1948.' *Journal of Southern African Studies* 29(2), pp. 373–392.

Giliomee, H.B. 2010. *The Afrikaners: Biography of a People*. Charlottesville, VA: University of Virginia Press.

Giliomee, H.B. and Schlemmer, L. 1989. *Negotiating South Africa's Future*. London: Macmillan Publishers Limited.

Gilroy, P. 1993. *The Black Atlantic: Modernity and Double Consciousness*. Cambridge, MA: Harvard University Press.

Gordon, C. 1980. Afterword. In Foucault, M. *Power/Knowledge*. New York: Pantheon.

Gramsci, A. 1971. *Selections from the Prison Notebooks*. Hoare, Q. and Smith, G.N. eds. New York: International Publishers Co.

Grant, L. 2014. 'Research Shows Sharp Increase in Service Delivery Protests.' *The Mail and Guardian Online*. [Online] 12 February. [Accessed 22 February 2014]. Available from: http://mg.co.za/article/2014-02-12-research-shows-sharp-increase-in-service-delivery-protests.

Greenstein, F.I. and Polsby N. W. eds.1975. *Macropolitical Theory: Handbook of Political Science Volume* 3. New York: Addison-Wesley.

Grobler, F. 2009. 'Service-delivery Protests a "Warning Sign" for Government.' *The Mail and Guardian Online*. [Online]. 20 July. [Accessed 15 February 2014]. Available at: http://mg.co.za/article/2009-07-20-servicedelivery-protests-a-warning-sign-for-govt.

Guha, R. 1997. *Dominance without Hegemony: History and Power in Colonial India*. Cambridge, MA: Harvard University Press.

Gunner, L. 2008. 'Jacob Zuma, the Social Body and the Unruly Power of Song.' *African Affairs* 108(430), pp. 27–48.

Hagopian, F. 2000. 'Political Development Revisited.' *Comparative Political Studies* 33(6-7), pp. 880–911.

Halisi, C.R.D. 1999. *Black Political Thought in the Making of South African Democracy*. Bloomington, IN: Indiana University Press.

Hall, S. et al. eds. 1996. *Modernity: An Introduction to Modern Societies*. Cambridge, MA: Blackwell.

Hall, S. 1996. 'The West and the Rest.' In Hall, S. et al. eds. *Modernity: An Introduction to Modern Societies*. Cambridge, MA: Blackwell, pp.184–227.

Hassen, E. 1998. *The Soul of a Nation*. Cape Town: Oxford University Press.

Hirson, B. 1979. *Year of Fire, Year of Ash*. London: Zed Press.

Horrell, M. 1968. *Bantu Education to 1968*. Cape Town: South African Institute of Race Relations.

Hough, M. 2008. 'Violent Protest at Local Government in South Africa.' Revolutionary Potential? *Scientia Militaria: South African Journal of Military Studies* 36(1), pp. 1–13.

Huntington, S.P. 1965. 'Political Development and Political Decay.' *World Politics* 17(3), pp. 386–430.

Huntington, S.P. 1968. *Political Order in Changing Society*. New Haven: Yale University Press.

Huntington, S.P. 1987. 'The Goals of Development.' In Weiner, M. and Huntington, S.P. eds. *Understanding Political Development*. Boston, MA: Little Brown and Co, pp. 3–32.

Huntington, S.P. 1991. *The Third Wave: Democratization in the Late 20th Century*. London: University of Oklahoma Press.

Innes, D. 1984. *Anglo-American and the Rise of Modern South Africa*. Johannesburg: Ravan Press.

IOL Online. 2009. 'Blu-Light Car Blamed as Pedestrian Killed.' *IOL Online*. [Online]. 2 February. [Accessed 5 September 2010]. Available from: http://www.iol.co.za/news/south-africa/blue-light-car-blamed-as-pedestrian-killed-1.432995#.VWyv9eexyi4.

James, A. B. and Hardgrave, R.L. 1981. *Comparative Politics: The Quest for Theory*. Landam, MD: Bell and Howard Company.

Jansen, J. 2010. 'Sing of Life or Sing of Death.' *The Times*. 7 April 2010.

Jessop, B. 1982. *The Capitalist State: Marxist Theories and Methods*. New York: New York University Press.

Johnson, R.W. 2009. 'False Start in South Africa.' *New Left Review*. 58(July–August), pp. 61–74.

Johnstone, F. 1970. 'White Prosperity and White Supremacy in South Africa Today.' *African Affairs* 69(275), pp. 124–140.

Jones, M. and Mtyala, Q. 2010. 'PIC: Zuma Cops Lock Up Jogger.' *IOL Online*. [Online]. 17 February. [Accessed 25 November 2011]. Available from: http://www.iol.co.za/news/politics/pic-zuma-cops-lock-up-jogger-1.473729#.UyZ2L1742UY.

Kadalie, C. 1970. *My Life and the ICU: The Autobiography of a Black Trade Unionist in South Africa*. New York: Humanities Press.

Kalyvas, A. 2009. *Democracy and the Politics of the Extraordinary: Max Weber, Carl Schmitt, and Hannah Arendt*. Cambridge, England: Cambridge University Press.

Kane-Berman, J. 2012. 'ANC Knows Delivery Protests Signify a Broader Popular Revolt.' *Business Day*. [Online]. 6 August. [Accessed 11 May 2013]. Available from: http://www.bdlive.co.za/articles/2010/05/24/john-kane-berman-anc-knows-delivery-protests-signify-a-broader-popular-revolt.

Kane-Berman, J. 1978. *Soweto: Black Revolt, White Reaction*. Johannesburg: Ravan Press.

Karamoko, J. and Jain, H. 2011. 'Community Protests in South Africa: Trends, Analysis and Explanations.' *Multi-Level Government Initiative*. [Online]. [Accessed 25 November 2012]. Available from: http://www.mlgi.org.za/publications/publications-by-theme/local-government-in-south-africa/community-protests/Community_Protests_SA.pdf.

Kasfir, N. 1998. *Civil Society and Democracy in Africa: Critical Perspectives*. Portland, OR: Frank Cass.

Kaufman, S. 2012. 'The End of Apartheid: Rethinking South Africa's "Peaceful Transition".' [Online]. [Accessed 12 October 2013]. Available at: https://www.sas.upenn.edu/polisci/sites/www.sas.upenn.edu.polisci/files/kaufman.pdf.

Kaviraj, S. 2000. 'Modernity and Politics in India.' *Daedalus* 129(1), pp. 137–162.

Kaviraj, S. 2009. 'The Post-colonial State: The Special Case of India.' *Critical Encounters*. [Online]. [Accessed 13 May 2010]. Available from: http://criticalencounters.net/2009/01/19/the-post-colonial-state-sudipta-kaviraj.

Kaviraj, S. and Khilnani, S. eds. 2001. *Civil Society: History and Possibilities*. Cambridge, England: Cambridge University Press.

Kayser, R. and Adhikari, M. 2004. 'Land and Liberty: The African Peoples Democratic Union of Southern Africa During the 1960s.' In South African Democracy Education Trust. eds. *The Road to Democracy in South Africa: 1960–1970*. Johannesburg: Zebra, pp. 319–339.

Keegan, T. 1997. *Colonial South Africa: Origins Racial Order*. London: Continuum.

Keegan, T. 1996. *Colonial South Africa and the Origins of the Racial Order*. London: Leicester University Press.

Keniston, B. 2014. *Choosing to be Free: The Life Story of Rick Turner*. Johannesburg: Jacana.

Kesselman, M. 1973. 'Order or Movement? The Literature of Political Development as Ideology.' *World Politics*, 26(01), pp. 139–154.

Kgosana, C. 2009. 'SACP Slams Malema.' *IOL Online*. [Online]. 24 August. [Accessed 14 March 2014]. Available from: http://www.iol.co.za/news/politics/sacp-slams-malema-1.456095#.UyMB5YVqP_Q.

Khoapa, B.A. 1972. *Black Review 1972*. Durban: Black Community Programmes.

Koeble, T. 1998. *The Global Economy and Democracy in South Africa*. New Jersey: Rutgers University Press.

Kohli, A. 1990. *Democracy and Discontent: India's Growing Crisis of Governability*. Cambridge, England: Cambridge University Press.

Krasner, S.D. 1984. 'Approaches to the State: Alternative Conceptions and Historical Dynamics.' *Comparative Politics* 16(2), pp. 223–246.

Kuhn, T.S. 1970. *The Structure of Scientific Revolutions*. Chicago: University of Chicago Press.

La Capra, D. 1983. *Rethinking Intellectual History: Texts Contexts Language*. Ithaca, NY: Cornell University Press.

Laclau, E. & Mouffe, C. 2001. *Hegemony and Socialist Strategy: Towards a Radical Democratic Politics*. London: Verso.

Lane, J.E. & Ersson, S. 1997. 'The Probability of Democratic Success in South Africa.' *Democratization* 4(4), pp. 1–15.

Lasswell, H.D. 1968. 'The Future of the Comparative Method.' *Comparative Politics* 1(1), pp. 3–18.

Latour, B. 1993. *We Have Never Been Modern*. Cambridge, MA: Harvard University Press.

Legassick, M. 1974. 'Legislation, Ideology and Economy in Post-1948 South Africa.' *Economy and Society* 3(3), pp. 5–35.

Lembede, A. 1996. *Freedom in Our Lifetime: The Collected Writings of Anton Muziwakhe Lembede*. Edgar, R. and Ka Msumza, L. eds. Athens, OH: Ohio University Press.

Lenin, V. I. 1999. *Imperialism: The Highest Stage of Capitalism*. Sydney: Resistance Books.

Leon, T. & Mbeki, T. 2000. 'HIV/AIDS: Thabo Mbeki vs Tony Leon.' *Politicsweb*. [Online]. [Accessed 13 January 2011] Available from: http://www.politicsweb.co.za/news-and-analysis/hivaids-thabo-mbeki-vs-tony-leon.

Lipton, M. 1986. *Capitalism and Apartheid: South Africa, 1910–1986*. Aldershot, England: Wildwood House.

Lodge, T. 1983. *Black Politics in South Africa Since 1945*. New York: Longman.

Lodge, T. 1992. 'The African National Congress in the 1990's.' In Moss, G. and Obery, I. eds. *South African Review 6: From 'Red Dawn' to Codesa*. Johannesburg: Ravan Press, pp. 44–78.

Lodge, T. 1998. 'Poltical Corruption in South Africa.' *African Affairs* 97(387), pp. 157–187.

Lodge, T. 1999. *Consolidating Democracy: South Africa's Second Popular Election*. Johannesburg: Electoral Institute of South Africa and the Witwatersrand University Press.

Lodge, T. 2009. The Zuma Tsunami: South Africa's Succession Politics. *Representation* 45(2), pp. 125–141.

Lukes, S. 1986. *Power*. New York: New York University Press.

Lundahl, M. 1999. *Growth or Stagnation? South Africa Heading for the Year 2000*. London: Ashgate Publishers.

Macey, D. 2000. *Frantz Fanon: A Life*. London: Granta.

Maharaj, M. 2008. 'The ANC and South Africa's Negotiated Transition to Democracy and Peace.' [Online]. [Accessed 13 August

2010]. Available from: http://www.berghof-conflictresearch.org/documents/publications/transitions_anc.pdf.

Makgethla, N. 2005. 'A Developmental State for South Africa?' *Cosatu*. [Online]. [Accessed 30 December 2006]. Available from: https://amadlandawonye.wikispaces.com/SA+developmental+state+query,+COSATU+CC,+2005.

Mamdani, M. 1996. *Citizen and Subject: Contemporary Africa and the Legacy of Late Colonialism*. London: James Curry.

Mandela, N. 1994. Inaugural Speech. [Online]. [Accessed 6 December 2012] Available from: http://www.africa.upenn.edu/Articles_Gen/Inaugural_Speech_17984.html.

Mandela, N. 1994. *Long Walk To Freedom: The Autobiography of Nelson Mandela*. New York: Random House.

Mandela, N. 1964. 'I am Prepared to Die.' In Sheridan Johns and R. Hunt Davis Jr., ed., *Mandela, Tambo and the African National Congress* (New York: Oxford University Press, 1991), pp. 115–33.

Manuel, T. 2011. 'Trevor Manuel's Open Letter to Jimmy Manyi.' *IOL Online*. [Online]. [Accessed 14 March 2014]. Available from: http://www.iol.co.za/news/politics/trevor-manuel-s-open-letter-to-jimmy-manyi-1.1034606#.UyMElYVqP_Q.

Marais, H. 1998. *South Africa: The Limits to Change*. London: Zed Books.

Marks, S. 1986. *The Ambiguities of Dependence in South Africa: Class, Nationalism, and the State in Twentieth-Century Natal*. Baltimore, MD: John Hopkins University Press.

Marks, S. and Trapido, S. eds. 1987. *The Politics of Race, Class and Nationalism in Twentieth Century South Africa*. New York: Longman.

Martineau, J. 2009. *The Life and Correspondence of the Right Hon. Sir Bartle Frere, Bart., G.C.B., F.R.S., Etc.: (V.1) (1895)*. New York: Cornell University Library.

Marx, K. and Engels, F. 1978. *The Marx-Engels Reader*. Tucker, R. C. ed. New York: W.W. Norton.

Mazower, M. 2013. *Governing the World: The History of an Idea, 1815 to the Present*. London: Penguin Books.

Mbeki, T. 1999. 'South Africa: Two Nations.' In Hadland, A. and Rantao, J. ed. *The Life and Times of Thabo Mbeki*. Rivonia. Johannesburg: Zebra Press, pp. 184–193.

Mbeki, T. 1999. Mbeki Speech at the Opening of Parliament, 1999. [Online]. [Accessed 12 May 2012]. Available from: http://www.dfa.gov.za/docs/speeches/mbeki.htm#1999.

Mbeki, T. 2004. 'Aluta Continua!' *ANC Today*. 47(26 November to 2 December). [Online]. [Accessed 12 May 2012] http://www.anc.org.za/docs/anctoday/2004/at47.htm#preslet.

Mbeki, T. 2007. I am an African. [Online]. [Accessed 12 May 2012] Available from: http://www.anc.org.za/show.php?id=4322.

Mbembe, A. 2012. 'The Spear that Divided the Nation.' *Amandla*. [Online]. [Accessed 6 September 2013]. Available from: http://www.brettmurray.co.za/the-spear-opinions/26-may-2012-amandla-magazine-professor-mbembe-the-spear-that-divide-a-nation/.

Mda, A.P. 1947. The Late A.M.Lembede, MA (Phil), LLB. Ilanga Yase Natal, September 27. [Online]. [Accessed 6 September 2011]. Available from: http://pzacad.pitzer.edu/NAM/newafrre/writers/lembede/lembedeS.htm.

Melber, H. 2009. 'Southern African Liberation Movements as Governments and the Limits to Liberation.' *Review of African Political Economy* 36(121), pp. 451–459.

Migdal, J.S. 1988. *Strong Societies and Weak States: State-Society Relations and State Capabilities in the Third World*. Princeton, NJ: Princeton University Press.

Migdal, J.S. 1983. 'Studying the Politics of Development and Change: The State of the Art.' In Finifter, A. W. ed. *Political Science: The State of the Discipline*. Washington D.C., VA: American Political Science Association, pp. 309–338.

Migdal, J.S.1994. 'The State in Society: An Approach to Struggles for Domination.' In Migdal, J.S. et al. eds *State Power and Social Forces: Domination and Transformation in the Third World*. Cambridge, England: Cambridge University Press, pp. 7–34.

Mirsepassi, A. 2000. *Intellectual Discourse and the Politics of Modernization: Negotiating Modernity in Iran*, Cambridge, England: Cambridge University Press.

Mitchell, T. ed. 2000. *Questions of Modernity*. Minneapolis, MN: University of Minnesota Press.

Mngxitama, A. 2009. 'We Are Not All Like That: Race, Class and Nation After Apartheid.' In Hassim, S. et al. eds. *Go Home or Die Here: Violence, Xenophobia and the Reinvention of Difference*, Johannesburg: Wits University Press, pp.189–205.

Monare, M. 2006. 'Vavi Moves on "Plot to Kill Him".' *IOL Online*. [Online]. 17 August. [Accessed 14 March 2014] Available from: http://www.iol.co.za/news/politics/vavi-moves-on-plot-to-kill-him-1.289787#.UyMAeIVqP_Q.

Moore, B. 1993. *Social Origins of Dictatorship and Democracy: Lord and Peasant in the Making of the Modern World*. Boston: Beacon Press.

Motlhabi, M.B.G. 1984. *The Theory and Practice of Black Resistance to Apartheid: A Social-Ethical Analysis*. Johannesburg: Skotaville Publishers.

Munck, G.L. and Snyder, R. eds. 2007. *Passion, Craft, and Method in Comparative Politics*. Baltimore, MD: Johns Hopkins University Press.

Murray, B. 2012. *The Spear Opinions*. [Online]. [Accessed 16 February 2013]. Available from: http://www.brettmurray.co.za/the-spear-opinions/.

Murray, M. 1987. *South Africa: Time of Agony, Time of Destiny: The Upsurge of Popular Protest*. London: Verso.

Naipaul, N. 2010. 'How Nelson Mandela Betrayed Us, Says Ex-wife Winnie.' *London Evening Standard*. [Online]. 8 March. [Accessed 14 August 2015]. Available from: http://www.standard.co.uk/news/how-nelson-mandela-betrayed-us-says-ex-wife-winnie-6734116.html.

Nash, A. 1999. 'Mandela's Democracy.' *Monthly Review* 50 (11 April). [Online]. [Accessed 27 July 2015]. Available from: http://archive.monthlyreview.org/index.php/mr/article/view/MR-050-11-1999-04_2.

Ndebele, N. 2009. 'Of Pretence and Protest.' *The Mail and Guardian Online*. [Online]. 23 September. [Accessed 17 March 2014]. Available from: http://mg.co.za/article/2009-09-23-of-pretence-and-protest.

Ndenze, B. et al. 2015. 'Still Blowing Cash.' *The Times*. [Online]. 4 June. [Accessed 17 June 2012]. Available from: http://www.timeslive.co.za/thetimes/2015/06/04/Still-blowing-cash.

Neocosmos, M. 2006. *From 'Foreign Natives' to 'Native Foreigners': Explaining Xenophobia in Post Apartheid South Africa: Citizenship and Nationalism, Identity and Politics*. Dakar, Senegal: Codesria.

Neocosmos, M. 1998. '"From Peoples" Politics to State Politics: Aspects of National Liberation in South Africa.' In Olukoshi, A. ed. *The Politics of Opposition in Contemporary Africa*. Uppsala: Nordic Africa Institute, pp. 195–241.

News24. 2014. 'Zuma Vows ANC Will Rule "Forever".' *News24*. [Online]. 8 December. [Accessed 17 May 2015]. Available from:

http://www.news24.com/SouthAfrica/Politics/Zuma-vows-ANC-will-rule-forever-20140108.

OAU. 1989. ANC Harare Declaration. [Online]. [Accessed 12 June 2011]. Available from: http://www.anc.org.za/show.php?id=3856.

Odendaal, A. 1984. *Vukani Bantu! The Beginnings of Black Protest Politics in South Africa to 1912*. Cape Town: David Philip.

O' Meara, D, 1997. *Forty Lost Years: The Apartheid State and the Politics of the National Party, 1948-1994*. Johannesburg: Ravan Press.

O' Meara, D. 1982. 'The 1946 African Mine Workers Strike and the Political Economy of South Africa.' In M. Murray, ed. *South African Capitalism and Black Political Opposition*. London: Schenkman, pp. 361-396.

Osterhammel, J. 1997. *Colonialism: A Theoretical Overview*. Princeton, NJ: Markus Wiener Publication.

Ottaway, M. 1991. 'Liberation Movements and Transition to Democracy: The Case of the ANC.' *Journal of Modern African Studies* 29(1), pp. 61–82.

Owen, K. 2009. 'Excesses of a Damaged Generation.' *Business Day Live*. [Online]. 22 September. [Accessed 15 March 2014]. Available from: http://www.bdlive.co.za/articles/2009/09/22/excesses-of-a-damaged-generation.

Parsons, T. 1968. *The Structure of Social Action: A Study in Social Theory with Special Reference to a Group of Recent European Writers*. New York: Free Press.

Paton, C. 2008. 'Inside the ANC's Brutal Contest for Power: The Battleground. Leader.' [Online]. [Accessed 27 July 2010]. Available from: http://www.leader.co.za/article.aspx?s=6&f=1&a=827.

Paton, C. 2012. 'A Looter Continua.' *Financial Mail*. [Online]. 02 April. [Accessed on 27 July 2015]. Available from: http://www.financialmail.co.za/fm/2010/05/20/corruption.

Polity. 2015. '"Protests Linked to Fruitless, Wasteful Government Expenditure": IRR.' *Polity.org.za*. [Online]. [Accessed 05 June 2015]. Available from: http://www.polity.org.za/article/protests-linked-to-fruitless-wasteful-government-expenditure-irr-2015-05-26.

Powell, D.M. et al. 2014. 'Civic Protests Barometer 2007–2014.' Cape Town: MLGI. [Online]. [Assessed: 13 July 2015] Available at: http://mlgi.org.za/talking-good-governance/20150219%20Civic%20Protest%20Barometer%20Published%20%20DP.pdf.

Price, R.M. 1991. *The Apartheid State in Crisis: Political Transformation in South Africa, 1975-1990*. Oxford: Oxford University Press, pp. 28–78.

Przeworski, A. and Teune, H. 1970. *The Logic of Comparative Social Inquiry*. New York: Wiley-Interscience.

Putnam, R. 1993. *Making Democracy Work: Civic Traditions in Modern Italy*. Princeton, NJ: Princeton University Press.

Pye, L.W. 1966. *Aspects of Political Development*. Boston, MA: Little, Brown, and Company.

Ramos, M. 1997. 'In Defence of Gear.' *Indicator South Africa*. 14(3), pp. 37–40.

Randall, V. and Theobald, R. 1985. *Political Change and Underdevelopment: An Introduction to Third World Politics*. Durham, NC: Duke University Press.

Rantele, J. and Giliomee, H. 1992. 'Transition to Democracy Through Transaction? Bilateral Negotiations Between the ANC and the NP in South Africa.' *African Affairs* 91, pp. 515–542.

Reddy, T. 2005. 'The Congress Party Model: South Africa's African National Congress (ANC) and India's Indian National Congress (INC) as Dominant Parties.' *African and Asian Studies* 4(3), pp. 270–300.

Riggs, F. 1981. 'The Rise and Fall of "Political Development".' In Long, S. C. ed. *The Handbook of Political Behaviour.* Vol 4. New York: Plenum Press, pp.282–348.

Robins, S. 2012. 'The Spear that Divided the Nation.' *Amandla.* [Online]. [Accessed 10 June 2014]. Available from: http://amandla.org.za/the-spear-that-divided-the-nation-by-professor-robins/.

Robins, S. 2013. 'How Poo Became Political.' *The Cape Times.* [Online]. 2 July. [Accessed 10 June 2014]. Available from: http://beta.iol.co.za/capetimes/toilets-that-became-political-dynamite-1089289.

Rostow, W.W. 1962. *The Stages of Economic Growth: A Non-Communist Manifesto.* New York: Cambridge University Press.

Rousseau, J.J. 1968. *The Social Contract.* Harmondsworth: Penguin Classics.

Roussouw, M. et al. 2009. 'In Black and White.' *The M&G Online.* [Online]. 24 September. [Accessed 11 May 2011]. Available from: http://mg.co.za/article/2009-09-24-in-black-and-white/.

Samāddāra, R. 2010. *Emergence of the Political Subject.* Los Angeles: SAGE.

Sartori, G. 1970. 'Concept Misformation in Comparative Politics.' *The American Political Science Review* 64(4), pp. 1033–1053.

Sartori, G. 1976. *Parties and Party Systems: A Framework for Analysis.* Cambridge, England: Cambridge University Press.

Saul, J.S. and Gelb, S. 1981. *The Crisis in South Africa: Class Defense, Class Revolution.* New York: Monthly Review Press.

Schrire, R. 1996. The Myth of the "Mandela" Presidency. *Indicator South Africa* 13(2), pp. 13–18.

Scott, D. 1999. *Refashioning Futures: Criticism After Post-Coloniality.* Princeton, NJ: Princeton University Press.

Scott, J.C. 1985. *Weapons of the Weak: Everyday Forms of Peasant Resistance.* New Haven: Yale University Press.

Seegers, A. 1996. *The Military and the Making of Modern South Africa.* London: I. B. Tauris.

Seekings, J. 2000. *The UDF: A History of the United Democratic Front in South Africa, 1983–1991.* Cape Town: David Philip.

Seky-Otu, A. 2003. 'Fanon and the Possibility of Postcolonial Critical Imagination.' *Codesria Symposium on Canonical Works and Continuing Innovations in African Arts and Humanities.* Accra, Ghana: Codesria. [Online]. [Accessed 12 December 2013]. Available from: http://abahlali.org/files/Sekyi_Otu.pdf.

Sellström, T. and Nordiska Afrikainstitutet, 1999. *Liberation in Southern Africa: Regional and Swedish Voices : Interviews from Angola, Mozambique, Namibia, South Africa, Zimbabwe, the Frontline and Sweden.* Uppsala: Nordiska Afrikainstitutet.

Sharma, S.D. 1994. 'Review Essay: Indian Democracy and the Crisis of Governability.' *The Fletcher Forum* Winter/Spring, pp.147-157.

Shepperson, G. 1953. 'Ethiopianism and African Nationalism.' *Phylon (1940–1956)* 14(1), pp. 9–18.

Simons, H.J. and Simons, R.E. 1983. *Class and colour in South Africa, 1850–1950.* London: IDAF.

Sisk, T.D. 1995. *Democratization in South Africa: the elusive social contract.* Princeton, NJ: Princeton University Press.

Sklar, R. 1993. 'The African Frontier of Political Science.' In Bates, R.H et al. eds. *Africa and the Disciplines.* Chicago: University of Chicago Press, pp. 83–110.

Skocpol, T. 1979. *States and Social Revolutions: A Comparative Analyses of France, Russia and China.* Cambridge: Cambridge University Press.

Smart, B. 1983. *Foucault, Marxism and Critique.* Boston: Routledge.

South African Communist Party. 1981. South African Communists Speak 1915–1980.

London: Inkululeko.

Southall, R. 2006. 'Introduction: Can South Africa be a Developmental State?' In Buhlungu, S. et al. eds. *State of the Nation: South Africa 2005-2006*. Cape Town: HSRC Press, pp. xvii–xlv.

Southall, R. 2003. 'The State of Party Politics: Struggles within the Tripartite Alliance and the Decline of Opposition.' In Habib, A. et al. eds. *State of the Nation: South Africa 2003-2004*. Cape Town: HSRC Press, pp. 53–77.

Southall, R. 2009. 'Understanding the "Zuma Tsunami".' *Review of African Political Economy* 36, pp. 317–333.

Stadler, A. 1987. *The Political Economy of South Africa*. London: Croom Helm.

Steenkamp, L. 2010. 'Political Hyenas in Feeding Frenzy Vavi.' *News24*. [Online]. July 26. [Accessed 15 May 2013]. Available from: http://www.news24.com/SouthAfrica/Politics/Political-hyenas-in-feeding-frenzy-20100826.

Stepan, A. 2001. *Arguing Comparative Politics*. Oxford: Oxford University Press.

Stepan, A. 1988. *Rethinking Military Politics: Brazil and the Southern Cone*. Princeton, NJ: Princeton University Press.

Suttner, R. 2004. 'Transformation of Political Parties in Africa.' *Transformation* 55, pp. 1–27.

Suttner, R. 2009. 'The Zuma Era: Its Historical Context and the Future.' *African Historical Review* 41(2), pp. 28–59.

Tarrow, S. 2011. *Power of Movement: Social Movements and Contentious Politics*. New York: Cambridge University Press.

Terreblanche, S.J. 2002. *A History of Inequality in South Africa, 1652-2002*. Pietermaritzburg: University of Natal Press.

Tilly, C. 1985. 'War Making and State Making as Organized Crime.' In Rueschemeyer, D. et al. eds. *Bringing the State Back In*. Cambridge: Cambridge University Press, pp. 169–191.

Tilly, C. 1993. 'Social Movements as Historically Specific Clusters of Political Performances.' *Berkeley Journal of Sociology*. 38, pp. 1–30.

Torfing, J. 1999. *New Theories of Discourse: Laclau, Mouffe and Zizek*. Oxford: Blackwell.

Trepido, S. 1971. 'South Africa in a Comparative Study of Industrialization.' *The Journal of Development Studies* 7(3), pp. 309–320.

Truluck, A. 1992. *'No Blood on our Hands': Political Violence in the Natal Midlands 1987-Mid-1992, and the Role of the State, 'White' Political Parties, and Business*. Pietermartizburg: Natal Midlands Region of the Black Sash.

Tutu, D. 2004. We Need a New Quality of Society. *The Cape Times*. [Online]. 24 November. [Accessed 20 July 2012]. Available from: http://www.iol.co.za/capetimes.

Waldmeir, P. 1998. *Anatomy of a Miracle: the End of Apartheid and the Birth of the New South Africa*. New Brunswick, NJ: Rutgers University Press.

Walsh, A.P. 1971. *The Rise of African Nationalism in South Africa: The African National Congress, 1912-1952*. Berkeley, CA: University of California Press.

Weber, M. 1958. 'Politics as a Vocation.' In Gerth, H. and Mills, C. ed. *From Max Weber: Essays in Sociology*. Oxford: Oxford University Press, pp. 77–128.

Weber, M. 2001. *The Protestant Ethic and the Spirit of Capitalism*. New York: Routledge.

Webster, E. ed. 1978. *Essays in Southern African Labour History*. Johannesburg: Ravan Press.

Welsh, D. 2009. *The Rise and Fall of Apartheid*. Johannesburg: Jonathan Ball.

Wiarda, H.J. and Skelley, E.M. 2007. *Comparative Politics: Approaches and Issues*. Lanham, MD: Rowman & Littlefield Pub.

Williams, G.F. 1905. *The Diamond Mines of South Africa*. New York: B.F. Buck.

Wilson, M. and Thompson, L.L. 1971. *The Oxford History of South Africa*. Vol. 2: South Africa 1870–1966. Oxford: Oxford University Press.

Wolpe, H. 1972. 'Capitalism and Cheap Labour Power in South Africa: From Segregation to Apartheid.' *Economy and Society* 1(4), pp. 425–456.

Wood, E. M. 2003. *Empire of Capital*. New York: Verso.

Worby, E.et al. 2008. *Go Home or Die Here: Violence, Xenophobia and the Re-invention of Difference in South Africa*. Johannesburg: Wits University Press.

York, G. 2014. 'Vigilante killings on the "Field of Death" in South African Township.' *The Globe and Mail*. [Online]. [Accessed 16 March 2014]. Available from: http://www.theglobeandmail.com/news/world/vigilante-killings-on-the-field-of-death-in-south-african-township/article17052460.

Yudelman, D. 1983. *The Emergence of Modern South Africa: State, Capital and the Incorporation of Organized Labour on the South African Gold Fields, 1902–1939*. Westport,CT: Greenwood Press.

Zuma, J. 2014. State of the Nation Address 13th February 2014. Presented at the Opening of Parliament, Cape Town. [Online]. February 13. [Accessed 27 July 2015]. Available from: http://www.thepresidency.gov.za/pebble.asp?relid=16912.

Index

Abdurahman, Abdul, 116
Adam, Heribert, 163, 165–6
administration, 'science' of, 54
Affirmative Action policies, 21, 177–8, 180, 183, 190
Africa, third wave democracy literature, 28
African Americans, struggle influence, 116
African Claims and Freedom Charter, 64
African mineworkers: Mineworkers and Construction Union, 12; 1946 strike, 105, 122
African Peoples Organisation, 115–16
African Renaissance, 81, 155, 170
Africanism, 179, 180; as consciousness-raising, 124; ideology, 125–6
Afrikaner Nationalist Party, 102, 134–5, 162, 166
Afrikaners, Great Trek, 55; republics, 93
Agamaben, Giorgio, 8, 12, 30, 35, 37, 39, 51, 60–1, 69, 83, 88, 99, 106, 134, 187; 'bare life', 13; *homo sacer*, 15, 31, 38, 148, 151; precariousness, 16
Aids, denialism, 173
Ake, C., 161
Albert Luthuli Municipality, 168
Alexandra, Johannesburg, 20; bus boycott, 125
All African Convention (AAC), 120, 127, 139
Almond, G.A., 47–50
Althusser, Louis, 72, 169
AmaZondi clan rebels 1906, 114
ANC (African National Congress), 2, 12, 23, 63, 65, 79, 117, 133–4, 145–6, 149, 152, 155, 165–6, 172; African Claims document, 118, 121; Africanists opposed, 126; armed struggle relation, 135; civil rights element, 115 complexity of, 26; 'decisive moment', 143; disintegration, 150; dominance, 164; elites subaltern classes mobilization, 15; factionalism, 33, 156, 167, 174–5; Freedom Charter 1969, 160; historical composition, 25; history of, 120; Inkatha Freedom Party clashes, 141; institutional resilience, 159; institutional weaknesses, 188; liberal-democratic tradition, 70; Morogoro conference 1969, 179; national bourgeoisie representation, 190; neoliberal policies, 180; non-racial tradition, 64, 68; patronage relations, 153; 'people's war', 137; Programme of Action 1949, 125, 127; race question, 178; sports representation emphasis, 184; state arrogance of, 18, 162; *State and Transformation*, 159; 'strategic' armed struggle, 64; Youth League, 122–3
Anderson, Benedict, 191
Anglo-American Mining Corporation, 105
Angola, 24–5; camp mutiny, 26
Anti-Republican Day celebrations, 130
Apartheid regime/state: bankrupt, 162; big capital influenced, 105; capitalism contradictions, 83; corruption, 176; international campaign against, 140; labour regulation, 103; layers of humiliation, 104; leadership, 64; migrant labour policy, 142; social planning intensification, 128
Arendt, Hannah, Hannah, 3, 15, 35, 37, 56, 58, 106, 187; refugees, 38, 164
Arian, Alan 164
Aristotle, 37
'armed struggle', 24
Arms Deal 2001 scandal, 156–7, 174–6
Armstrong, J.C., 88–9

Asian 'crony capitalism', 181
Azanian Peoples Organization, 130, 139
AZT, 173

Bali, 160
Ballinger, William, 120
Bambatha revolt, suppression of, 116
Bandung moment people's visions, 46; socialist ideals, 36
Bantustan project/system, 104, 144; Bantu Education Act, 87; creation of, 105; independence strategy, 102
bare life, politics of, 8
Barnes, Samuel, 164
basic resources, common grievances, 16
Beinart, W., 103
Benjamin, Walter, 45
Berlin, Isiah, 27
Bhabha, Homi, 71, 73, 74, 76; ambivalence celebration, 75; postcolonial theory version, 73
Biko, Steve, 1, 30, 63, 64, 66, 68, 72–3, 77, 129–30, 180, 187, 189; national struggles criticism, 67; *see also* Black Consciousness
biopolitics, 37, 98
Bisho shootings, 146
'Black Consciousness', 1, 26, 30, 63, 65, 68, 75, 114, 130, 180, 189; ANC attacks, 26; 'formation schools', 129; mobilisations, 128
Black Economic Empowerment, 21, 79, 155, 177, 180–1, 190; Mbeki defence of, 157
black middle class, 12, 71, 78, 106
black workers; miners 1946 strike, 122; 1973 strikes, 101
Bloemfontein, 118
Boer Republics, 93
Boer War, 93
Boipatong township, 145, massacre, 138, 146
Botha, P., 176; security state, 105
Botswana, 105
Boucek, F., 174–5
bourgeoisie: nationalist, 110, 112; opportunist class, 80

Bratton, Michael, 27
Brazil, 50, 89
British parliament, SANCC delegation to, 117
bureaucratic rationality, discourse, 152
business class, 'de-racialization', 181
Buthulezi, Chief, 139, 144, 165

Cabral, Amilcar, 104
Cambridge, Alexander, 94
Camus, Albert, 58
'capacity lack', 18
Cape Colony, slave society, 88
Cape Constitution 1853, 90
Cape Town, 88
Cape Frontier Wars, 113
capitalism, accumulation-war link, 91; racialized, 4, 11; universal process, 86
Chakrabarty, D., 52, 58–9, 86
Champion, George, 120
charisma: and symbolism discourse, 151–2, 164; political use of, 161, 163
Chatterjee, Partha, 3, 8, 12, 31–7, 108, 111–12, 115, 147, 154, 187
Chief Bambatha, armed revolt, 114
China: communist-led struggles, 121; immigrants from, 19
Christianity, 116; African intellectuals, 114; conversion to 113, 115
Cillie, P., 102
Ciskei Bantustan, 145
civil service: preserved, 158; redeployment, 166
civil society: definitions of, 27–8; discourse of rights, 68, 121; state relationship, 3, 29, 31
Clapham, C., 160–2
CODESA I, 138, 144, 145
Cold War, end of, 5–6
colonialism, 54; Apartheid re-invigoration, 7; British, 92; bureaucratised violence, 109; distinctive racism of, 56; hidden 'spirit' of, 53; types of, 55; unspoken trauma of, 76; 'of a special type', 126–7; state war-making expansion, 95; violence reliance, 98; World War II impact on, 121
Coloured People's Organisation, 166

Coloureds, racial classification, 72, 183
Columbia University, 116
community protests, 1990s, 16
comparative politics, 57; conventional paradigm, 6; field of, 41
'comprador class', 104
'compatibility thesis', 51
compromises, elite, 143
Congress Alliance 1950s, 166
Congress of Democrats, 166
Congress of the People, South Africa, 24, 175
corruption, 27, 191; large-scale, 156; regional instances, 176–7
Cosatu, 23, 160, 166–7, 172, 175
crime, drastic increase in, 178
Cronin, Jeremy, 1
'crony capitalism', 181
cultural humanism, modern African, 77

D'Urban, Benjamin, 94
DA (Democratic Alliance party), 173
Dahomey, 89; Dahomian people Ivory coast attacks on, 81
Davenport, T.R.H., 92
De Beers, labour surveillance, 100
De Klerk, F.W., 138, 140, 144–5, 154, 176
de-education, Bantu Education policy, 103
decolonisation, comprehensive need, 76–9
democracy: ANC view of state, 159; conventional theory, 3; radical meaning loss, 51; rights discourse, 136
Derrida, J., 'floating signifier, 74
'development state', idea, 160
diamonds and gold, nineteenth-century discovery of, 85, 93
discourses: modernist, 73; nationalist, 111; relational nature of identities, 71; settler colonial, 74; struggle, 112; symbolic political, 165
'dividing practices', 97
division of labour: colonial, 88; racial, 99
dominant party thesis, 164, 188
'double consciousness', 65, 72; African Americans, 30

Du Bois W.E.B., 30, 65, 72
Dube, John, 115
Durban, 2015 street battles, 19; national conference 1991, 140
Durkheim, E., 49, 59
Dutch East India Company(DEIC), 88; settler farmer conflict, 90; slave importing, 89

Easton, David, 46, 48–9
Eastern cape protests, 17, 130
Eber, Max, 51
Economic Freedom Fighters, 24, 31
education, integration process, 154
Egypt, 42
elites: 'backward' masses need, 117; Cape black, 117; colonised, 107; criminality accusations, 13; defeated African, 95; leadership, 68; mass demobilization desire, 10; -masses alliances, 113; nationalist, 11, 24, 34, 118; negotiating, 146, 153; political conflicts, 27; -subaltern relations, 31, 131
Employment Equity Act, 1996, 182
Enlightenment, the, 59
Erwin, Alec, 1
Ethiopian Church of Pretoria, 114
'Ethiopianism', 114
ethnic identities, black African, 12
Europe: bourgeois accumulated capital, 79; fascist ideology, 43; ideal universal standard discourse, 8
evaluation, conflict over establishing criteria, 4
Evaton, bus boycott, 125
exile, politics of, 156
extraordinary politics, normalised, 38
Eze, Emmanuel, 54, 189

factionalism: ANC, 18; degenerative, 175
Fanon, Frantz, 8–9, 12–13, 15, 22, 30, 37, 39, 53, 56–7, 61, 63, 65, 68, 70–4, 80–3, 86, 95, 97–8, 108–12, 124, 127, 131, 137, 147, 158, 160, 162, 167, 170, 187, 189; analysis of power, 35; *Black Skin, White Masks*, 67; concept of violence, 69; 'decisive moment', 140, 142, 190; decolonisation project, 75–6; 'geog-

raphy of power', 96; 'Manichean' society, 66; modernity ambiguity, 78; Negritide critique, 77; *The Pitfalls of National Consciousness*, 79
Farlarn, Ian, 12
Fatton, Robert, 128–9
fear, 73; sustained trauma of, 70
finance capital, power of, 105
First, Ruth, 163
Fischer, Bram, 163
forced resettlements, Stalin induced, 55
Forman, L., 89
Foucault, Michel, 12, 32, 35, 37, 66, 77, 83, 95, 98, 100, 118, 187; Enlightenment critique, 97
Free State province, protest numbers, 17
Freedom Charter, 125, 166, 171, 179
Freedom Front, 165
Frere, Bartle, 92–3
Friedman, S., 164
'Frontier wars', 92
Fukuyama, F., 45

Gandhi, M., 116
Garvey, Marcus, 114
Gauteng, 176; political violence, 141; protest numbers, 17
Geertz, Clifford, 160
genealogy of emergence, 96
Germany, 92
Gerschenkron, Alexander, 160
Giliomee, H.B., 93, 103
Gilroy, Paul, 30, 65, 83
Ginsberg, Ruth Bader, 42
Glen Grey Act 1894, 99, 113–14
GNU, multiparty composition, 165
Goldstone Commission, 145
Goodman Gallery, Johannesburg, 14
Grahamstown, 94
Gramsci, Antonio, 3, 5, 8, 12, 29, 31, 35, 39, 70, 154, 187; 'trench warfare', 12
Groote Schuur mansion, 138
Group Areas Act 1950, 103
Growth Employment and Redistribution (GEAR) policy, 166–7, 169; language of, 168; unemployment growing, 170

Guha, R., 32, 83
guilt, 68

Hagopian, F., 61
Hall, Stuart, 8, 52, 58–9
Hani, Chris, assassination, 146, 159
Harare Declaration 1989, 139
Hegel, G.W.F., 37, 53
hegemony, 70
Herbert, Henry, Lord Carnarvon, 92–3
Heroes Day, 163
historical narrative, Eurocentric, 57
'historicist' viewpoint, 51, 56, 59
HIV/AIDS, 172–3; Mbeki attitude, 155
Hobbes, Thomas, 27, 37, 49
Hogan, Barbara, 174
Holomisa, Bantu, 174
hostel migrants, 'mini-wars' against, 142
housing crisis, Tutu critique, 156
Human Rights Day, 163
Huntington, 46–7, 51, 61, 161; authoritarian regimes tolerance, 52

identity: discourse, 124; politics, 121, 16
'illegal immigrants', official discourse, 20
imbizo, 168
Imbumba Yama Afrika, Port Elizabeth, 115
Immorality Act 1950, 103
imperialism: centre historic moves, 44; violent core, 54
'imperial gaze', 48
imvo Zabantsundu, 11
indentured workers: Chinese and Indian, 55, 116
Independent Labour Party, England, 120
Independent Tembu National Church, 114
India: Communist Party, 34; Congress Party, 34; immigrants from, 19; postcolonial studies, 53
Indian Congresses, 115–16, 119, 125
Indians, South African racial classification, 72
indigenous societies, colonial knowledge of, 97; kingdoms defeats, 109
Industrial Commercial Union, membership surge, 119; political approach, 120

inequalities, reproduced, 13
'informal settlements', 16
Inkatha Freedom Party (IFP), 138, 142, 144, 162, 165
ANC violent attacks on, 26
'interest aggregation', 49
intellectuals, colonised, 78
Ivanov, Victor, 14

Jabavu, John Tengoimvo, 115
Jagersfontein, 118
Jamaica: 'nationalist-modern' project, 36, 63; nationalist elite, 187; politics, 7
Jansen, Jonathan, 177
Japan, 58
'jobless growth', 170
Johannesburg, street battles, 19
Johnstone, Frederick, 85
Joint Franchise Action Committee, 125
Jordan, Pallo, 179

Ka Seme, Pixley, 115
Kadalie, Clements, 120
Kalyvas, Andreas, 3
Kant, Immanuel, 'racial theories', 59
Kasfir, Nelson, 27–8
Kaviraj, Sudipta, 28–9, 87
Kenya, 54–5
Khayelitsha squatter camp, Cape Flats, 19
Khilnani, Sunil, 28–9
Khoi people, 88–90, 113, 171
Khutsong township, extended protest, 18
King Zwelithini, 19
Kliptown, 125
Kohli, A., 33
Kuhn, T., 43, 44
Kwa-Zulu Bantustan, 142, 144
Kwa-Zulu Natal province, 130; protest numbers, 17

'labour aristocracy', white, 99
Lacan, Jacques, subject identity notion, 74
LaCapra, D., 49
Land Act 1913, 100, 113
landless peasantry, creation of, 99

Lasswell, Harold, 43–4
late modernisers, 58
Latour, Bruce, 45
law, -violence line blurred, 69
Leballo Potlako, 125
Lembede, Anton, 122–5, 191
Lenin, V.I., 109; Ivanov portrait, 14
Leon, Tony, 173
Lesotho, 105
liberal democracy, 'Western', 6
liberalism, 45; Victorian, 116
Limpopo province, protest numbers, 17
'living wage' demand abandoned, 169
Locke, John, 27, 37, 49, 59
Lodge, Tom, 25
Lomnin mine, strike and massacre 2012, 11–12, 26, 32, 39, 80, 107–8, 151; Commission, 190
Lukes, S., 50
Luthuli, Martin, 115

Macaulay's Minute, India, 87
Macey, D., 78
Machiavelli, 37
Macozoma, Saki, 181
Madikzela-Mandela, Winnie, 22
Madzunya, Josias, 125
Makone, Mangena, 114
Makwetu, Kimi, 191
Malan Accord 1991, 135
Malawi, 105
Malema, Julius, 178; accusations of, 179
Mamdani, M., 54, 161–2
Mandela, Nelson, 2, 22, 107, 123, 135, 140–1, 145, 147–8, 152, 154–5, 163, 166, 167–8, 170, 172, 174, 185; charisma, 165; release of, 144; Rivonia Trial speech, 64–5; symbolic modernist discourse, 177
Manichean society, 158; irrational generalisations produced, 77
Mantashe, Gwede, 179
Manuel, Trevor, 183
Manye, Jimmy, 183
Marikana, Lonmin mine strike and massacre 2012, 11–12, 26, 32, 39, 80, 107–8, 151; Commission, 190

martial law, Apartheid state, 133
Martineau, J., 93
Marx, Karl, 4, 6, 37, 45, 49, 59, 68, 77–80, 86–7, 109–10, 192; critical tradition, 76
Marxism, 45, 50–1, 95; neo-46
mass/subaltern politics; disciplining, 149; 'irrational' label, 141; 'passive support' role, 163; strategic tool, 146; *see also* subaltern
Mazwele, Chumani, 162
Mbeki, Thabo, 16, 151–3, 156–8, 160, 163, 166–8, 170–1, 173, 175, 179, 181, 185; African Renaissance vision, 155; identity approach, 172; Presidency loss, 174; structural adjustment program, 147; -Tutu debate, 152–4
Mbeki, Moeletsi, 12
Mbembe, Achille, 14–15, 34
McBride, Robert, 135
Mda, Ashley Peter, 122–3, 191
MDC, 155
Melber, Henning, 23–5
'mental emancipation', 124
Mexico, 50
Meyer, Roelf, 145
Mill, John Stuart, 49
Mineworkers: Marikana massacre, *see above*; National Union of, 12; strike 1946, 122
mining, 4: capital/capitalists, 105–6; coercive labour, 99–100; global trading network, 5; racial division of labour, 84–5; Transvaal province industry, 142
Mitchell, T., 58, 98
Mixed Marriages Act 1949, 10
Mngxitama, Andile, 19
'mob', ideological view, 151
modernisation theory, 7–8, 41, 45–6, 53, 57; Eurocentric assumptions, 50; 1950s, 6; revival of, 61; stability bias, 48; third wave democracy influence, 41
modernity(ies), 6, 87: colonial, 56; European nationalist, 111; European, 'consent' of the governed, 71; global story of, 192; non-Western role silenced, 57; political linear narrative, 4, 42; settler-colonial imposed, 4–5, 8–9, 11, 28, 32, 69, 71, 84, 99
Moraka, James, 125
Motlanthe, Kgalema, 182
Mozambique, 24, 25, 105; RENAMO, 24
Mpumalanga province, protest numbers, 17
multiparty conference, National Party proposal, 144
Murray, Brett, Zuma portrait, 14–15

Naipaul, Nadira, 22
Namibia, 24–5
Nash, Andrew, 165
Natal: colonial government poll tax, 114; political violence, 141; University Medical School, 129
National Forum coalitions, 30
National Liberation Movements (NLMs) Southern Africa, 23–6
National Party, 134, 143
National Peace Accord, 141, 143
National Prosecuting Authority, 175
National Union of Mineworkers, 12
National Union of South African Students, 66, 129
'national' territories, imagined, 83
nationalism: elite, 107; nativist, 167
nationalist bourgeoisie, 13, 110, 112: accumulated capital lack, 80; anxieties of, 21, 27; crisis of, failures of, 79; political dominance of, 81
nationalist elite(s), 8, 25, 78, 117, 133–4, 142, 163; discourses shift, 141; liberal democracy model, 148; mass participation used, 136; pacts entered, 150; personal gain, 33; political rationality claim, 137, 147–9; uncritical solidarities' need, 178
nationalist struggle paradigm, 6
Native Education Association 1884, 115
Native Electoral Association 1884, 115
native intellectual, 110–11
Native Land and Trust Act 1936, 100
Native Representative Councils, 117, 136, 139
Ndebele, Njabulo, 13, 77, 108

necklacing, 20
Neoscosmos, M., 54
negotiation process 1990–4, 133, 137; differences over, 139; narrow agenda, 143; track dominated, 140
negritude: Fanon's problem with, 77; Senghor's idea of, 70
Nelson Mandela Memorial Lecture, 154
neo-patrimonialism, 50, 161
NEPAD, 155
New Formations, 73
Newlands, Cape Town, 21
Ngonyana, Smuts, 24
Nieztsche, F., genealogy of, 96
Nigeria, 50, 53–4
Non-European Unity Movement (NEUM), 120, 122
North America, universal standard discourse, 8
North West province, protest numbers, 17
Northern Cape, protest numbers, 17

O'Meara, D., 105
OECD, 180
Operation Vula, 135
Osterhammel, J., 54–6, 189
Otherness of Self, 74
Ottaway, Marina, 23
Oupa Gzoqo, 145

Pakistan, immigrants from, 19
Pan Africanism, 114, 124–5
Pan-Africanist Congress, 122, 126, 128, 138–9, 179, 191
parastatals, tendering, 177
Parsons, Talcott, 47–9
particpatory democracy, absence of, 168
passes: British laws 1896, 95; laws, 102; women burning 1918, 118
Paton, Carol, 176
patriarchy, 15
patrimonial state: conception of, 160; pre-modern, 161
Patriotic Front, demand for, 139
peasantry, radical goals, 78

Pelem, Meshach, 115
Phosa, Mathews, 174
plantation economy, 55; class tensions, 116
Plato, 37, 60
politics/political: acceptable limitations, 135; -'criminal' binary, 134, 138; development, idea of, 47; development modernisation discourse, 41, 47; electoral, 147; mass, 68; mobilized, 11; modernity historicist notion, 87; new expert language, 136; of the extraordinary, 151; political prisoners issue, 135, 138; 'poltical socialisation', 49; subaltern alienation, 36, 108, 134
Polokwane conference, ANC, 156, 175
'Poo wars', 37
Population Registration Act, 103
populations, classification, 97
Port Alfred, 1854 workers strike, 118
postcolonial situations, questions of modernity, 3
post-structuralism, 95
Powell, G.B., 47
power-knowledge relationship, 96
Pretoria Minute, 135, 138
'progress' accepted metaphor of, 45
protests: numbers, 17; South African Police wordings of, 17
'public-private' partnerships, 169
punishment, practices of, 97
Putnam, R., 34
Pye, Lucian, 47, 53–4

race: ethnic consciousness encouraged, 104; groups classification, 103; racialised property issue; ignored, 136; 'scientific' racism, 70; South African hierarchy, 95
Radebe, Mark, 115
'rainbow nation', 97–8, 177
Rally for Democracy and Progress, Zimbabwe, 24
Ramaphosa, Cyril, 12, 135, 145, 174
rape, cases of, 156
rational-bureaucratic discourse, 153, 168

rationalist-modern discourse, 163, 167, 170
Reconstruction and Development Program (RDP) fund, 166, 168; abandonment of, 169
'regimes of truth', 59
'repertoires of contention', theory of, 31
res nullius principle, 59, 93
resistance, 75, 98, 163; dominant narrative of, 112; South Africa history, 108; to colonialism, 77; violent, 76
Rhodes, Cecil, 99
Riebeeck, Jan van, 113
Riggs, F., 44
Rivonia Trial, 141, 148
Robins, Steven, 14–15
Robseon, Paul, 120
Rondebosch, Cape Town, 21
Rousseau, Jean-Jacques, 27, 37, 49, 60, 73
Rugby World Cup 1995, 165, 177
rural-urban subjects, separation, 54

Said, Edward, 48, 51; *Orientalism*, 46
San people, 88–90, 113, 171
Sanlam insurance company, 105
SASOL, 183
Schlemmer, L., 103
Schmitt, Carl, 3
school boycotts 1980, 130
Scott, 35, 37, 187
Scott, David, 7, 12, 35–7, 63, 187
Scott James, 119
self-policing, 98
Seme, Pixley Ka, 116, 123
Senghor, L., 70
Separate Ameneties Act 1953, 103
separateness, geography of, 72
service delivery protests, 16, 27, 39, 108
settler colonialism, 4–5, 11, 15, 52, 70, 98
 Sc, 101, 117; abiding influence of, 31–2; civilized/savage dichotomy, 101; class formation, 80; compartmentalised worlds, 72; inherent violence, 69; modernity(ies) of, 41, 151, 187–9; power operation mode, 53, 148; racialised organisation of labour, 102; racism, 71; specificity of, 30; violent legacies of, 23

Sexwale, Tokyo, 156, 174
Shaik, Shabir, 175
Sharpeville massacre, 104, 108, 126, 131, 136; mobilisations up to, 190; -post period, 65, 128
Shepstone, T., 93
Sisulu, Lindiwe, 179, Walter, 123
skin, 75
slavery, 54–5; Cape colony uprisings, 89
slippage, 76
Slovo, Joe, 145
Smith, Harry, 94
Sobukwe, Robert, 191
social mobilisation, 'new' post-2009, 17; increased, 18
social science, USA political use of, 45
South Africa, 53–5 Auditor General, 2007-8 report, 177; democracy conventional approach, 7; Department of Home Affairs, 20; Department of Labour, 182; economic growth 1960s, 106; historicist analysis, 60; increasing inequality, 188; influx control laws 1952, 95; Labour Court, 183; land grab expansion, 90;'liberalisation' economy, 169; Local Government Association, 16; Manichean world, 189; Marxist approaches, 84; monopoly capitalist phase, 105; nationalist elite, *see above*; new constitution praise, 2, 42; 'patterns of politicization, 33; Portfolio Committee on Sport, 184;
'race-consciousness' politics, 57–8, 66; resistance history, 108; settler-colonialism dynamics, 52,63, 82, 123, 151; state formation, 92; studies of democracy, 62; 'Two civil societies', 30; Western discourse mimicking, 15
South African Communist Party (SACP, ex-CPSA), 23, 122, 126–7, 137, 145, 166–7, 172; formation of, 119
SASA, 175
South African Council of Sport, 184
South African Institute of International Relations,
South African Labour Party, 119–20

South African Native National Congress, 115–119
South African Police Service, 182
South African Students Organisation, 66, 129
Southall, Roger, 23
Soweto, 82; Afrikaans language science teaching, 130; 1976 revolt, 26, 63, 102, 130
SSRC, Committee on Comparative Politics, 44
state, the: Apartheid, 105; colonial, 98; European history, 90; European model, 45; four conceptions of, 152; idea of, 109; monopoly of violence, 5, 91; neoliberal policy, 32; notions of 'neutral', 160; of exception, 69, 106; popular pressure resistance, 52; settler colonial, 84
Statutes of India 1642, 89
Stellenbosch conference 2002, ANC, 175
Stepan, Alfred, 27–8
strikes, 101, 118, 121
structural functionalism, 44, 47–51
struggle: discourses, 128; narratives, 112
subaltern masses: control 'culturalism' use, 14; everyday policing of, 42; mobilisations, 21, 63; nationalist elites control failure, 32; politics of, 8; spontaneous, 118; township, 122
superstructure, -base reversal, 86
Suttner, Raymond, 26. 164
Swaziland, 105
symbolism, discourse of, 16; -modern, 163

Tanzania, ANC camp mutiny, 26
Tarrow, Sydney, 31
The Spear (Zuma portrait), protests against, 11, 39
'theatre state', 160
'third force', 135, 142
third wave democracy discourse, 6, 30, 42, 58, 87, 188; Africa literature, 28; modernisation approaches, 11, 41; studies scientific pretence, 43; violence history excluded, 83
Third World: comparative study desire, 43; conventional approach to politics, 8 failed modernity discourse, 7
Thompson, Leonard, 92

Tile, Nehemiah, 114
Tilly, Charles, 31, 91–2
Tloome, Dan, 123
Transvaal:, annexation, 93; Republic, 99
TRC (truth and reconciliation) process, 154; report, 172
Treatment Action Campaign (TAC), 173
Tri-Cameral parliament, 144
'tribalism', 50; mineworkers divided, 101
Tripartite Alliance, 13, 23, 168
Tshabalala-Msimang, Manto, 173
Tshwete, Steve, 174
Tutu, Desmond, 152; -Mbeki dispute 154–8, 170

Ubuntu, 20, 81
Umkhonto we Sizwe (MK), 64, 144–5, 179
'uncritical solidarities', 13, 77, 108, 178
Union 1910: establishment of, 115; non-whites, 113
United Democratic Front, 30, 130
Unity Movement, 136, 139, 179
universities: Cape Town protests, 180, 191; neoliberal conception, 184; proposed autonomous, 124; social sciences departments, 45
urban black world, mass mobilisation, 106; rapid wartime growth, 122
USA (United States of America), 25; Political Sciences departments, 46; social science use, 45

Vaal uprisings 1984, 130
Vagrancy Act 1889, 115
Van Riebeeck, Jan, 88
Vavi, Zwelinzima, 160
Ven der Stel, Adriaan, 89
Verwoerd, H, regime of, 102, 104; ideological phase, 176
Vietnam, ISA defeat, 46
Viljoen, Condtand, 165
violence: black-on-black, 134, 142; community, 20; continued State, 83; efficient colonial use, 109; material and psycholgical, 70; South African culture of, 2; 'structural', 135; 'vigilante, 19

Vitor Verster Prison, Mandela's walk from, 2
Voltaic people, Ivory Coast attacks on, 81
Vorster, J., 176
voting rights, limited African extension, 117
'vulgar tribalism', 81

Waldmeir, Patti, 22–3
Walshe, Peter, 116
Walzer, Michael, 27
Weber, Max, 3, 48–9, 59, 87, 91, 94, 163
Wessels, Allison, 120
'West and the Rest', discourse of, 58–61
Western experience, as universal model, 60
Western Province, protest numbers, 17
Whites: informal identity privileges, 85; miners 1922 strike, 101; power structure; reproduction of, 66–7, 136; supremacist discourse legalising, 102; supremacist policies, 5
Williams, Gardner Frederick, 100
Wilson, Monica, 92
Witwatersrand Native Labour Association, 100
Wood, Ellen, 59, 88, 93

Worden, N.A., 88–9
World Cup (football) Stadiums, 177
World Economic Forum, 191
World Trade Centre, December 1991 conference, 144

xenophobic attacks, 11, 19, 21, 39, 81; mass mobilisations, 20, 190
Xhosa people: nineteenth-entury wars against, 90, 92; King Hintsa beheaded, 94; 'tribalist' label, 183
Xuma, Alfred, 125

Zimbabwe, 24–5, 105, 155; crisis, 157; ZANU-PF, 155
Zulu Kingdom, 93; King Solomon ka Dinuzulu, 94
Zuma, Jacob, 1, 12, 14, 42, 162–4, 170, 172, 175, 185; cabinet composition, 178; Nkandla house scandal, 176, 191; non-racialism emphasis, 179; State of the Nation speech 2014, 21; tired nationalist narrative, 22